To Joyce & Jerry —

More cherished memories —

Lois Costomiris

Some day you'll have cherished memories to set down for family -- Don't put it off too long.

Best wishes —

Aunt Lois

WINDMILLS WASHBOARDS & WHIPPERSNAPPERS

The Legends Live on in Hamilton County, Indiana

Lois Kaiser Costomiris

Illustrations by Richard Day

Guild Press of Indiana, Inc.
Carmel, Indiana

 Published in the United States by Guild Press of Indiana, Inc., Carmel, Indiana.

Library of Congress
Catalog Card Number
98-72778

ISBN 1-57860-067-7

Manufactured in the United States of America

Cover art by Richard Day
Text designed by Sheila G. Samson

ALSO BY LOIS KAISER COSTOMIRIS:

Rail Fences, Rolling Pins & Rainbows (1994)

MORE *Rail Fences, Rolling Pins & Rainbows* (1995)

To our grandchildren, to remember how it was back in Grandpa's and Grandma's day:

Angie, Andy, Christopher, and Nicholas John; Rebekah Holmes; Kim, Kris, and Joshua Boone; and our new great-grandson, Nathan Watson.

Contents

Preface

MY FIRST TWO BOOKS, *Rail Fences, Rolling Pins, & Rainbows* and MORE *Rail Fences, Rolling Pins, & Rainbows*, received a wonderful response. So, the Hamilton County, Indiana, legends continue.

Windmills, Washboards & Whippersnappers contains more memorable excerpts from my huge collection of stories and interviews that I wrote for the *Tri Town Topics*, the community newspaper for Cicero, Arcadia, and Atlanta area in Hamilton County.

We are living in a mobile society, and often family members live hundreds of miles apart. It is unfortunate that most of our Heartland, USA, early history is recorded only in the minds of old folks. My husband, Bud, and I are asked several times a year to be interviewed by middle school, high school, and college students for oral history assignments, so they can learn how life was "back then." These young folks have an intense interest in the past.

Because of this, I came to realize the importance of my stories as research materials. A good example is one of the stories in this book, "Pauline's Poultry Paradise." The secrets of hatching and raising poultry aren't being passed on from generation to generation as it was in the old days before the poultry and egg market became the huge industrialized operations that exist nowadays. Textbook-like accounts of facts, figures, and dates alone would be boring reading, as dry as dust. In Pauline's story, sandwiched between the factual items are the interesting and often humorous accounts of day-to-day life on a poultry farm, bringing the experience to life. These warm and enjoyable stories of common folk, living ordinary lives, are too precious to let disappear.

Also notable in the stories is how local dialect has changed since the early 1900s—even since I started writing these stories in the early '70s. I enjoyed so much the countless conversations, clothed with colorful colloquialisms, all stitched together with Hoosier idioms, jargon, cliches, and euphemisms. These too are being lost! But I can honestly say, "Yes, that's just how it was then!" Bud and I lived through many of the experiences.

Tri Town Topics publisher Vaughn Rathbun was generous with the space he gave me in the newspaper. Often my stories were in two or three installments. Sometimes, after someone's account ran in the paper, I'd get calls back from them: "I forgot to tell you . . ." Even at funeral home visitations folks would volunteer anecdotes. Readers would call or write in saying, "That story reminds me of when . . ." Each person had his own bag of memories that enriched these stories.

As with my first two books, the stories are full of names from the past and the present. Be sure to check the index at the back of the book—your name might be there!

Lois Kaiser Costomiris
June 1998

Acknowledgments

AGAIN, SPECIAL THANKS to my storyteller husband, Edward "Bud" Costomiris, who was born with one foot in the past. He's been my life partner for fifty-seven years, and my business manager with my books, making local deliveries, collections, banking, and endless other details. Bud and our daughter, Toni Boone, a first-grade schoolteacher, are my diligent proofreaders.

Thanks to the many wonderful folks—most of whom are "Up There" now—who so happily gave me their accounts for my newspaper column of fifteen years. And to those who still fill in unknown gaps when I'm rewriting.

Several of us bandied around ideas for a title for this book before we happily settled on *Windmills, Washboards & Whippersnappers*, suggested by our grandson-in-law, Kenneth Watson III, a first-grade teacher at Hamilton Heights Elementary.

Thanks also to Guild Press of Indiana publisher Nancy Niblack Baxter, who, with editors Jenny Larner and Sheila Samson, worked to produce another top-quality book; and to artist Richard Day for the beautiful cover art and illustrations. He possesses a genuine knowledge of olden times.

And finally, thanks to the many businesses in Hamilton County who carry my books: Bargin Bob's in Atlanta; the many Community Banks in Cicero and Noblesville; Lea's Hallmark in Cicero; Book & Pub Book Store and Barbara Adams' Country Store, both in Noblesville; McDonald's Hardware Store in Sheridan; and Antiques Galore and More in Westfield.

I'm now in the jumping-off years myself. Hopefully, the Good Lord will let me keep my health and mind long enough to get all the accumulated stories into print for an enduring record of Hamilton County's bygone days.

George "Speed" Flanagan

Speed Flanagan and His Dance Band

I became acquainted with the very friendly Speed and Dugan Flanagan in their dry-cleaning shop in Cicero.

NOTHING EVER TOOK ME from home on the night of Red Skelton's radio or, later, his TV programs. *Nothing*! He was a "Back Seat Performer" before he ever became famous.

Red was once in my dance band!

Whoa now, I'm way ahead of my story. You want to hear of my exciting years with a dance band? Later, I'll tell you all about Red.

The popular dance bands—oh boy, that was a great time to be alive. Everyone having a big time!

Ma was a local "country girl." Pop came from afar with his "city ways," they told me, but I don't recall where. My father, James A. Flanagan, was a tailor. I was raised in the clothing business. His store was in where Dud Purkey's Barber Shop is now. He could identify every man's coat or trouser size as he passed through the door. I should tell you about Pop's stirring life, too.

Pop was a fastidious dresser. He'd been a tailor for as long as I can remember, and he made a good living for us all. Most folks around Cicero assumed he was well-heeled. Ready-to-wear clothing wasn't easy to buy if you weren't the perfect size, and who is?

Expensive, yes. Naturally, Pop dressed well to show off his profession. I guess I took my appearance from him. He always said, "When I take my family out, I want them to look as snappy as a band on parade." We always did.

Pop took Ma regularly to the beauty parlor in Noblesville to have her hair dressed. How exciting—ladies just *never* did that around little ol' Cicero. And what *man* would think of doing that? He took her to dances but she never could get the hang of it, she said. So she didn't dance. She spoke, using language so polished you could skate on it, folks said. I guess I took after Ma in that respect.

I'd often ponder, when I was young, what I'd do for a living when I grew up and had a family. Pop laughed and gave me one of his slow smiles and said, "Don't ever take ahold of anything with a handle." Meaning, I guess, tools for physical labor: a shovel, hoe, rake, pitchfork, paint brush. I'm sure he wanted me to follow in his footsteps and join him in his tailoring business. I liked tailoring, but I loved *music*!

I, George Flanagan, was known as "Speed" in the music circles, and "Sport" by my family and friends. Some said I looked like the Arrow Collar Man in newspaper and magazine advertisements.

My oldest sister, Dorothy—"Doll," we called her—she wrote to her beau in Indianapolis when I was born, telling him that Ma had a new baby boy. He came up, took one look me and said, "Hello, Sport!" And "Sport" stuck.

Same way with Lula, my wife. She got her nickname "Dugan" when she was born. Ferd Laudig, living on a farm out there by them, came over to see the new baby. He looked down into the cradle at her and said, "Hello, Dugan Punch!" They called her "Dugan" the rest of her days.

When I dated Dugan, her parents had two pianos. She and her brother, Bruce, could make the music go! That was real unusual—*two* of those high-back pianos. Most folks saved and saved, just to have one. Her ma said she never had to make either of them practice.

Dugan and I started married life with a Ragtime Band, with the beat in our blood!

A dance band is the easiest way there is to make money. Play till past midnight, then we'd all go eat and visit. Sleep till noon. It gets to be a habit. From then on, I always liked to stay up late at night and sleep in.

People were forever asking me, "When are you going to go to work?" I'd say, "Work? What's all this talk about *work*? I work, don't I? That's what I call it. I play at work and I work at play!" If people, early in life, would find an exciting profession, their work *would* be play!

I married Dugan Hartley, daughter of the Mark Hartleys, when I was twenty-one. I am eighty-one now and still going. Dugan's gone. Oh, how I miss her! We have three married daughters: Maxine, Bonita, and Isabelle.

You probably remember Dugan's father, Mark Hartley. For several years he was grand marshal at the Fall Festival. He rode way up there on his big white stallion, wending through crowded streets, loudly announcing the attractions through his megaphone for everyone to hear. The crowd parted to let him through.

Every so often a mother would cry out to a child, "Better look where you're going!" Even though children were accustomed to animal droppings, in the excitement of that beautiful horse and the man with the megaphone, they only looked *up*. What a beautiful sight—little children watching with wide, excited eyes.

Each year Cicero's main street turned into a midway when the annual Fall Festival and Homecoming got underway. Many a young boy yearned to grow up and ride a big white stallion down the major drag during "Cicero's Big World's Fair," as everyone called it—just like Mark Hartley!

Dugan got her musical ability from her dad. Her mother, just like my mother, didn't have music in her. She claimed she had a tin ear, couldn't toot a hoot! I never saw her even pat a foot to the rhythm of a band or snap her fingers—she just did not have it. She was glad Dugan and her brother, Bruce, took after their father.

When Dugan was dating, she asked a close school friend if he'd like to go to the Saturday night dance that week. He said, "I cain't dance. Nobody ever learned me. Why, I cain't even carry a tune in a Easter basket! What's the sense of puttin' on the dog a-goin' to those things?"

Her friend hated dances and dressing up. Didn't much like women either. He said it didn't bother him in the least if all the other guys and gals were a-swingin' all over the floor. Just leave him be! But he was a respectable and resourceful fellow, or her parents wouldn't have allowed her to go with him. Dugan would coax, saying, "The music's fantastic! Come on. You'll never learn to dance by sitting there like a stuffed owl!" He was never convinced.

Mark Hartley said when he was a young man, songs spoke of the secrets of the soul: human loneliness, death and melancholy love. They didn't appeal much to him. But it's surprising how many songs were written about fallen women and roving males. "She Is More To Be Pitied Than Censured" is the tale of a girl who had fallen to shame. The ill-fated heroine was being mocked by some young fellows when an elderly lady reminded them: "a man was the cause of it all." And there was "Bill Bailey, Won't You Please Come Home?" and "Where Is My Wandering Boy Tonight?" Most of these songs sent out honorable messages.

Ma said I kept time to music before I could walk. I hummed tunes before I could talk and sang all the time except when I was asleep. Even when I was older, Pop maintained that I half-sang in place of snoring. He'd say, "Boy, for the love of life and liberty, will you *stop* that noise? You sound like the squallin' of a stepped-on cat!"

When I was a little tyke in the high chair, I'd beat out tunes with my spoon to sister Doll's singing. Sometimes I turned the washpan or dishpan over and tapped on them. My feet were always on the go.

At school I was a drummer without a drum. A pencil in each hand, I'd sing and thump along to the music on my desk while the students were singing. Teacher didn't mind. In fact, she encouraged it, except when I was supposed to be writing out an assignment for arithmetic or spelling. She'd be drilling one of the other grades—eight in our one-room school—and instinctively I'd start tapping out a tune or rhythm that came to my mind. She didn't scold me; she kindly frowned and shook her head.

Our school had a kitchen band. I'd beat my drumsticks on the bottom of the school's old washpan, or I'd run my drumsticks up and down the washboard—an old thing someone had brought from home. There were toots from an empty jug and bottles; a boy played the tunes on his comb; someone had a harmonica—a mouth organ; and a girl beat a tune out with metal kitchen spoons. Oh my, what else? All the boys envied me, the drummer!

I always wanted a drum so bad. Kept hoping I'd find one under the Christmas tree some year, but I knew that was impossible. Just no money now that everyone was suffering through the Depression. I was wearing out two pencils instead of the one I was allowed for my school work. Ma complained about that expense. So I whittled myself a couple of drumsticks from a hickory limb. I went to playing on Ma's turned-upside-down galvanized washtub.

The whole family attended the Saturday night dances. I'd beat out tunes on my washtub, accompanying the piano and usually a fiddle or a guitar, banjo, mouth organ, or other musical instrument. It held everyone spellbound! They stood around, watched, then cheered. A kid sure loves that kind of attention, and I never outgrew it!

When I was older, I had an unquenchable urge for partying and dancing, and was always stage-struck. I'd rather dance than eat! We'd gather around in one another's homes, roll back the carpet, and start in. Dance faster and faster, until the dishes rattled in the cupboard! All those family pictures on top of the piano jiggled around and had to be moved. The whole houseful of kids whirled in happiness! Now, that's fun! Fit for the gods!

One time, dancing away like that, it shook the parlor stovepipe loose. It fell, spraying ashes and soot all over. Oh, the smoke—whew! We big boys grabbed gloves to hold the hot pipe and hurried to put it back in place. The girls rushed in with the broom and dustpan and swept up the mess. The dancing continued.

Midnight, when the last dance was approaching, the aroma of hot coffee, made by a parent or an old-maid aunt in the kitchen, would seep into the room. Too soon, it seemed, it was time to waltz to "Home, Sweet Home." Then the young ladies got busy bringing out the food while the fellows rolled the carpet back into place and arranged the furniture.

When Dugan was a high-school girl, whenever she'd show up at a friend's home, it didn't take her long to find the piano and start playing and singing. She'd fill the room with her bouncy tunes and catchy lyrics. Hers was an interesting style—she played with all those flourishes up and down the keyboard. That was a show in itself.

I had my eye on her way back then. She kept everyone happy with her music, but, as accomplished as she was, she complained—she loved playing the piano but she never got to dance! Later, a few families were buying Victorolas, so she got her chance to dance.

I remember when she and I first started keeping company—she always smelled of clean, freshly ironed clothes. Oh boy! Said she put them away in drawers scattered with rosemary leaves from her neighbor's garden.

Many people frowned on dance halls. At a family dinner once, my aunt and uncle were quarreling. "I wish," said my uncle, "they'd close up those danged places, tear them down or burn them. If one of our kids ever went in a dump like that, I'd kick 'em out and disown 'em. Goin' on a Saturday night to those sinful, evil places . . ." My aunt answered snidely, "It's *not* a dump; it's respected. There are a lot worse things our kids can do than be caught at that dance hall. While they are dancing, they aren't tempted into disgraceful behavior." She had in mind her sons a-boozin' and crawling under girls' skirts.

One of the cousins said later that her mother told the daughters over and over: "Keep dancing, girls. When you're dancing, you're not doing other things that could get you into trouble."

After Dugan and I were married, we moved from Cicero to Terre Haute. We both sang and she played the piano for the silent movies at the Gem Theater, to illustrate slides on the silent screen. A sheaf of music came with the can of film. We'd go to the post office to get it and then practice at the theater, so that we could accompany the film that night. I'd turn the pages. We had to be on the alert every minute to keep up: runaway horses with their shootin' cowboys, Southern belles dancing the minuet, gigolos with enough Vaseline on their hair to grease a fat hog.

In a dance band like ours, the pianist plays orchestrations; you have to be able to read music. Dugan could. There are a lot of good piano players who can't. They can sit down and play any song title that's called out, but put music in front of them and it's like a foreign language. I never could read music. I always played by ear, and it worked out fine.

Then we left Terre Haute and went to Olney, Illinois. We would sing duets at the theater at night and press clothes at the cleaning shop during the day.

Later, we left Olney, moved to Indianapolis and started a dance band. Dugan was the pianist, I was on the drums, and we had a sax player. We bought our sheet music at the five and ten. Dime stores all over carried the latest tunes, and most of them had someone who'd sit down at the piano and play the newest popular music for you. Dugan could look at the score and play it right off!

Reminds me of the time a fellow asked me for a job. When I

showed him what we'd be playing, he replied, "Don't know nothin' 'bout no notes. Couldn't tell one from th'other. I jist play it. I play the guitar, banjo, fiddle, mandolin an' mouth harp." Then he proved it to me. He sure could make music!

We played in Indianapolis for three years. At that time Dugan and I had a baby girl and another in the oven. Then we went back to Terre Haute, formed a ten-piece band and played at the Trianon Dance Palace for two years. We started out with a three-piece band, then added a banjo and kept on adding pieces until there were ten. I've played music to many different dance crazes. There was the waltz, two-step, ragtime, polka and jazz.

Later on, we couldn't leave our home and go on the road like the big bands were doing, because we were thinking ahead to the time our daughters would be ready to start school. So I booked dances all around Terre Haute and Decatur, Illinois. In Terre Haute, it cost each couple ten cents a dance. We'd play a verse and two choruses. The crowd then left the floor and another bunch was let on. We played four hours.

I had a musician that was bigger than I. He lived near the train depot and carried the drums till we got on the train. Later I bought a seven-passenger Hudson. We put the instruments in the back and I drove to the dance halls.

A band always played on Saturday night and maybe a night or two through the week. On the side, to meet expenses, Dugan and I were pressing at a cleaners, making around seventeen dollars a week. That doesn't sound like much, but we only paid four and a half dollars a month rent for an apartment. Our little girls went along with us to the dry cleaners. When we were entertaining at night, we paid the going rate, fifteen cents an hour, for a baby-sitter.

Next, we moved to Mattoon, Illinois. I bought a bicycle. We lived a-ways from town, so I'd put Bonita on the handle bars and hold the younger one, Isabelle, in my arm, and I'd ride them to the baby-sitter. Then I'd go home and get Dugan; she'd sit on the handlebars and I'd pedal her uptown. In town, we'd get on a train and go on to our destination. I did this winter and summer and only once had a spill. It was icy-slick that day. Going over a railroad track, the wheel went out from under me. It didn't hurt anybody, though. I weighed only 128 pounds.

Maxine, our oldest daughter, lived with Dugan's folks after we left Cicero. They loved her so very much and she was a lot of company to them. They missed us all when we moved away.

Dugan and I decided Maxine should come and live with us to start school. So Mother Hartley brought her on the train. She stayed with us for two weeks. All that time, Mother Hartley was very depressed, became downright surly. We tried to ignore her feelings as we discussed our plans for Maxine. But she wore her feelings all over her face—looked like an old rag doll that had been thrown into a forgotten corner. Her eyes resembled two black buttons. Such an awful sense of hopelessness. Whenever she did enter into conversations, her voice was packed with misery. She acted like a hen being pushed off her nest.

Her despair was more than I could bear. "Mother," I said to her, "you might as well say what's on your mind. You aren't your usual happy self. It hurts us to see you this way."

She threw one hand up in desperation, shrugged, and was about to speak, but her mouth shut like a steel trap. My words were cutting straight through to her heart, I could see that. So I went on, "Mother Hartley, Dugan and I have been thinking—how would you like to take Maxine back home with you to go to school?"

"Oh! Oh!" She cried tears that had been building up for the last two weeks. She dabbed her red eyes with her lacy-edged handkerchief. When the girls came running into the room, she kept hugging them all. Her expression had changed into a glow; she was her happy self again!

Now, to Red Skelton! I could play all the instruments. If, for some reason a musician didn't show up—sick or whatever—I called Red Skelton to take my place on the drums, and I'd fill in for the sick man. A fine fellow Red was, and a good drummer—redheaded and freckled and one of our best friends.

He was always comical, good for a laugh—just like on TV—a very enterprising person with a most active and progressive mind. He bristled with ambition and talent—a sweet-natured, childlike clown who made everyone laugh wherever he went. He had a full head of red hair and freckles *all over*! On one of his Tuesday night TV programs, when he was a lot older, I remember him saying, "I used to use Head and Shoulders; these days it's Mop & Glow!"

I could take you right to the place where he lived in Vincennes . . . if it hasn't been torn down. His father died two months before he was born, and his mother raised four boys by working as a cleaning woman. She taught him an appreciation for the arts. Music and entertaining were in his blood—just as it is for me. He had run away from home, so from age ten on, he traveled with a medicine show, minstrels, circuses, burlesque, showboats, vaudeville—all those things.

Red always got an enthusiastic reception wherever he went. America's classic clown. He had so many funny jokes—all of them clean. Said that was because he had respect for his audience. Red liked the sayings of little kids. Here are some I remember:

> *A little kid kept wanting something and his mother would hurry and get it for him. He wasn't satisfied. She'd hurry for something else to give him. He'd whine and whine. She finally cried out in desperation: "Well, what* DO *you want?" He squalled, "I want something I can't have!"*

> *Preacher: "Do you say your prayers at night, little boy?" Jimmy: "Yessir." Preacher: "And do you always say them in the morning?" Jimmy: "No, sir. I ain't scared in the daytime."*

Preacher: "Good morning, Betty. I hear God has given you little twin brothers." Betty: "Yessir. And He knows where the money's coming from, too. I heard Papa say so!"

A father was passing his son's bedroom and overheard him saying his nightly prayers: "Dear God, make me a good boy. But it's all right with me if you take your time about it!"

A little boy had to be bribed to be good. His mother would say, "If you are a good boy today, I'll give you a penny." One day, the infuriated mother cried, "Why is it that you will only be good for a penny. Why aren't you like your father—good for nothing?"

A minister once asked a lad, "Sonny, who made you?" The boy replied, "To tell you the truth sir, I ain't done yet."

And he had jingles like this one:
"Ailing on Monday, bed on Tuesday, bad on Wednesday, dead on Thursday, sad on Friday, buried on Saturday, forgotten on Sunday."

But there I go, getting ahead of my story again. As we traveled to our destination, two of the boys and Red sat in the seat behind us—Dugan and I in front, instruments on back. That's when I had five pieces and we were driving fifty to sixty miles to a dance. The three boys put a curtain between the front and back seat, and they'd make up a show while we were driving along. Then they'd open that curtain and start performing—some of the funniest things you've ever heard!

Red kept an entire cast of characters in his head, trotting them out to entertain us. I can still hear the "here-we-go-again-kid a-whoop-te-do!" and we knew the belly-laughs were starting. With a theatrical flourish of his hat, he would call out, "It is good to see you all, folks. If you want to dance, get out and shake a leg!"

Even back then, he had his favorite characters—the same

ones he portrayed on radio and TV—a laugh riot that never let up. Junior, Da Mean Widdle Kid, with his baby talk, was one of my favorites; Clem Kadiddlehopper; Freddy the Freeloader; Cauliflower McPugg; and Bolivar Shagnasty. I think the funniest on TV was The Fuller Brush Man.

At one of his performances, out on the stage, he whirled his imaginary partner across the floor, dipped her way down, then pretended to drop her. You should have heard the crowd roar!

DUGAN WORE A FORMAL, and the band members and I wore tuxedos. She had more long gowns and I had more tuxes than we had street clothes. Women dancers came in their beautiful evening gowns that swept the floor, and men were dressed in their Sunday suits, white shirts and ties. Everyone looked so handsome!

We were the ideal couple—enjoying our work and family. But I remember one time when a streak of jealousy hit Dugan right between her bright blue eyes and threatened our happiness. She kept treating me very coolly. She was *not* loving our music, or me, as she always had. I could see she was like a cauldron ready to boil over. Finally I pinned her down. "What's the matter? You aren't your playful self!"

Dugan was livid. "It's that dishy chick. She's a designing hussy, and I should like to tell her to her face. She's out to get Speed Flanagan—playing up to you right before your wife's eyes! Can't you *see it*? You won't—you don't even want to! Every girl had her hat set for Sport Flanagan before we were married, but I didn't think I'd have that worry now! I've been so careful never to let myself go to seed, so you'd be ashamed of me."

As she sobbed, I tried to ease her sorrow by kissing her a lot. She kept twisting her apron in frustration and pushing me away. Her features were pinched; she had a red, shiny nose and great dark circles under her eyes.

Dugan continued tiredly, letting it all pour out. "She's trash. Nothing more than a snake, fallin' in love with a man she wants mostly because he belongs to someone else. And . . . she's a golddigger. She sees you—*money*. Always throwin' her hips around like a saloon doxie. She doesn't even dress decent. She's a greedy, selfish bitch who should have been drowned at birth.

"How would you feel if the shoe was on the other foot? What if I was a pushover for a feather-headed, woman-crazy guy who'd want to meet for stolen pleasure? I've been propositioned more than once—yes, *since* we've been married! You never gave it a thought that I'd be desirable to someone else, did you? If any man had persisted, I'd a put a knife to his private parts, you can be sure. I value my husband's and daughters' love too much to stoop that low. The Devil attacks marriage, and I won't let him kill mine!"

The "chick" had been coming to our dances, all rouged and powdered, in her drop-shouldered gowns, the most daringly cut of any lady's dress in the room. Her voluptuousness captured every man's attention and every woman's annoyance. She was one of those women who didn't like women, only men—preferably *married* men.

I began to see through her. She'd come shining in like a summer breeze, holding onto her beau's arm with a show of wide-eyed innocence. Then she'd ditch him and sally up to any man, single or married—made no difference to her. She thought she raced the blood of them all. I wasn't about to give her that satisfaction.

Pop once warned me of such women during one of his numerous lectures, after I whistled softly at a female going by. I said, "Wow, looky a-goin' there! Twists like a snake on a hot rock!" He clamped his teeth down on the butt of his cigar and said, "Now there's a woman bears watching. She's evil—no lady! Stay away from that kind. Yes, they are pretty if you like another man's castoffs. Damaged goods. When you're a man, you have only one thing to remember: *Be* a man. Look after yourself and don't go spending time or money on loose women. They can be predators.

"I don't like a fellow who forgets he's engaged or married every time he sees a pretty face. There's no brains between a man's legs. A woman can either make or break a man. There's been men who have lived a lifetime of regrets and unhappiness from a night of playing a bedroom game with a fiery little no-good bed-warmer."

This "dishy chick," as Dugan called her, took advantage of every opportunity to flirt with me. When dancing, she and her partner would waltz back and forth in front of the band. She'd catch my eye and give me a big wink, being overwhelmingly showy, then watch for Dugan's disapproving expression. I ignored her. It would be insensitive and arrogant for me to cast aside my wife's feelings.

One of the men dancers said the chick attended all the dances when other bands played here. She was forever flirting with him when his wife went "out back."

"At first I thought she was just fantasizing about romance," he admitted. "But she was persistent—even in my wife's presence. Thank goodness I got my eyes open. Just shows what a fool a man can be. Maybe she thought—that is, if she had a brain in her head—that I was a pushover and would encourage her, just to make my wife jealous. Some men-skunks do, then go bragging about it.

"I learned later she gave her favors to many men, even had a woods-colt and didn't make no bones sayin' so. Never mind whose toes she walked on or whose home she wrecked. Her next biggest joy was breaking up an engaged couple.

"The poor guy that gets her, does he foresee what life will be like? A real handful! No vittles in the house; no food on the table, or never on time anyway. Children—he'd wonder whether they even his—running the neighborhood like stray cats; and her off traipsing up and down Heaven-knows-where. Sure my wife was jealous. Wild mad! A bird always fights when her nest is threatened. Ma reminded me, 'The greatest gift a father can give his children is to love their mother, and show it in front of them.' And that's what I try to do."

Well now, I had this weighing on my heart. Had it not been for my feelings for Dugan, I may have felt flattered, even responsive. The old adage about being known by the company one keeps came flashing through my mind. Why should I ruin my good reputation? What would the folks back home think of Sport Flanagan? Look at the hearts I'd break. Divorce in our town was as odd as a purebred dog.

I took Dugan into my arms and said, "I don't have any time or inclination for a backstairs romance with a flip. I am under the impression my reputation is without blemish, and I intend to keep it that way. Just look what I'd lose if I had a fling: the love of my life—you, Dugan—and our partnership in music and family."

We made up and had a big cry. I told her how very sorry I was that I had unknowingly let her suffer through those weeks with her heart hurting so. Harmony was restored. The rest of the day we went fluttering about the house, laughing and crying by turn, remembering before we were married, walking hand and hand at the Fall Festival or to church, and our school-day fun.

I had difficulty locating my spine in order to stand up to the trollop, but I did! Why no, I didn't tell her it was making my wife jealous; that would be a coward's way out. I cornered her. She gave me one of her slow smiles and a wink. I'm sure she thought I was going to ask her for a date, but I said, "You've been making a play for me. I don't like it at all. If you can't come to the dances and be a lady, like the other women here, you can go elsewhere for your entertainment. I will stand for *no one* to ruin the respect Dugan and I have for each other, our band and our dancers. I run an honorable establishment here—one that folks are happy to attend."

She went stomping out and never came back.

Reminds me of when I was working with Pop, when he was teaching me his trade. A well-dressed man, wearing a derby hat and smoking a cigar, came in to order a ready-to-wear winter suit. In the course of the conversation he boasted, "I've pulled many a blind down in bedrooms around town—been in more homes and turned more doorknobs than a traveling salesman."

I could tell that infuriated my father. After the man left, I got my first lesson in sex education, as they call it today. That reputation, being easy to lose and, once lost, all but impossible to regain, must be guarded as zealously as life itself.

"Someday," he explained, "you'll hope to amount to something, and the time to start protecting your good character is before you even have one. Don't play around with anybody you wouldn't want to live with. You don't ever want to be seen in the company of a woman of questionable virtues. Trouble is, that woman hasn't a moral to her name. Her kind always smells like a perfume counter and wears clothes that fit her like skin on a sausage. Usually a bottle-blond with more tits than brains. Spending more time on her back than on her feet. There's a line between being a lady and being scum, and you know the difference! You have to be able to look past her to her heart and soul."

I was shocked! *Never* had I heard him speak so frankly. Then he went on to explain about the self-centered customer who'd just left.

"Why that pompous fool!" he almost shouted. "There are those kinds of men, too, but people don't recognize them like the hussies. He'd just love to start gossip going around, most of the time untruths, about an innocent young lady or wife and his and her escapades. Why, it'd ruin her life! A husband will often believe a scoundrel before his wife, sometimes to salve his conscience of his own misdeeds."

Another time, Pop pointed to a charming lady entering her husband's business, carrying his noonday lunch to him. Then he told me about this wife who took her umbrella, hooked it around the neck of the giddy woman standing there, and she cried out to her husband, "I'm not sitting back while this upstart hijacks my husband and causes a scandal, her a-coming in here flirting all the time. She's nothing but a low-down dirty alleycat!" The wife gave the umbrella a jerk—she meant business! The woman winced, but said nothing. This businessman's wife—she had class! And the alleycat didn't step inside that store again.

Now, back to my band. Nearly all musicians are temperamental. After a while you fire them or they quit. The hardest musicians to keep are those who have to blow hard over long periods of time: the trombone, cornet, reed . . .

Once we had a lot of agitation going and I couldn't put my finger on it. Someone was always nitpicking. One man, Jerry, lied, telling the other musicians that I paid him more than the others. He'd complain all the time that I wasn't paying anyone enough. Naturally, the whole bunch got sore at me, and I didn't know why until one of the players finally told on him. I up and canned Jerry. He said, "Why, you have to give me a week's notice. I'm a member of the union." I just reached into my pocket and paid him.

Earl, another musician, complained about his wages. I said, "What's the matter—I'm not paying you enough? I'm paying you the union scale." He said, "That ain't enough. I want a fifth of the intake." I said, "All right, if you're not satisfied, just quit. Don't play for us anymore." Bullheaded, he left.

Wherever I took the band I'd have to pay all their expenses, furnish transportation, their eats, hotel rooms, and buy their music. It took a good deal of money to run a band. They all knew I had to pay that, but some people are greedy.

Every band member that hit town came to my tailoring shop to loaf. Earl came in one day, says, "Speed, I'm just so hungry and I got no place to stay and I ain't got no money and I don't know what to do." I knew he had to be desperate to come crawling back. I said, "Earl, we're playing at Decatur tonight. Would you like to go with us? You'll get fifteen dollars." He jumped a foot high, yelling, "Oh boy, would I!"

He told Dugan later, "I found out who was doing the agitatin'. It was that Jerry."

Now, the whole story finally was out. I went down there to Jerry's rooming house and, boy, did I romp on him. Told him to get out of town and I never wanted to see him again!

On the way home from the dances, one or two o'clock in the morning, Dugan always went to sleep with her head lying on my shoulder. I wouldn't let anyone else drive my car—nobody else except Dugan, of course.

She was such a good mother to our children. She sewed all of our daughters' clothes. She'd make a coat for Maxine, hand it on down to Bonita, and when she outgrew it, Isabelle would wear it. Same with the dresses. Sometimes the younger girls got new dresses and coats.

When they were small, I'd play tiddleywinks, Old Maid, jacks, and all those kid games with them. We both enjoyed our daughters—we were together all day. Children need love as flowers need sunshine. It didn't take much sleep for Dugan or me.

I booked a job in Streator, Illinois. By now, we had a seven-passenger Buick with side-curtains and oh! it was cold. We were to play at Ashkum on Saturday night, then go 125 miles to Streator on Sunday night. Ashkum was a little town—smaller than Cicero. They had a large dance hall and people came from miles around to dance every Saturday night.

My trombonist wanted to play a job in Chicago. I gave him permission, provided he'd be back on Saturday night to play with us. He promised.

Driving to within ten miles of Streator, we ran out of gas. I walked to a farmhouse but nobody was home. I looked all around and there was no gasoline barrel anyplace. I saw a coal-oil tank, took some, left the amount I owed with a note weighed down with a rock. Then I poured the coal oil into the car and drove back to return the can. It got us into Streator in a trail of smoke! Phew! Oh, we were terribly cold. We had wrapped paper around our shoes to keep our feet from freezing, and we had big sheepskin coats on.

A huge, strapping Indian owned the Streator Hall. Big sign out front: INDIAN ACRES. A very large, red-hot, potbellied stove warmed the room. We were just about froze, so we stood around it to warm ourselves.

A lady came and called out: "Mr. Flanagan? I want to talk to Mr. Flanagan!"

"I'm Flanagan!"

"Well, Omer Sammy, the manager, wants to see you." And I said, "I'll go right to him." The office was out a-ways from the dance floor. Nobody was supposed to go back there a-tall. That was his private office.

Omer Sammy jerked up his big ol' head, cigar stub bobbin' like a conductor's baton, and yelled to me, "Flanagan! Open that gate and come in here!"

His voice then settled down somewhat. He stopped talking, stood, and put out his hand. "Howdy, Mr. Flanagan! Mighty proud to make your acquaintance. Now, I want to give you a little instruction on how you're to play tonight. First, I want you to start with waltzes. There will be a lot of old people here. Give them sweet, slow music—two-step, one-step—just for the old folks. But do 'em nice and *slow*. Then, ten o'clock intermission, when the old folks go home, I want you to romp on it!"

He'd been having big bands out of Chicago, like Coon Sanders and Darberger. Omer Sammy dressed so he looked like a mail-order catalogue on foot.

"Well, Omer Sammy," I said. "We're supposed to play at eight-thirty and it's now eight. I couldn't bring you but five pieces." Right then I could see he was a driven, demanding man with no patience for mishaps. His face looked like it was carved in wood. Certain lines around his mouth indicated that he was not accustomed to smiling very much.

Before I had a chance to explain, he jumped to his feet, and that old Indian went up in smoke. His big bushy eyebrows climbed to his bald spot and I felt he was going to pop me then and there. His neck corded. The scars on his face turned purple. He swore for ten minutes without repeating a word, which shot like bullets

Speed
FLANAGAN

through his gritted teeth: "What'll we do? What'll we do? #!#&! They'll run you outta here! They'll throw eggs atcha! #!#&! Ever'thin'! Dammit now, I've done swallered my cud!"

All this talk went into my heart like a sharp-pointed knife. To tell the truth, he had me scared to death. I said, as calmly as I could, "The trombonist promised he would, but he didn't show up. Here we are. I brought you five pieces and it's too late for you to get anybody else 'cause it is pert near time to start. The thing to do is to give us a try!"

I told the band of our conversation, and I stuck an extra trombone in. Musicians always could play other instruments when we needed them to. They were afraid they'd make big mistakes. Well, we played the sweetest waltzes, nice and slow, and the old folks all danced till ten, then most of 'em left.

Our band was always considered wild, and we really put on a performance that night. The younger couples came onto the floor like a big, screaming wave. Then the jazz, the rousing, foot-stomping rhythms, and our exhibition acts.

The sax player was over in the corner of the room a-playin'. The fill-in slide trombonist was a-hangin' down from a rafter in another corner, blarin' out the music, instrument a-flashin'. We others joined in during the chorus. Two of 'em drew together, playin' and bouncin' around like a coupla chickens in high rye. Each one of us had an act specialty—every imaginable trick—and all the time, loud and fast!

The kids were having a rollicking good time. As the night wore on—it was a hot one with windows and doors open wide—the shedding of clothes began. Men took off their suit coats first and piled them on benches along the walls, and then they loosened their ties and rolled up their sleeves. But they never stopped dancing, even when they were drenched with perspiration and their shirts were plastered to their backs.

I had one flashy drummer—Ralph Swisher was his name. He was better than me. I wasn't the flashy kind. I kept good time and rhythm for dances, but not showy. Ralph was light-footed and light-spirited. He came cartwheeling from the back room, along the dance floor and up onto the stage. He assembled his drums together and started in with all his favorite drumstick gymnastics. The crowd went wild! A sea of faces closed in to watch the exhibition.

During the breaks, the kids flocked around, cheering us on. All through the evening, whenever the dancers paused to change partners or to catch their breath, I would boom out, "Now, girls . . . you aren't going to let that floor get cold are you?" I knew, if the girls kept the boys a-dancin', they wouldn't be looking for trouble behind the dance hall.

So the good-time sounds lasted far into the night. The frolic over, the fellows would take the girls on home. We played at respectable places. What went on afterwards, we weren't accountable for. However, we did learn that the stork sometimes forgets to look for a marriage certificate.

Everyone left. We were all scared to death, wondering if we would get paid, much less, be asked to return. I walked into the office. Omer Sammy yelled—sounded *mean*!—"Flanagan, come in here!" I was so nervous, wondering how I'd pay my band if I didn't get a check. That's the experience you go through. You just never know.

He yelled again. "Flanagan, open that gate and come in here!" I walked in easy-like and sat down. He didn't mince words. "Flanagan, you got a durn . . ." But he used stronger language. I thought he was going to say durn rotten, but he said, "Flanagan, you got a durn *good* band here. You brought down the house. A real crowd pleaser! Do you want to come back next week?"

I swear I was so taken aback I like to choked. "Well, I'll have to look at my book to see if I have an open date," I said. 'Course I did have, I knew, but I got my book out and thoroughly studied it.

We went back there and played for a long time—all those kids a-dancin' the night away, dancin' like their feet were on fire! The

Indian never did have any of the big-name Chicago bands back as long as we were performing for him.

I fired that trombone player who hadn't showed up. He heard of our reputation up in Chicago, and he was mighty sorry he didn't fulfill his promise to us that night.

Once we scheduled to play in a park in Terre Haute. It just poured and poured on Saturday night. Two couples showed up. Went back on Sunday night. Rain. No crowd. Just four or five couples.

I saw the manager going through the cash register. And, as we were talking, I watched him take a handful of bills out and put them in a pigeonhole in the desk. He said, "Well, it rained and no one came. I don't know how I'm going to pay you." He pointed to the empty drawer. "Well, that's too bad," I said, "we had a contract and my band played."

"I didn't have a crowd!" he complained.

"I agree. You didn't have a crowd and the weather was against you, but you better get the money 'cause I've got to have it to pay my boys. They played. I saw you put some money up in the pigeon-wing of your desk. How about *that?*"

"Oh, I forgot all about that." He got it, counted the bills and handed it over to me.

We played a lot on college campuses. Oh, that was fun! Some of the popular tunes of those days were: "My Gal Sal," "St. Louis Blues," and "When My Sugar Walks Down The Street."

I have all kinds of records our band cut.

When radios became more common in the homes, dance bands gradually lost their popularity. So Dugan and I came back to Cicero and went into the cleaning, pressing, and tailoring business. People said they knew I was back to stay when they saw me wearing a cloth tape measure around my shoulders!

Even though we had our own business, we still had our band on Saturday night—four pieces: Dugan played piano, I was on the drums, a sax, a trombone, and our daughter, Isabelle, our youngest one, she sang. We played for the American Legion and for square dances at Odd Fellows Halls, the Grottoes in Indianapolis—lots of places down there.

I always hoped someday I'd have a chance to visit with Red again. I'm sad to say, I never did. But I tried never to miss one of his programs.

Dugan assisted at our cleaning shop—always. Couldn't keep her away. She loved people. I had the cleaning done wholesale in Tipton. Take it up in the morning, go back after it in the evening, and we'd press that night to have it ready for the next day. We gave good service. I'd see Dugan sit for an hour and half, sewing on a man's coat all along the ripped lining and under the arms, and she'd not charge a penny extra!

I had made-to-order clothes to sell, and I still have made-to-measure clothes.

We just never knew who was coming into our place of business. Dugan would go home and start supper, I'd step out to go to the post office for about ten minutes, leave the door open, get back, and there'd be two or three bundles of clothes with tickets all made out as to whose it was and the price marked. We had good, honest customers.

Old Loring Foster started opening up for us in the morning and he stayed till we appeared 'cause we still liked to sleep in—not as late as when we had the band though! Loring, an old bachelor, was a wonderful worker, dependable.

We never did hire help to do the work around our home. Dugan and I, we worked together. On weekends I'd sweep the rugs, mop the floors, wash windows, and take all I could off her. She worked for me during the week, so I thought that turn about was fair play. Well, back then, couples just never did work that way—together. Most men were afraid they'd be caught doin' *woman's work* and be considered a sissy—it was unmanly.

One morning, when I was seventy-one, I got up and never felt better in my life—like I was forty again! I always drove my car to work so I'd have it to drive to Tipton to pick up the cleaning. But this morning I felt so good, I walked. I altered pants in the back room between customers.

Along about three o'clock, I got a lady's cleaning off the rack to give her and laid them on the counter. My lips started to tremble. I couldn't hold them. It was just terrible. I thought it wouldn't amount to anything. 'Bout that time, Bob Payne came over and I was telling him how I was feeling. He's the druggist. He said, "Better get right over to Doc Havens!"

I didn't pay no attention to him, went ahead and finished the alterations. It kept getting worse till time to close, to go home to supper. My lips still quivered all over. Dugan was sitting on the front porch and saw me coming home, staggering like a drunk. Out she came running and got me up as far as the door that went onto the porch. She had to drag me into the house.

She put me to bed and called Doc Havens. He came running over when she told him about me. He took my blood pressure and said, "Sport, you've had a light stroke. Don't go down to your shop a-tall. If you don't want to stay in bed, just stay at home. But don't go to work!"

I stayed there for three months. Dugan ran the store, took care of everything perfectly. I walked with a cane. When I got better, we took a trip to California.

Dugan and I got along good for fifty-seven years. Live with a man for that long—or vice-versa—both has to be right. Everybody has their spats. We had ours—little ones that don't amount to anything. Then we'd be right back on good terms again, and later laughing about how silly the disagreement was.

We had a very nice time all of our married life—all fifty-seven years. And then she was gone. Gone—just like that. Saddest day of my life. I've been so lonely ever since, but I've kept working here in my tailoring shop. I miss her. We always worked so well together. We both liked doing things to make each other happy.

To me, the final act says so much about the human spirit. You live out your dreams until the end. Life is a series of challenges. And it's too bad when people think the challenges and adventures are over and you're just waiting to die. I want to continue to keep busy. If I had it to do all over again, I'd do it just the same way!

People can make the most or the least of what they are born with. I believe that all men are created equal and that everyone has within himself the power to make this a better world.

I once heard that there are two kinds of talents—man-made talent and God-given talent. With man-made talent you have to work very hard. With God-given talent, you just touch it up once in a while. I'm sure my talent and Dugan's were God-given, but we did a lot of touching it up!

Tri Town Topics, November 23 and 30, 1972
Cicero, Indiana: 1834–1984

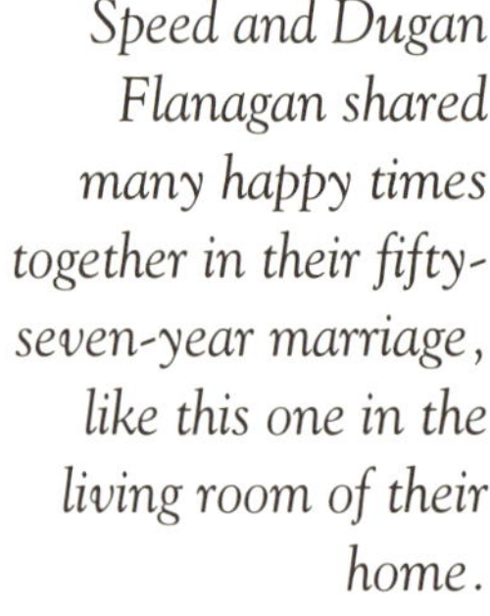

Speed and Dugan Flanagan shared many happy times together in their fifty-seven-year marriage, like this one in the living room of their home.

Lois Costomiris

Grandpa Lost His Funnybone Twice a Year — Spring and Fall

I loved listening to my husband Bud's family stories. This one especially I related to. When I was a little girl, I longed to live in a candy house like the Costomiris family—Dad (Sam), a candy maker; sisters, Helen and Georgia; and Bud. Sam owned a confectionery store. Many will remember his Sweet Home in Noblesville. Bud's mother died when he was seven. Sam never remarried. My fantasy was somewhat fulfilled—being the recipient of many boxes of chocolate candies—but I became a farmer's wife. "Puttin' up the stove—or takin' it down" was my favorite story when I joined the family, an anecdote that will probably linger for many generations!

FARM COUPLES WEREN'T KNOWN to get divorces. Many have said that if they ever came near, it was through the ordeal of taking down the heating stove—or putting it up!

Taking down the parlor stove. This was a new experience for Ed and Lizzie Venable's grandson, Edward "Bud" Costomiris, named for his grandfather, age seventeen, a recent high-school graduate from Detroit, Michigan. He'd known only steam-heated apartments.

Bud was tall and dark, showing his Greek heritage. He was continually laughing, flashing prominent white teeth. He had rented acreage, and was purchasing farming tools and pursuing his life's ambition—farming. In his senior year of high school, each student was required to make a notebook about his desired vocation. Out of his class of 432, Bud had been the only one interested in agriculture.

Grandpa Venable was a wisecracking, bantering comic, thin as a pitchfork handle. He looked as though he could do with a square meal. Ed's bib overalls hung on his lean hips. He admitted his legs looked like hog-rubbed saplings. He grew old and toothless—had a face seamed with more than seventy years of outdoor farm work. His alert eyes had funny birds-foot wrinkles and happy lines at the corners. Life by him was richly enjoyed. His speech bubbled with wit—he spent half his life clowning. Seeing him and his wife together, this ditty came to mind: *Jack Sprat would eat no fat, his wife would eat no lean. Betwixt the two, they licked the platter clean.*

Ed unmercifully teased and pestered his serious-minded, hardworking wife, Liz. Folks said she was a woman who knew the value of a dollar. Grandpa would laugh and say, "Liz watches a nickel to make sure the buffalo doesn't ride away with it!" He had a live-and-let-live philosophy. "We can't do anything about yesterday," he'd say, "but we sure can spoil today by worrying about tomorrow."

He was as lively and mischievous as an old rooster, and whenever anyone asked him how he felt, he'd break into a jig to demonstrate his health and vitality. "Oh, waltz me around again, Nellie . . ." he sang and did a fast two-step around the kitchen, grabbing the broom for a partner.

He never crossed his wife, never argued with her in any way but jovially, and he never lost his temper, except over political issues, or the heating stove—but we'll get to that. He laid everything at the door of the politicians and lawyers. He told anyone who'd listen where the fault lay: "It's them durn lawyers and Washington crooks. The whole dang shebang!" He, like so many others in this all-Republican Hamilton County, Indiana, thought a Democrat was one who crawled on his belly.

Grandma was a short, pudgy, dark-haired, careworn little farm lady, neat and clean, energetic but humorless. A go-getter. An apron covered her colorful cotton house dress. Her mercerized, tan cotton stockings were knotted at the knees. Liz spent her time hustling about, keeping everything inside the house, and out, in spotless order. She was intolerant of wasting time in fun-making.

"Now, Liz," Ed would often say when she continuously worried about family finances, crops and trials, "can't you ever see the funny side of things? I reckon Heaven will be all gold and wings and harps and pearly gates, but you can enjoy some of that here on Earth!" She'd answer, "One thing it *will* be—no scrubbing floors, washing dishes, making beds or carrying out the pot."

Grandpa had a digestive rumble in his stomach at the beginning of every meal. He'd pat it and say, "Worms, be still!" That was so funny to young kids sitting around the table. When Bud was a little fellow, he wished his stomach would growl like Grandpa's. Grandma would say, "Ed, take a bite or two to settle your belly down. It's a-carryin' on like two cats in a fight on the back porch."

The Costomiris children went to school in Detroit during the winter months. Just as soon as it dismissed for summer vacation, the three boarded a bus for Indianapolis, then took an interurban to Cicero. As soon as it stopped and unloaded passengers, the three took off in a mad run to their grandparents' farm—a couple of miles from town. On the way, they stopped at childless Orin and Carrie Brown's for handfuls of cookies and a drink of cold water from their pump. They joyously spent the many weeks ahead living and working in fresh country air, eating nourishing farm meals and enjoying entertainment that was much different than they had in the city.

As a little fellow, Bud followed in his grandpa's footsteps everywhere—trying to stretch his little legs to step in his grandfather's tracks across the barnyard. Behind them, Collie barked and bounced from one track to the next.

Grandpa operated on this theory: All you need is a roof over your head, a shirt on your back, and something in your belly. "I'm kinda content," he'd say, "lovin' God, my fellow man, and the good earth!" Heaven, to Ed Venable, was eighty acres, a good wife, a dependable team of horses, and a hot meal three times a day. He never desired to be rich. "Don't worry and don't complain; hard work never strains the brain," he'd say.

He'd warble favorite tunes as he went about his work: "It came to my window one morning in spring, / A sweet little birdie, she came there to sing. / The song that she sang was prettier by far / Than ever was played on a flute or guitar."

While doing his farm work, he wore patched, faded-blue bib

For Ed Venable, Heaven was eighty acres, a good wife—Lizzie, pictured here with him—a dependable team, and a hot meal three times a day.

overalls—like all farmers—and a blue denim work shirt over his union suit. The stringy column of his neck looked like a plucked turkey's, thrust out of the top of his underwear.

Bud had graduated from high school and moved down to the farm. He also wore bib overalls and blue denim shirts—but no long underwear all summer, like Grandpa.

But Grandpa Venable lost his funnybone twice a year: spring and fall, when he had to take down the sitting-room stove in late April and put it back up in early October. He had all but used the divining rod in search of a way out, but to no avail. This circulating heater, at those two times, was an intruder that disrupted the tranquility of the whole home.

It all started in late spring—housecleaning time—on the morning when Grandma, tying her apron strings in back, announced in her kindest manner: "It's such a gorgeous, warm day; let's take the sitting-room stove down this morning before you and Bud go to the field. Then I can get my housecleaning started."

Ed's jolly, sunny disposition turned sour. Grandpa, a masterhand at joking, had no stories to banter today. To any and all who would listen, he let them know that housecleaning was more than he could bear. He roared, "I despise havin' the house torn up, an' you know it! Hate takin' down the stove. Have to set in the kitchen, the only warm room in the house on cool evenings. Have to hunt all over the house for my rocker. Haphazard meals." He was probably thinking, until this housecleaning jig was finished, there'd be no fresh-baked pies every day like he was accustomed to. Yes, he liked a slice of pie for breakfast, too!

Take down the stove! Grandpa's prominent Adam's apple worked up and down like the plunger on the kitchen pump as he reached for his cup of coffee. He flushed an angry red, and his chair slid back with a bang! "Hells bells!" he shrieked up an octave. "I got work waitin' out there. You think all I have to do all day is set in the house and look at my navel?"

Grandpa's Adam's apple. When he was just a little fellow, Bud would crawl up on his grandpa's lap and feel up and down his neck. "Tell me a story, Grandpa." Grandpa bounced him on his knees as he sang a ditty, then said, "I can't tell stories, but I might lie a bit." Bud would laugh and say, "Aw, Grandpa, you're funnin' me. When I get old, I'm gonna have a *big* Adam's apple, just like yours." Grandpa laughed. "You hear about Stringfellow? He had the longest neck of any man in town. His Adam's apple made only two trips a day!"

While Bud was reminiscing, he realized a respectful silence had fallen over the room. A kitchen that always smelled of sugar cookies or fresh-baked applesauce cake, now held no scent to savor. Grandpa's bald pate popped out with sweat. Everything but the teakettle held its breath; it sang and hissed merrily at the pronounced doom. Grandma's canary tucked her head under a wing.

He set his jaw and bellered: "Do you have to git in sich an all-fired hurry? Come blackberry winter and you'll wish you'd left 'er up! 'Sides, I have to go over to help Bub Welsh work on his pigs this mornin'." From that moment, Grandma took command of the situation. "That beats all," Grandma challenged. "You know the cookstove will give enough heat for the three-day, early-June spell. Bub Welsh can wait another half hour till . . ." She placed the food on the table.

"Bud," Grandpa motioned, "pass the sow belly an' eggs and reach over there for the cow grease, jelly an' toast. Help yourself first." Then he groaned, "Why cain't y'jist leave 'er up year 'round? Other people do. Don't cart 'er off to a shed." Grandma was unyielding. "Lawsy mercy, how do you think I'd clean the rug? It's easier to roll the stove out and take up the rug, than to try and prop the stove and pull it out from underneath!" Bud's grin widened as he listened to his grandparents rant and rave.

Grandpa was taking his time drinking his second cup of coffee. Grandma busied herself in the sitting room, placing papers all around the stove to keep the black soot from falling onto the rug when they took down the pipe. Even though the rug was winter-dirty, soot made a very stubborn, greasy stain and was hard to clean up.

She took out the ash-pan and set it beside the back door, its dead ashes to be scattered later. Then she followed the two men into the sitting room.

"I just read in *Prairie Farmer,*" Bud said, "the easy way is to take the stovepipe down all in one long section, turn it to the side, and ease it out the door . . ."

Grandpa pulled on his old, battered felt hat and yelled, "Who elected you boss of this outfit, you young pup?" He jerked the stovepipe from the wall and showered himself full in the face with fine ashes. He was not a profane man, but he had a rather tightly controlled bag of colorful words which he reserved especially for these drastic occasions.

Grandma stood back and watched, all the time advising: "Hold it tight . . . Don't sift soot and ashes all over everything on the way out . . . Watch when you go around that corner an' don't knock it apart an' dent it . . ."

As Grandpa and Bud lay the pipe down in the grassy backyard, she continued: "See that rust hole? Be sure and buy a new section . . . Clean all the ashes and soot out and oil it good, so it won't rust . . . Try and remember which sections go together after you take 'em apart, so you won't have such a hard time gettin' 'em back next winter . . ." But, even as she spoke, she knew it would do no good.

"On a rainy day, Liz," he promised with an exasperated sigh. Her advice was seldom followed. Most farmers had a bad habit of putting off repairing their farm tools or anything else until they were badly needed.

Back inside they all came. A gush of wind suddenly blew down through the chimney hole, scattering ashes and soot. Grandma grabbed the flue stopper. Grandpa reached up and slapped it into place until Grandma had time to clean out the hole properly. He scrubbed his hands on the sides of his overalls, then worked a fresh

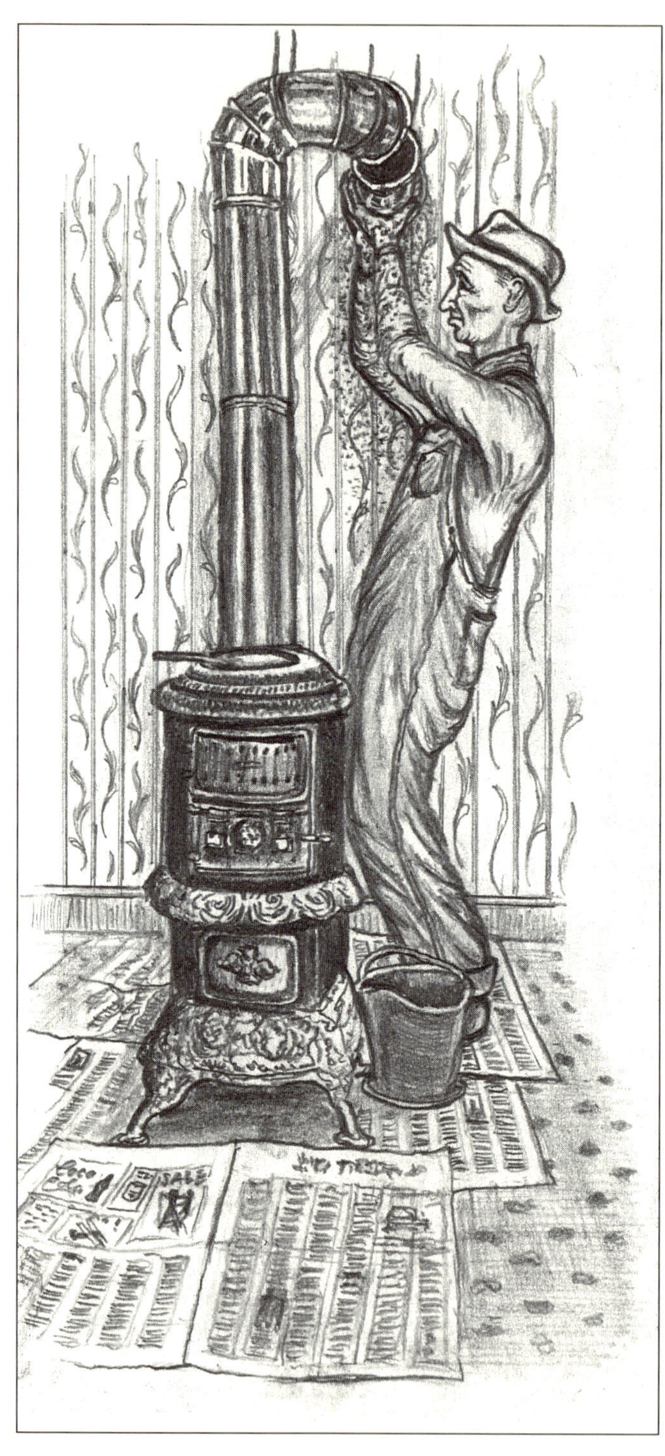
SALE

cud of tobacco around his mouth from one cheek to the other. Grandpa shot a look at Bud: "Don't stand there with your mouth open. A bird might drop in. Get a wiggle on. Go bring the stove trucks. Be back before your dust settles . . ."

The trucks were borrowed from Blann-Boone Hardware Store in Cicero and were used to take the stove to the storage space in the smokehouse. On their next trip to town, the trucks would be returned.

Bud still remembers the day Grandpa went to Cicero for them. Grandpa hitched his team to the wagon. Down the road, he picked up an elderly, arthritic Mr. Whitesell. Mr. Whitesell'd always remind Grandpa, "You'll have to lift me up there, Ed. When we come home, I can fall off! These pegs o' mine—they's a-gittin' weaker and hurtier as the days pass. I'm as slow now as a man with the seven-year itch an' six years behind on his scratchin'!"

Mr. Whitesell was a Civil War veteran. When he was younger he rode on the rear gate, his legs dangling, like an overgrown boy's. Nowadays, anytime Ed went to Cicero, he'd pick up Mr. Whitesell and set him up there on an age-worn chair. The old man, who smelled of liniment, rested his hands and chin on the handle of his cane. Ed grabbed the lines and clucked at the horses, Maude and Lori. "Giddy-ap!" The team took off.

"Neighbor," motioned Mr. Whitesell, "scootch over here closer t'me so's we can wind on the way to town." He held up a kitchen match and struck it with his thumbnail to light his pipe. Both men liked to talk about the olden days.

Bud brought the stove trucks in. Grandpa snapped, "Stand back till I have 'er set!" He worked furiously. "Buggered if I know what's the matter with this consarn thing—it won't lift. Here, young rooster, go get a brick and a long board. We'll have to pry 'er up. And make your heels fly!"

Bud was back. Grandpa pushed the plank under, then rested it on the brick behind the stove. He leaned heavily on the plank gently—oh so gently—then the catch caught. "Watch, it's gonna go over!" Grandma yelled as everyone grabbed to hold the stove upright.

When Grandpa was rolling the giant hunk of iron recklessly out, Grandma cried, "Don't scrape the floor . . . Watch the wallpaper—don't scratch it . . . Don't bang the woodwork . . . Be careful goin' down them steps . . ."

And so the stove was put away for the summer. But Grandma wasn't through with Grandpa yet. And there was no way for him to avoid the next trap: to take up the rug and carry it to the clothesline to have its accumulated winter dirt beat out.

Grandma swept off the brown, four-foot-square, asbestos-metal-covered stove board, making it ready to take outside to be scrubbed and put away with the stove. Underneath that board, the clean square rug area looked up righteously. As all of the carpet wore and became permanently discolored from use, this spot remained new-like.

Grandma and Bud hurriedly moved all the furniture to the next room, out of the way, so the carpet could be taken up. Grandpa, again, turned into a demon at work, rushing about like his britches were on fire. He took the tack claw and furiously pried up each carpet tack. They were spaced closely along the four sides of the rug to hold it securely stretched.

"Liz, why can't *you* take out these gol-durn tacks, and we can roll 'er up and take it to the line at noon?" Grandpa asked. "I gotta git goin'. Time's a-wastin'!" Grandma raised her finger to her lips warning Bud to be silent. Of course Ed knew why. The rug needed to be beat with strong arms and the rug beater, then hang all day to air.

She frowned as she watched her husband snap off some of the tack heads—those couldn't be used again. Bud offered to do it but Grandpa shoved him aside. Grandpa got off his knees and went to the corner where the rug was nailed down with a shingle nail to keep the rug from working loose, but it wouldn't give. His rough hands could chop a cord of wood, give the gentlest caresses to a little child, but could not manage this household task.

"Now wait a dang minute," Grandpa complained as he studied the carpet. Then he took hold of it and, with all his might, he yanked it up the length of the room, leaving a string of carpet yarn all along the sides. The air filled with flying tacks, dust and unprintable language. Grandma almost exploded. Bud's shoulders shook with a fit of laughter. "Jist go ahead and laugh," Grandpa gasped. "Hit ain't no joke to me!"

Grandpa skinned his knuckles, bruised his fingers and got a sliver of wood under his thumbnail. He took his old sweet time digging the splinter out with his pocketknife, then sucked at the blood, continuously making verbal observations about the weather outside and his work still waiting. Grandma, too, worried about the weather. That's why she chose a sunny day. She didn't want it to rain on her rug hanging on the line when the men were in the back fields.

"Oh, sin!" Grandma bawled—as near as she ever got to a cuss word. "Why, I never in my life heard anything equal to it." She picked up stray tacks and put them into the saucer with the others to be used again.

Bud, on his knees, was ready to help Grandpa roll the carpet and carry it to the clothesline—one man on each end. Grandpa, with his puffs, pants and groans, was heaving up his end when he expelled a big blast of wind—the result of yesterday's navy bean-and-cornbread meals. He stood straight, rubbed his tense back muscles, stomped his foot hard and yelled, "Holler if you're lost!" Bud about choked laughing.

As Grandma picked up tacks, she told Bud about little three-year-old Mary Emma Illyes. Mary Emma, watching as her mother put carpet tacks to her lips—in handy reach when tacking down the rug—imitated her mama with tacks in her little mouth. Before Mother Ada could rescue her child, a tack slipped down Mary Emma's throat. Mary Emma came up choking and crying!

Sam and Ada Illyes rushed their daughter to the doctor. Doc

wasn't too concerned, said, "You go home and feed her mashed potatoes with torn-up cotton mixed in with them. Then watch her movements till she passes the tack." Ada found the well-wrapped, cotton-covered tack sometime later.

When he was a little fellow, Bud was always fascinated by the way Grandpa's mouth sprouted nails while he hammered. They were easy to get when he was repairing roofs or loose barn siding. Now, Grandma's mouth sprouted carpet tacks!

"Ed," Grandma yelled, painfully aware he was testing her patience all the way, "you're tearin' those papers!" Feet that could lightly dance a jig at the first suggestion of a tune and could swing all over the floor like a puppet on a string during a Saturday night barn dance, were now awkward and clumsy.

Grandma was glad for these gray felt strips that were made special to lay under carpets. They padded the rug, kept out drafts from the cracks in the floors and were supposed to make the carpet wear longer. Years before, she'd used a padding of a heavy layer of clean straw from the strawstack, as all ladies did. With constant traffic, the straw would mat down, then crumble, causing dust and chaff underneath. Mice would work under and make nests in it. When newspapers were more plentiful, she layered *them* beneath it. And now, all these years later, her wonderful felt strips! Grandma carefully rolled up the yard-wide felt ribbons, took each to the yard and unrolled them, to be swept off with the broom later.

How proud all the ladies were when the Olson Rugs, patterned on both sides, came into style. One side for spring, the other for fall—double the wear! Two prominent colors in the patterns—green for summer, brown for winter. These rugs came in two sizes: eleven-feet-three-inches by twelve feet, or nine-by-twelve feet. Most women bought the smaller, cheaper size.

Women boxed old wool rags—suits, coats, pants—and sent them to the Chicago factory with their Olson Rug Catalogue order. With each pictured design, the rag poundage was stated. There was also a cash payment. The rugs were easily affordable and just as pretty and more durable than most store-bought ones. Some ladies now had the linoleum, board-patterned strips lying along the sides of the room to give a polished-floor effect.

As Bud and Grandpa went out the back door with the rolled-up rug, Grandma was reminding: "Don't break it in the middle . . . Push up the line-prop, so the carpet won't drag the ground . . . Here's the beater—watch along the road for anyone coming, so they won't see . . ." At that, Grandpa expelled a held-in breath, "Drat it all!"

In the country, as in town, the housewife didn't want her neighbors to see how dirty her carpet was. Even though it was swept with a broom each morning, much of the soil was walked down through it. Town ladies often had their husbands hang the rug out on a clear night to get a good beating after dark when no one could see all the dirt fly with each lick of the wire rug beater.

The weight of the rug pulled the clothesline down almost to the ground. They placed a prop on each end of it, pushing it up higher so air could circulate better. His manhood asserted, Grandpa plowed right on. His muscular arm, taking swooping whacks, wielded the beater mightily. His blows hid the sun behind the clouds of dust. No matter where he stood, he always seemed directly in the path of that dirty fog. He beat! Beat! Wham! The dust mushroomed! Grandpa coughed, choked and sneezed, but refused to surrender the beater to his grandson.

Grandma picked up an old tin bucket and a shovel, then she headed to the emptied room. She crawled up on a stool to scoop out ashes and soot from the flue. She had part of a roll of matching wallpaper and a small batch of paste to paper the chimney wall that had been stained by heavy rains seeping down through.

Finally, a quiet calm settled all around. Grandma realized the men had finished and were probably out harnessing the horses to take to the field. All day long she worked, taking time out only to hastily prepare the noon meal, which was eaten in subdued quiet.

As soon as Bud and Ed returned from the field in the evening, they brought in the rug. In no time, the room was back in order with a clean, tacked-down carpet, soap-shined woodwork, sparkling windows, freshly washed, starched, and stretched curtains, and polished and positioned furniture.

After the milking was done, the men came into the kitchen to good supper odors. "Beans 'bout ready?" Ed asked. He and Bud went in and looked the room over with pride, before sitting down to eat. A network of wrinkles shone at the corner of Grandpa's amused eyes as he said, "Y'got everything lookin' as fine as a butterfly's behind, Liz." They all laughed.

ALONG ABOUT THE MIDDLE of October—a threat of snow in the air, sounds carrying unusually well—the serenity of the household was again blown sky high with Grandma's announcement: "Let's put the stove up this morning before the weather sets in."

Grandpa, with a face as long as a hoe handle, gave her a polite, quick freeze as she donned her dust cap, pinned a cloth around the business end of the broom and headed into the sitting room to sweep away any errant cobwebs along the walls.

Bud hurriedly got to work, getting things ready, hoping to appease Grandpa. He knew the stove's heat would feel mighty good when they came in from a long, cold day of corn shucking.

Bringing the stove back in—it wouldn't go through the door like it had gone out, even with a desperate sort of manipulations. They jiggled and joggled and then tried brute force to push it through. Grandma screamed that the men were scraping paint off the door jamb. Then it was decided that they should take the door off its hinges. The fact of the matter is that they had never been able to get it back through without taking the door from its hinges. But they had never been able to resist trying.

And so, the process was repeated in reverse from spring. Grandpa complained: "Why couldn't we have rolled 'er over into a corner and thrown an old quilt over 'er like some people do?"

Bud continued to serve as a shock absorber between the two. As he hurried around helping, he'd hear Grandpa occasionally shout, "Don't tell me how!"

Both men followed each other from the smokehouse with pipe joints to put together out in the yard. The stove had been thoroughly checked for rust, cobwebs, bird droppings and dirt-dauber nests that had accumulated out in the smokehouse during the summer. The damper was scrutinized.

There was a cry from Grandma: "Ed, I thought I told you to clean out those pipes when you put 'em away! How often do I have to spell it out!" She could be thankful he hadn't brought them inside the house to put them together on her still-clean rug! Ashes, left in the stovepipes for the summer months, drew dampness and rusted the pipes quickly. They would probably have to be replaced—an expense that could have been avoided.

Grandpa strained and swore as he and Bud started to match stovepipes and fit the end of one pipe inside the other, just right. Then they carried them through to the sitting room. Carefully they positioned it, twisting and squaring the elbow joint around.

Grandpa yelled, "The danged blasted thing ain't right. We'll have to take 'er out an' start the whole shebang over!" Ed always said the Devil invented stovepipes just to try a man's patience. Sometimes, when the stove was all set up, Grandpa had to wear mittens for three days because the palms of his hands were so sore.

As they took the stovepipe out through the door, Grandma cried, "There's a bad section. I thought you were going to buy a new one!" Grandpa muttered, "Everybody to his own taste, said the old lady as she kissed the cow." He let her fuss on and on. All the while, the new one was lying outside in the grass. Sometimes she knew he was being spiteful just to hear her fume.

"Bud," Grandpa ordered, "go out in that old cow manger and get me some bailin' wire so I can wire this gol-durn pipe together here. Get the wire cutters and tin snips out of the shed on your way." Bud came back: "I can't find the . . ." Grandpa cut in, "It's there, plain as the wart on a billy goat's nose. They was a-layin' right there on the . . ." Bud knew his grandpa was careless about putting away tools when he was finished with them. "I looked there and I looked where you used them last time we . . ." Grandpa's graying eyebrows wiggled like hairy caterpillars as he grumbled out of sight. "If y'want anythin' done 'round here, jist as well go yerself!"

Grandma was telling Bud she was glad they didn't have a stovepipe that stretched far out into the room like in some homes, schoolhouses or churches. They had to be anchored with wire to the ceiling in several places to keep it from falling apart. What a task it would be installing *that*!

Bud's bedroom was upstairs. A floor register allowed heat to flow to it. The chimney wall was always warm. He remembers many a morning he'd wake up with snow on his covers.

Most houses had high ceilings—ten or twelve feet up. Women recognized the reason tall husbands were always complaining about the heat. Standing on a footstool to hang curtains—oh, it was so much warmer up there! Years later, folks lowered their ceilings with sectioned plasterboard.

When all was in place, Grandma eyed the stove and pipe to see how it lined up. "Oh my, look at that stove board—it's whopper-jawed." The stove board had to be set just so—straight, squared off—then the stove could be put into place. It probably shifted when the trucks let the stove down.

Grandpa gave a slight lift with the trucks. Under his breath he said, "So danged pertickler." Bud, on his knees, eased the board back into place. Grandpa said, "Better make a nice fire now. You go hustle somethin' up, *Costa-smear-butt*." It was Grandpa's affectionate nickname for Bud. Grandpa had his good humor back and was chanting: "She could sing and dance and flirt / But she could not sew a button on her old pappy's shirt . . ."

Bud brought cobs, kindling, coal oil and wads of newspaper to start the fire. That afternoon Grandma had polished and shined the Base Burner with stove polish until she could see her reflection in it. The old stove stood grinning with shiny satisfaction. Bud put a match to the paper and kindling, then he added coal. The stovepipe ringled with expansion. The heat from the stove and pipes filled the room with familiar eye-burning, smoky smells as the polish burned off. "I'd better open the doors to let it air out in here," Grandma said. "I can hardly breath."

"Yeah, and waste all that fuel, even before we start heating for winter. You women and your noses!" Grandpa snorted as Grandma fanned the smoky air out the door with a dishtowel.

The first fire built in the heater was probably the most cherished one of the entire winter. Grandpa always started a corncob-and-kindling fire in the cookstove each morning before he and Bud went to do the milking and other barn chores. He'd shake down clinkers in the Base Burner and add a bucket of coal. He took the ashes from each stove outside and emptied them.

After supper, on a real cold night, the feel of snow in the air, Grandpa would say, "Good night to crawl between the kivers with my favorite she-pup!" He'd dance in from the kitchen carrying a dishpan of popcorn and a bowl of Jonathan apples, singing, "Say good-bye, say good-bye, say good-bye to the old apple tree. / If my Pappy had of knowed it / He'd be sorry that he growed it, / For they hung him on the old apple tree . . ."

Some stoves were set quite a ways from the wall, and the space behind it was the warmest in the house. Here, a daybed or pallet was usually kept, reserved for a sick child or an adult's afternoon nap. But at Grandma's, the stove set too close to the wall for a daybed. In the wintertime, Grandma put up a folding wooden clothes rack back there. The warm heat dried long underwear, flannel shirts, overalls, or diapers when grandbabies made visits.

It was a favored spot for small grandchildren, since it was always draft-free and warm back there. They'd play with their dolls and wooden blocks or they'd build clothespin log cabins. A newborn baby could sleep comfortably in its bassinet, away from drafts. It was also a good place to take Saturday night baths or to dress on a frigid winter morning.

This warm spot near the stove was often the bed of the family dog. But not at Grandma's. The dog wasn't allowed in the house.

Grandpa and Bud wished the whole house could be this cozy-warm. Grandma was always fanning and wiping away perspiration, even in the coldest winter. She couldn't understand why her hot flashes lasted into old age! Bud couldn't understand how Grandpa could wear his long underwear year-round. Whenever Grandpa got a new pair to start a winter out, he complained, "The wrists of these gol-durn things are so tight I can't push 'em up to scratch!"

Nighttime, Grandpa hung his overalls and shirt on the back of a chair near the side of the stove. One morning when he was putting his clothes on, a mouse—no doubt sleeping cozily all night in the warm overalls—ran up Grandpa's leg! Grandpa yelled, clutched at his pants and slapped at the overall leg, dancing all around the room on one foot. Grandma and Bud came a-running—was he *hurt*? Grandpa grabbed the mouse, held it tight while he was taking his pants off, then handed the overalls to Bud to shake the mouse out the back door.

A special coal for the Base Burner had to be purchased—no wood was burned in it, like in some circulating heaters. It took a lot of time and hard work to cut and bring in wood for their cookstove. Liz conserved heat by letting it die down after each meal. So up on the flat top surface of the Base Burner, she cooked pots of ham an' beans, hominy, stew, or soup. The coffee pot always held hot coffee.

Outdoors was a two-room coal house. One side was filled with coal. The other room had corded wood for the cookstove and a large pile of cobs and kindling for starting fires. A filled coal house gave a secure feeling.

There were the lazy men who cut only enough wood on Saturday to last the week. The whole neighborhood worried for that family when they knew a big snow was coming, except, of course, *that man*! His wife was a bundle of nerves and generally out there wielding the ax. Occasionally, a competent man cut wood a year ahead. It dried out good and burned better. At the beginning of winter, his wood house was stacked full!

To many men, the stove served as a dandy spittoon when their thick dark tobacco juice rolled into the ash pan. Some—smoking cigars, cigarettes, or pipes—opened the door to shake off the ashes. But not at Grandma's!

Throughout the winter there were admonishments: "Look at the way that stove's a-smoking! You forgot to open the damper! . . . I'm cold. Open the damper! . . . Yeah, open the damper and let the heat go up the flue and waste all that fuel!"

Grandma moaned. "If only we were rich and had a furnace, I'd not have to sweep and dust every single day. There'd be no ashes to carry through the house. Yes, sweeping and dusting ever' blessed day! A good furnace and we wouldn't have to wallpaper so often, or clean it every spring." Only the few rich town people had furnaces, but it was every woman's fantasy.

"Oh, tarnation!" Grandpa roared. "Wish in one hand and shit in the other an' see which fills up the fastest! Why didn't you just marry a rich guy?"

More than anything, Lizzie, as a schoolgirl, had wanted a high-school education and to be a schoolteacher, but her father was dead set against it. In his mind, schooling was a complete waste of time for a girl. She'd only get married anyway, he'd say. So Elizabeth Berg went to grade school and then married Edward Venable.

The warmth from the stove on that first fall night brought back memories to relate to and laugh at. "Ed Griffin," said Grandpa, "before his marriage to Mary, Liz's sister, he told everyone, 'Nothin's runnin' 'round our yard after we're married but a black iron fence!' They filled their house and yard up with ten children."

Grandma laughed. "One time the Griffin children had cousins

a-visiting them. Some of the younger ones spent long, fascinated hours lying on their stomachs on the rag rug in front of the stove, turning the pages of the Sears Roebuck or Montgomery Ward catalogues.

"Anna, the Griffin's oldest daughter, was to entertain her sweetheart that evening. She worked all day getting the house in order. Her dad teased her, 'Beaus don't go where cobwebs grow! Who you swappin' spit with tonight? You know that'll give ya hydrophobia!'

"In due time everyone went on to bed. The young girls—Anna's sisters, Margaret and Katherine, and cousin Helen Costomiris—high-tailed it upstairs ahead of the younger boys and got into their winter flannel nightgowns. Katherine said, 'Let's nib! Do you suppose he'll get fresh with Anna?'

"Sometime later, downstairs, where Vaughn Seeright and Anna were sitting on the brown leather davenport, something broke the silence. There was a sporadic sizzling sound. Another. They both listened. Again. Again. Vaughn went to the stove and opened the door and looked inside. Nothing. Above the stove, out the corners of their eyes, they saw a string of water dropping and splashing onto the hot stovetop with a sssizzzlle. Then Anna, with a knowing smile, excused herself and went upstairs.

"There, three heads on the register—bodies spread out on the floor like spokes of a wheel—lay the peeping girls. The warm air from the stove, the golden glow from the dimly lit lamp, vapors from the steaming teakettle, and the quiet mumblin' had anesthetized them and they had fallen fast asleep. Saliva slipped from the corners of their mouths, dripping onto the hot stove below. Anna, laughing and shaking her head, helped each of the girls, with their register-imprinted faces, to their feet and on to bed."

One woman told about a man taking down his stove. This guy always had a bad temper whenever anything went right *or* wrong. The stovepipe had rusted almost through. When he pulled it from the flue hole, it broke in two where his hands held it. He was so mad, he proceeded to stomp each section flat, right in the room! Listening to the story, Grandpa put on his most foolish grin.

Fires! There was a constant worry in every family of the house catching on fire when using stoves of any kind. In 1934 Guy Gilkey's house burned. They said Glen Miller's house burned one winter night when it was colder than the Devil. The fire was caused by a faulty furnace.

Lightning struck Henry Heinzman's house with such force that it caused combustion—blew it all apart before it caught fire. The lightning caused so much heat that every place where there were nails on boards that hadn't burned, there were burned places. Neighbors from all over gathered to help the old folks, Mary and Henry, and their daughter, Louise, safely out. This was the second time the Heinzman's lost their home by fire. The first occurred because they lived so close to the railroad tracks. Sparks from the train ignited their shingle roof and burned the house to the ground.

John and Cora Kepner's house caught fire one hot fall day and burned down. The two heard the rumbling as they were eating dinner at noon. The flue burned out, spraying live sparks all over the dry shingles.

William Boatright's house was struck by lightning and burned down on a hot summer day. Neighbors from all around came and carried out what little could be saved.

The house on the Pet Buzan farm burned. (Farms always retained the long-ago owner's name.) Mrs. Wright, the owner at that time, built a new, modern, ten-room, full-basement house. She and her son and family, the Maurice Lyles, all lived together. On the enclosed back porch was a coal-oil stove they used in the summertime to cook meals, and for canning and heating water on wash day. The stove was the cause of the fire. A new porch was built on and you can't tell the difference today.

Mrs. Wright told Bud and Lois Costomiris about the fire when they bought the farm in 1946. Mrs. Wright didn't believe in electric wiring in the barn—a fire hazard. Most people felt safer with lightning rods on their buildings; others thought they'd only attract lightning.

Many of the neighborhood barns burned—either from hay combustion or lightning: Bert Mosbaugh's, Wib Davis', Hez Webster's, Lacy House's. Most buildings had wood-shingle roofs. If the fire hadn't gotten too big a start, men formed bucket-brigades and took water to douse it out.

Stoves, be they the kitchen cookstove or the sitting-room heater, served a vital role in the home. Besides their usefulness and cheerfulness, the Base Burner, the Warm Morning or Airtight stove was delightful for daydreaming. The mind goes traveling while the body remains watching—comfortable and entranced.

Today, all these many years later, Bud remembers walking a mile to see neighbor Bob Gilkey on a cold winter's night. Coming back home, he'd see the lovely red-glowing isinglass windows of the big Base Burner! He looked forward to its pleasant warmth which would bring feeling back into his cold fingers and toes.

When he'd drive home from a ballgame on a dark winter night, he'd see the bright white light from Grandma's Aladdin lamp and the flickering flames from the stove.

Aside from the turmoil it caused, the sitting-room stove furnished a cozy warmth throughout the long, cold, dismal days.

This twice-a-year chore that disrupted the tranquility of the home, stood in penitence through the winter, radiating a warm glow for everyone to enjoy.

Tri Town Topics, November 7, 14, 1974
Good Old Days, May 1981
Cicero, Indiana: 1834–1984

Jean Groves and Jane Hadley

The Hello Girls

When I wanted a telephone-operator story for my newspaper column, our local ladies had passed on, but these two in Arcadia happily obliged. Jean and Jane were telephone operators in Arcadia, Indiana. Jean started work in 1939, and Jane came in 1950.

THE TELEPHONE OPERATORS were the best-posted women in the neighborhood. They were considered the heartbeat of the community. Nothing would have uprooted them from their stools, nor would fire or flood have found them fleeing their posts.

In the days before radio and television, the spoken word was a vehicle for news, gossip and the telling of tales. Back then, someone said that a small town is where the telephone operator gives you the right number when you ask for the wrong one.

There was a lot of teasing about "The Hello Girls." People joked, "Anytime a woman suffers in silence is when her telephone is out of order" and "An executive knows something about everything, an expert knows everything about something, but a switchboard operator knows everything about everything!" And the kids' favorite: "The three modes of communication are the telephone, telegraph, and tell-a-woman."

JEAN AND JOAN DESCRIBED what it was like to be a Hello Girl:

Our job—the telephone operator, or "Central" as most called us—consisted of not only answering calls, but also blowing the noon whistle and the curfew whistle at nine every night.

We memorized all local numbers and learned to recognize voices. This was more advantageous to the subscriber than to the operator. If the party being called failed to reach the phone before the caller hung up, we usually knew by the voice who the person was and we'd promptly ring them back.

All flashes of lightning sounded on the telephone wires—a sharp click that made us hold our breath. A fire? When there was a fire, we hurriedly called the firemen. Our office was headquarters in times of disaster and need.

The telephone was a big wooden box that hung on the wall in the home, usually in a kitchen. The old phones had a receiver, a black mouthpiece, a transmitter, two batteries, and a crank to turn the magneto to ring Central. When it was cranked, a little jack or drop would fall down on the switchboard. The operator would pick up a cord and plug into the hole just beneath the drop. We'd push the key forward and say, "Number, puh-leese." Then we took the corresponding cord to match that number, bring it up and plug into the numeral you wished. We'd pull the key forward to ring into that home or business.

If you wanted somebody on your party line, you cranked them yourself. Need two longs and two shorts? You'd grind the crank two long sounds, then two short ones. There were phone numbers like 131AB and 131C. The letters designated the rings in the home.

Sometimes we'd have fifteen or sixteen people on one party line, and each had a different code. There were all kinds of rings:

one short and a long, two shorts and a long, two longs and two shorts, three shorts, and as high as five shorts and a long or one long and five shorts. All the neighborhood people were linked together. When it rang in one house, it rang in all the others. Your ear quickly tuned to it and readily recognized everyone else's ring. A new one? Immediately you're alert: Who has moved in?

The operator knew the history of every family plugged into her switchboard. Folks on the telephone would tell the neighborhood problems, all their troubles and cares and woes.

We could identify each voice. Some would always holler when giving their number and when talking on the phone, thinking, I guess, they couldn't be heard otherwise. Very early phones were often quite noisy and folks had to shout to be heard.

One woman was famous for her shouting. During her phone sessions, she would turn aside and speak in a lower tone to someone back in the room with her hand over mouthpiece. She never knew that her "asides" carried more clearly than her hollerin'.

One old farmer couldn't hear thunder, but we always knew who he was calling and we'd ring for him. If the line was busy, we'd try to get the message across. He'd get so mad: "Whadja say?"

Sometimes the rings came in fuzzy and were hard to distinguish, like when there was bad weather. This old guy would take down his receiver and ask, "Who'dja ring?" Even if the call was not for him, he'd stay on the line to see what it was all about. He'd get a loud report from another on his line: "Well, I hope that old goat gits his ears full!"

Most homes had a telephone years before electricity came through to our town. One old codger snorted gruffly, "That'll be a livin' nuisance! Terrible extravagance! Why, I can git in my buggy and go visit. I'd rather talk to somebody I can see. I already know what's goin' on in town 'bout as soon as it happens. I don't want nuthin around that'll electrocute me or my family!"

But before we knew it, he conceded its value. "Gosh, I never thought I'd see one of them things in this house. Just think, to talk with someone clear in town, without even having to saddle up a horse and ride the distance! All I had to do was ring up Central and tell her who I wanted. And just as easy as that, I had my party!"

After being hired in, we operators soon memorized all the numbers. But some, men especially, would never give a number—just, "Operator honey, ring up Maw on her telephony for me, please. How's things goin' with ya there in town?" One gruff old man went to his phone, turned the crank real hard and barked into the mouthpiece: "Operator, git me the bank! Number? Hell, lady, I cain't be bothered lookin' up numbers. *You* git it. Your job. There ain't that many telephones in town!"

A Cicero man was telling about when their phone rang the first time after it was installed—his wife hurried and changed to a clean apron and patted her hair into place before answering it, just as she did when a caller came to her door. Another man said his wife was as nervous as a witch, jumping every time the phone rang, which was constantly.

Often we'd get a neighborly call: "I'm going to be gone a while. If my ring comes in, you take the message for me."

One young mother stopped in Cicero's office to pay her phone bill. The operator asked, "Where are you going all dressed up this early in the morning?" She answered, "I'm driving to Indianapolis to shop for the day. There's some really good sales."

Sometime later that morning, the woman's very frugal grand-mother-in-law rang to visit with her. The accommodating operator laughed aloud. "You'll have to wait until evening. She's shopping in Indianapolis all day."

The operator left the grandmother to stew about such an uncalled-for trip—clear to Indianapolis, twenty-five miles away—and wonder how much of her grandson's hard-earned money she'd spend foolishly. But this was money she'd saved from her sewing jobs. She'd take advantage of the end-of-the-month sales to buy yard goods to make more clothes for her dressmaking customers.

"Number, please." Early telephone operators needed a number of skills, from handling all the equipment, seen here with "Hello Girl" Clara Boone, to being a public-relations specialist!

But Grandma wouldn't understand.

Every Monday, without fail, a bride from the city—now a farmer's wife—would ring in: "Operator, is it safe to hang out my wash?"

She called her mother-in-law one evening, just beside herself. "Ma! I was getting ready for the Sunday School class party and I cooked the spaghetti. I put the lid over the top and was draining the steaming water from it down into the slop bucket. The lid slipped, and spaghetti, water and all went into that mess. What will I do?" Usually no one bought extras of things like spaghetti, especially not a bride on a limited budget.

Her husband's mother answered, "Just put more water on to boil. I'll send Pop down with another package and my colander. You drain the spaghetti into it, over a stew pan this time! Now, settle down. You'll laugh about this fifty years from now."

With the daily regularity of a well-wound clock, she called her mother-in-law after breakfast every morning, asking about meal ideas or recipes, telling her what the new groom would be doing on the farm or asking about planting her garden or raising baby chicks. One day an irate farmer broke in on the conversation. He barked, "Who in Sam Hill cares if you washed your sheets and bedspread? My cattle got out and I gotta call someone to come and help me round 'em up!"

On top of everything else, we were supposed to forecast weather. Some farmers even called us for the cattle, hog, and grain market reports. Of course, we didn't know, but we'd plug them into the Farmers' Elevator.

No one ever rang in at noon for any reason short of a catastrophe. It was the time of day when everyone was busy with dinners for hungry farmers and field hands. Most town women had their men to cook for, too.

The telephone also served as a warning signal. A woman down the road would crank a continuous ring, which everyone would recognize as the sign of an emergency. She'd call if she saw a tramp sauntering by, a band of Gypsies, a big puff of smoke at a suspicious location, a threatening black funnel cloud, or the milk inspector. There were so few automobiles; any questionable one, they'd wonder—is it a salesman you want to avoid by not answering the knock at the door?

That milk inspector! Farmers sold either grade A or grade B milk. There were more stringent health regulations on grade A, and that milk brought a much higher price. It was quite a chore to keep the milk house and barn spotlessly clean, so this warning was much appreciated, especially if they hadn't had time to completely do up the morning cleaning.

This telephone office has always been in the same location, on the second floor of the Central Bank Building. Our cage had metal bars all around. We always kept the door closed and locked.

For anyone needing to come in, we'd push a button on the switchboard to open the door. Patrons had to walk up those steps to pay their phone bill. Also, there was a pay phone booth. Many, without phones in their homes, came up and used this one.

We realized that phone visiting was the only social outlet for some women. A few ladies were nosier and gossipier than others, but the right-minded operator courteously kept them under control. The telephone was no instrument for confidences for people in Arcadia, nor in any other small town, for that matter.

Infidelity was one of the favorite subjects for party-line gossips. They promptly lined up on the side of the "poor, wronged little wife," and groaned at the disloyalty of male deceivers. Or sometimes it was the other way around: "That little blond leech! I'm glad he had the guts to finally break loose!" or "The poor, helpless, innocent creature was conceived in sin."

"The number of married men who tried to date us was shocking!" Jane laughed. "These were guys who didn't know who we were or that we were happily married. I was tempted to make a date with one man I knew pretty well—just to see the expression on his face when he saw me!"

We recognized those with "secret affairs" who used the booth. When the man (or sometimes a woman) gave us the number, we knew instantly who he was calling. When this happened, we'd talk about it later, uttering no names: "One-forty is calling sixty-three!"

One married man, from a city a few miles away, had a sweetie here in town. He would come clear down to Arcadia to call her. "Oh, goodness," said Jane, "I'd get so nervous I could hardly plug in the right trunk!"

We had three shifts: 7 A.M. to 1 P.M.; 1 P.M. to 6 P.M.; and 6 P.M. to 7 A.M.

JEAN STARTED OUT WORKING NIGHTS. Later, she was mostly on the board during the day. Jane worked nights for a long time, then went in as bookkeeper and also worked nights.

Many remember these lady operators who worked different years after 1950: Mary Zeiss, Leurie Eller, and Mary Chenoweth. Bookkeepers were Emma Cunningham, Joan Rutledge, and Evelyn Pontius.

Sometimes there were two operators at the board at the same time, but not often. The head operator taught the learners on the other switchboard. Jean taught Jane when she came to Arcadia. Jane had worked in Noblesville and Cicero, so it didn't take her long to learn.

When someone called in a fire the operator always asked, "Which direction?" Each section of town had a designated ring: two blasts for northwest, four blasts for northeast, six blasts for southeast, and eight blasts for southwest. They still do it, but they send it out from the town hall now.

As soon as this fire whistle blew, the operator had to be on her toes! Seems all drops on the board would fall: "Where's the fire, Operator?" She could have plugged in a whole bunch and told them all at once through the open keys, but someone might be ringing in, not knowing there was a fire or maybe even for another emergency, like calls for an ambulance or a doctor.

Folks were trained not to bother Central about the fire's location for at least fifteen minutes, since some of the firemen further out would call her for the site of the fire and go directly there. These were all volunteer firemen. They usually lived and worked around town and were always faithful to the job.

There wasn't any rest during a storm. The lightning kept causing most of the drops to fall and the operator had to keep testing to see if someone might really need the line. The bell kept ringing as long as the drops fell, and she'd often get bad cracks in the ear from lightning.

In homes, families were warned to stay out of the room where the telephone was, because lightning could come in and give a shock. Some threw a feather pillow over the phone, thinking it would arrest the electricity. Lightning came in on the telephone at one house and set the phone afire. The husband pulled it loose and threw it out the door in a downpour of rain. It's been known to come in and blast the phone right off the wall! At one house, it blew a hole in the wall across the room.

Again, after a storm, people called in continually, reporting damages it caused, like downed trees, broken power and light lines and animals killed. They'd come to town to report their telephone was out-of-order.

Many other emergencies came through: a death, a very sick person, a lost child, farm accidents, a sick horse or cow, heart attacks, births, tornadoes, an occasional robbery, the cancellation of important events, and yes, we even had a suicide or two. In the middle of the night, when the whole countryside was asleep, the sound of a telephone came only to report sickness, fire, a baby on the way, or a death. We don't remember ever having a rule of "no calls after nine o'clock," as in a lot of places. People didn't ring in late; they knew we operators needed our sleep. Most folks were in bed by that time of night anyway.

If the ambulance went out with its sirens blaring, all the calls again: "Has there been an accident? Do you know who's sick? Who are they taking to the hospital?"

At night the operator actually went to bed, wearing her own pajamas and sleeping on her own bedding. She had a cot that pulled up under the switchboard, and all she had to do was raise up and turn around to take the call. It was set up so that when the operator went to sleep, if a call came in, the drop would fall and ring a bell to arouse her.

She took her bedding and pajamas home once a week, laundered and ironed them, and brought them when she came back to work. You can be sure she waited for a sunny day!

One couple had a new baby every two years. He'd go, in horse and buggy or auto, inform the doctor, then bring back their neighbor lady to help with the delivery—but he never phoned. He didn't want everyone listening in.

They had only one window and that was by the board, so we needed the electric light switched on all the time. The bookkeeper's desk was across from the board with a light over it.

"Was I ever scared at night?" Jane asked. "Sometimes people had to come up the stairway late to make a call, but it never alarmed me. An electric light, with a sixty-watt bulb, hung down from the ceiling on a cord out there. We had a steel door with bars, and it was locked, so no one could get in. But a paperhanger who lived on the other side of the steps committed suicide one night when I was working. *That* was scary!"

"I remember one midnight," Jean said, "I heard a commotion and I looked down on the street from my cot and saw two men, quite inebriated. One was hanging on the telephone pole, very sick, saying, 'I wanna go home!' The other one fussed with him. 'Why in the world do you want to do that? Aren't you having a good time?' He answered, 'I hafta pee!' The other man persisted. 'Then go out to that privy back there. By the looks of your pants, it's too late! You go home now and your ol' lady'll be waitin' fer you with her rollin' pin.' "

"One time," said Jane, "when I came to work, Jeanie could see I was so sick. She insisted she keep working the next shift. I was sure I'd be all right, so she went on home. The longer I sat at that board, the sicker I got. I called Jean. When she got back, someone was in the booth, trying to make a call to his folks in Tennessee and it was urgent. I just couldn't get the call to go through. Half the drops were down on the board. I don't remember how I ever got to that board to push the door button to let Jean in, but when she came, I was never so glad to see anyone in my life!"

One time, a hysterical mother was screaming, "Operator, my Billy just swallowed something out of a bottle Grandpa kept in the bottom of the cabinet, and I don't know what it is!" I said sternly,

"Stick your finger down his throat!" "What for?" she wailed. "Never mind what for! Just do it right now while I get the doctor for you!" The doctor went there immediately, but the danger was over. The child was sitting on her mother's lap, happily chatting and clapping her hands. Picking up the mysterious bottle, the doctor took a sniff and a taste. "Vodka," he said. "Tell Grandpa to hide his booze where the kids can't find it. This could have been a very sick child if you hadn't made him puke it up!"

"Years ago, there was a small switchboard at Deming," Jane said. "My niece, Ercel Kinder, worked there. I'd visit her and help run the board. We were never busy, so when we got bored, we'd call people we knew and sing to them. They liked it!"

Ercel always knew when a certain drop was showing up erratically—that child! "Betsy Sue," she scolded fiercely, "hang up your receiver this very minute and stay off the telephone!" The three-year-old was frightened by Ercel's voice. She dropped the receiver and ran away. Ercel would whistle loudly in the transmitter. "Bertha! Bertha! Keep your baby off the phone!" She yelled until the embarrassed Bertha would come running and hang up the receiver—without so much as a thank you.

There were times when kids annoyed the operator—usually when their parents had gone to town. They'd eavesdrop and then add unasked-for bits of naughty information.

One distraught mother, so terribly busy, let her unruly child keep playing with the crank, ringing the phone, to keep him from bothering her. Oh, sure we reprimanded the mother. That distraction was going in on all the phones on the line.

Camilla Axelrod's mother, Barbara Allen, was a telephone operator in Westfield for many years. As a small girl, Barbara would visit her Aunt Mollie McKinley, the operator at that time. Barbara would turn a cane-bottom chair on its side, take pencils, tie string to them like a telephone cord, and poke them into the caning. That was her "play switchboard." She'd carry on with her make-believe callers: "Are you having club today? . . . Is Mary at home? . . . Where's the fire? . . . Is your baby still teething?"

Jane laughed as she recalled an operator who worked a twenty-four-hour job from a small exchange at her home. The husband was the maintenance man—a husband and wife operation. Operator: "Lula, did you say two longs or three longs? . . . William, don't upset that pan of milk . . . Browns aren't home today. Call them when it is time to do the chores . . . Mollie, get William away from that pan of milk and go blow his nose . . . Do your kids all have colds, too? I think you might find Bessie at four-oh. Would you like me to ring her for you? . . . Mollie, see if that bread is ready to put in the oven. Don't bump it; it'll fall. And see if your little sister is still napping . . . Why, Sheriff, I haven't heard from you since Hector was a pup! Whatcha comin' out here for?"

One handsome bachelor always came in from the country and used the phone in the booth to call his intended. He claimed he had too many interested neighbors on his line and not only did he not want them to hear what he had to say, but with them all listening in, he couldn't hear—they all had their receivers off the hook.

And there was another man who came into town to call because he said he could drive to town and get through faster than if he waited for some old tongue-waggin' hens on the line to quit talking. Yes, we understood.

One fellow would come in and phone his ex-wife long distance. It went like this:

"Are you coming up?"

"Well, do you *want* me to come?"

"Well, do you *want* to come?" That's all they ever said, over and over, for about an hour, until he finally said, "Well, I guess I've bothered you long enough." Each time, when he hung up, he'd mutter under his breath, "She can just go stick her head in the rain barrel as far as I'm concerned!"

You see, the operator had to open the key intermittently to say, "Are you through?" to clock the caller's time when he finished talking, then disconnect the cords if he was. We had our own opinion of those two: she was a poor catch anyway.

Central generally knew about the conversations concerning a new baby, one expected, a thrilling romance or a wedding. We knew the high-school couples who were going steady and those who were getting more serious. Sometimes there was a call for help from a couple who'd gotten stuck in the mud down on Lover's Lane—their automobile had to be pulled out.

Tipton was the toll-center outlet for long distance calls. All of them going to Indianapolis, Chicago—all over—had to first go through Tipton. Most would never ring in for long distance, anything short of a death in the family or another difficulty. Even today, many of the older folks feel guilty making long distance calls unless they're for emergencies. In those days they were considered the height of extravagance, especially if they were longer than three minutes.

On Mother's Day and Christmas, it would often take many hours to make contact—if at all. Some calls had to go through several cities, and maybe the operator would almost get there and the last circuit would be busy. She'd have to wait, then start all over again. One from Maine to California required the services of eight different operators! Some folks were considerate—others impatient.

Even though we stayed busy, Christmas was still a joyful time for us. Folks brought in all kinds of cookies, candies and other gifts. As soon as one of us tried out a new recipe, we'd bring in samples to pass around.

Sometimes there were six or seven long distance calls going at the same time, and that many time-tickets to clock carefully. We had to be on our toes! "Your three minutes are up." We'd give that warning signal. Of course they could talk longer, but most wanted the time limit. During all of this, we were still busy putting the local calls through.

The operator had to watch the clock, to write the time down

on a little card when the conversation started and again when it'd finish. One lady fussed that she didn't talk overtime, 'cause she had her three-minute egg timer right there by the telephone!

Someone was always calling in for the time of day, especially of a morning when the kids were getting ready for school. They had forgotten to wind the clock the night before.

If school was called off—a snow storm or a flu epidemic—the board would be busy with kids calling each other reporting no school, to save them walking a long lane or from a far distance here in town.

Most everyone knew the telephone operator by her voice. Children associated her speech with the phone. They were astonished, if a mother brought them in when she paid her bill, to see a body was connected to it! Most adults would tell us our faces didn't look like how they had pictured us in their mind.

We could count on the board lighting up about the time a ballgame was over. "Operator, could you tell me the score of that game?" We were the source of all kinds of information: "Where's Book Club tomorrow?" or "When did so-and-so die and when's the funeral?"

Esther Correll, who's eighty now, started on the board here when she was sixteen. Her sister, Nell Marquis, was operator at the same time. They took Dr. Hicks' calls. He was single—no wife to take messages when he was out. Doctors and veterinarians always left word with the operator when they had to be away. The operator would write down messages and then report to him when he returned.

Eavesdroppers. There was always a telephone audience, although you never knew how many were in it. While everybody engaged in the practice, nobody intended to be caught. Usually the receiver was eased off the hook and a hand covered the mouthpiece. But sometimes it was easy to pick out who it was by the clock ticking, a baby playing nearby, or a rooster crowing just outside the kitchen window. Sure, most farmers had chickens, but they weren't allowed in the yard; only that one lady didn't mind them scratching around her flower beds.

There was Charlotte's singing canary and Betty's talking parrot saying continuously, "Hello! Hello!" and a parakeet chirping, "Pretty Baby! Pretty Baby!" One lady never bothered to replace her receiver on the hook gently. If something annoyed her as she listened in, she'd slam it down.

An old asthmatic lady would put her hand over the mouthpiece, but still we could hear her trying to get her breath. It was her only enjoyment—hearing about the church social, her sister's catarrh, or the winter weather forecast—so she was overlooked.

One lady listened with proper tongue-clicks, especially when overhearing about a husband's drinking problems, a wayward son, or a daughter's new beau she didn't approve of.

Without fail, if a mother wanted to listen in, or when she had a call, that's when the kids or house pets would start acting up. "Is that your dog barking?" one caller asked. The woman laughed, "Yes, Old Blue, that pest! He lays at the kitchen door all the time and keeps barking when I'm talking. He wants in!" Another lady had a house-dog and every time she was on the phone he'd drag out a shoe, magazine or something from the clothes basket and start chewing on it.

There was the bothersome caller who seemed to never have anything to do but hang on the phone. Goodness knows she could have been kept plenty busy making a path through the house if she had wanted to. It got so annoying. When one busy neighbor didn't want to waste her time talking to her, she would say, "I'm going to have to hang up. I'm coming down with one of those sick headaches." Another said she'd use the excuse, "I hear someone knocking at the door. I must go." But the caller would reply gaily, "That's all right. I'll wait."

At the meat market, the meat cutter got a phone call. It was his landlady, although she didn't identify herself. A customer asked him, "How'd you know—you didn't mention a name?"

Laughing, he told her, "She always calls me Shitass!"

Carrie and Orin Brown, a childless farm couple—one or the other sat near the phone and listened into every conversation. A salesman or peddler dropping by, Orin would continue with the receiver to his ear and chortle to himself, signaling for quiet.

This agitated Bub Welsh, a close neighbor. When Bub rang one of his farmer friends, he splintered the air with his abrasive speech and off-colored jokes. If Carrie was listening, she'd cut in, "Why Bub! You shouldn't be talking that way on the telephone!" He'd snap back, "And you, Carrie, shouldn't be listenin' in on the grapevine!'"

"When General Telephone took over in 1955," Jean said, "they tried to cut our wages. We said if they did, we'd have to strike, although we didn't believe in striking. Our wages were very low as it was. They said they didn't care if we did strike, because they had workers from Pendleton who could come in and take over and run it as smoothly as we did. So, we struck. Workers came and brought their own cots and bedding, to stay on until we came to terms.

"In about three days, they were out of their mind—said they'd never seen such a crazy board in all their life! It was mass confusion with wrong numbers, and everybody was complaining they couldn't get who they called. Such a mess! They had been used to a board that lit up, and these were drops. Folks knew of the strike and, just for meanness, some asked for a party by name, not number. The new operators were awfully glad to get us back on the job. And, I might add, we got a raise."

The switch from manual to dial was a sad moment indeed—not necessarily because our jobs were terminated, but because the very pulse of the community was abruptly suppressed. The old switchboard, that minutes before had been so alive, was suddenly a monstrous, blank, useless contraption.

"When the dial system went in," Jane explained, "and the dial tone replaced 'Number, please?' the closeness of the community was never the same. A lot of people said that when the telephone operator was gone, the heart of the community went with her."

Most women were proud of their desk dial phone, the black ones that replaced the big, old wall phone. Then gradually these were exchanged for colored ones.

There was a newspaper write-up of a retiring operator. She said, "It has been my privilege for the past forty-three years to have my ear on the heart of this town, and I shall never forget what I heard!"

Listening—or rubbering, as some called it—was a popular pastime. Then the radio came into the homes, and women heard the woes and wiles of Ma Perkins or Pepper Young's family—more important than hearing about someone in the family down the road.

"I think everyone felt just as I did," Jean said. "Something was being sacrificed to neon lights and supermarkets and dial phones. It was a farewell to the past that was filled with many unimportant but beloved little things too simple to survive in a complex world.

"We both just loved it all—working for the people and being such a vital part of the community. And I'd still like being an operator if there was a board around," Jane said. Jean nodded in agreement.

Phone Charges in 1926

Single-line business	$2.00
Party-line business	$1.75
Single-line residence	$1.75
Party-line residence	$1.50
Party-line rural	$1.50
Extension telephones	$ .75
Extension bells	$ .25

Add 25¢ if paid after 15th of month.

Arcadia Telephone Directory

Jean and Joan both have big collections of old Arcadia Telephone Directories. On the previous page and below are some interesting items from a book dated from the 1920s, when Arcadia was a busy, exciting place to live.

Tri Town Topics, March 27, April 3, 10, 1975
Cicero, Indiana: 1834–1984 and *Cicero, Indiana: 1835–1976*

Instructions to Subscribers

- One quick turn of the crank gets Central. Don't make a long ring; it hinders the operator.
- Hang up and ring off when through talking. (Most didn't do this.)
- Please answer your ring promptly. Operator will ring subscriber three times. Failing to receive an answer, party calling will be informed "will not answer."
- Do not attempt to use the telephone during a thunder or electrical storm, as the operators are instructed not to make connections at those times.
- The use of profane or obscene language over the lines is prohibited.
- Subscribers will be held responsible for all toll charges from their telephone. If your friends want to use your telephone to make a toll call, ask the operator for the toll charges, tell her it is OK, and then you collect from the friend.
- All long-distance talks are limited to three minutes; local talks to five minutes. (Usually these rules were not followed, except for costly long distance.)
- Answer your ring only.
- Do not take down the receiver during the conversations of other parties on the line. This weakens the connection and causes unsatisfactory service, besides exhausting the batteries on your telephone.

Arcadia Telephone Directory

Hello, Central!

Hello, Central! Give me Heaven,
For my Mamma's there.
You will find her with the angels
Sitting on the golden stair.
She'll be glad it's me who's speaking,
Call her, won't you please,
For I want to tell her
We're so lonesome here.

When the girl received this message
Coming o'er the telephone,
How her heart throbbed in that moment,
And the wires all seemed to moan.
I will answer just to please her,
"Yes, Dear Heart, I'll soon be home."
"Kiss me, Mamma, kiss your darling
O'er the telephone."

—Author unknown

Shelton Bishop

Operator, Send Out the Repairman!

Before my marriage, I was a telephone operator. It was there I realized the importance of the telephone repairman.

I GUESS I PROBABLY KNEW more people in this Tri Town area—Cicero, Arcadia, and Atlanta—than anyone in these parts!

I came to Arcadia on July 15, 1941. I hadn't been here three days when I knew it was going to be *home*.

I had worked to pay my way through high school in Hoopston, Illinois, during the Depression. I wanted to be a veterinarian but there was no money for that. So I got a job at the Arcadia Telephone Company.

I roomed and had my meals with Sarah and Nettie Bowser. Sarah told me one day, "There's a young lady next door I want you to meet." She took me to see Mildred Pettijohn. I didn't know anyone like Mildred existed. Right then I fell head over heels in love! And, I might add, it was a determining factor in Arcadia becoming my home.

Mildred had graduated from high school and then music college. She was teaching piano lessons and volunteering as director of children's choirs here in Arcadia.

We hadn't gone together three weeks when I asked her if she would marry me. She thought I was fooling, but I meant it! We were married November 2, 1941. We have a daughter, Nancy. Later, we raised Mid's niece, Grace McNew. Folks said Grace looked more like Mid than her own daughter. I guess Nancy took after me.

The Arcadia Telephone Company was established in 1904. It has always been in the same location, in the Central Bank Building here in town.

The telephone workers have had a lot of fun—from July 1941, to now, February 1975—forty-three years! I have so many fond memories.

The two-foot, wooden wall telephones weren't hard to service or install. Big, long screws fastened them to the wall. The plastering was pretty thick , so sometimes we had to make two or three tries to hit a lath to be sure it would be secure when it was hung. Most of the phones back then were put on an outside wall, and I'd go in with the wires to it.

I'd notice, when I was ready to install a new one, sometimes there were three to four coats of new-like wallpaper around the edges where I took the old one off the wall. Some wrote frequently-called numbers on the wallpaper next to the phone, or emergency ones, like the doctor's.

Tall telephone poles lined the streets in each town and all the gravel roads in our county. Some had weathered too many storms and leaned badly from age when I was first hired on. Several wires were strung along the tops of their crossbars. I had a big job facing me and I enjoyed it!

In town, it looked very complicated behind that switchboard, but all it really amounted to was a set of wires for each telephone in town and the country. Well, I guess that did mean there were a lot of them.

A note pad always hung at the switchboard. A trouble call, the operator would write it down for me. I would go the first thing in the morning, scan it and say, "I see trouble out west here at . . . and over east at . . ." There were no street addresses. "Go to Main Street—or Back Street, North Street, South Street—to the second house on the east side." I knew where everyone lived.

Each morning I went to work at eight o'clock. If there had been a storm, then I'd get out much earlier. I worked from eight to five—five and a half days a week.

Bernard Hill worked here when I came. Before him was Irie Trout. Bernard learned from him then shared his vast knowledge with me. Basically, the trouble was about the same as it is now: that is, broken wires, poles down, a tree or limb on the line. Wet trees would put a line out of order when they hung down on it. Repair work was done the hard way—by one man. I had to go out and try to repair the problem. If there was severe damage, help came in from away, on a line truck.

Telephone poles were placed at regular intervals along the road, and the wires that carried the voices were strung between them.

I dug the holes and set poles by hand, put up the wires, installed the phone and did the cable work. It was called a "one-man plant." I did everything. It was the same in all small communities. Shelton Bishop had to know it all or find out from someone on higher up.

When the day's repair work was done, I could find plenty of things to do—trim trees near wires, rebuild a line, replace insulators. And it is still that way, although one man doesn't have to do all that anymore. Of course there are more people and more phones now, too!

When I first started working here in 1941, I was paid ninety-five dollars once a month—not even twenty-five dollars a week! Later, I'd get a check twice a month. That ninety-five dollars made Mid and me a good living; we didn't want for anything. We had a big garden. Folks out in the country would give me meat when they butchered. I've come home with pumpkins, eggs, chickens, a piece of beefsteak, and fresh vegetables and fruit.

One time an old lady—she's gone now—said to me, "I've got too much stuff down in my cellar. If I give you some of it, would it insult you?" I laughed. "Well, I don't know why it should!" She gave me four quarts of sausage that had been fried down at butchering time and cold-packed, a peck of potatoes and several heads of cabbage. That tasted mighty good with hot biscuits and sausage gravy! So we always had plenty to eat and something to wear, and we had a savings.

The first thing after a stormy winter night, Mid and I would look out our front windows and see such a beautiful snowy landscape! The three wires, which were strung from one telephone pole to the others on down the street, sagged under the coating of ice and were a giant necklace of glass running along there. The buildings wore big caps of winter snow, and the trees bowed down with the weight of the whiteness. It was a pretty world.

"Yes, it's so beautiful," said Mid, but I could hear worry in her voice. "You'll have to be extra careful!"

I dreaded the day ahead of me—all those wet, slippery poles to climb! I can still see groups of kids on their sleds, happily sliding down that steep embankment at the edge of town.

Sleet and high, strong winds were my worst problem. Sleet doesn't bother so much anymore because all are underground cables, but it sure caused havoc back then. Kids liked to press their ears against the wooden poles in freezing weather and listen to the humming wires.

I dreaded all sleet storms, but this particular one was worse than any other. In just one hour it took all the telephone lines down that we had. Every one for miles around! I got Alvin Hunter and he took two men with him. He went one direction out of Arcadia and I took two men with me and went another direction. We worked day and night.

How could we get up those slick poles? It was always easy for me to climb them, but not after an ice storm! I put the safety belt around it first, as I always did before climbing, and it would slide right off. I kept hacking away at the ice with a small ax, and finally I balanced myself. Where poles had snapped off, we had to dig holes through accumulated ice and water to set the new ones. It took almost a month to get all the poles reset, the lines repaired and the phones back into service. Mildred worried until she saw me drive in safely at night.

Always, boys would stop and watch me climb a pole to fix wires, looking on in amazement, their eyes bright with envy. I knew what they were thinking—someday they could have a job like mine!

One little feller, the son of a rich couple, watched with snappy, bright eyes. He asked me, "Mr. Bishop, do you suppose Santy Claus would bring me a pair of shoes with cleats on them like yours?" I could see the excitement in his eyes, visualizing himself hurriedly climbing a pole with all his jealous friends looking on! I gathered the kids around and showed them how the cleats worked.

Boys'd provide much of their enjoyment playing with tin-can-string play phones, stretching their lines from the back porch to the wood shed, toilet, or barn. Or they'd walk along, throwing rocks at the blue glass insulators for target practice and marveling that one of those wires was his mother's party line—maybe she was talking to Grandma that very moment!

They'd use slingshots or shoot with BB guns to test their accuracy by hitting the humming wires, the insulators, or blackbirds sitting along the line. Sometimes, during their play, those wires would swing together and interlock, and then I had boys to scold. They'd see I was having a lot of trouble getting it corrected. I'd call the boys together and ask them to aim at pine cones on pine trees or tin cans—those kinds of things that aren't harmed. Today, boys, and even men, shoot through the cables for plain meanness.

Which reminds me, a little boy asked his grandpa, "Why do all those blackbirds always sit on the telephone lines?" Grandpa

laughed and answered, "They're listening in to your mother's and grandmother's conversations!"

Our worse danger, as always, is during a storm when power lines blow down across telephone lines. Sparks jump! A person can get killed. Before we do much after a storm, we usually ride the complete route to see if there's a power wire lying across a telephone line.

I was up a pole working on a line once, and I saw black clouds and lightning ten miles away. It hit the power wires and I saw a ball of fire coming right toward me! What to do? Just cut loose—*quick*!

My closest call came when I was working way up on a telephone line and the electric-light men were repairing their wires. One of those electric wires got away from them, fell and brushed me on the shoulder. My coat happened to be good and dry, and that saved me! The minute I felt the wire, I dropped to the bottom of the pole. Didn't hurt me, but it could have. When you're up there working, you watch what you're doing real close. If you don't, you'll be shuffling off into the Great Beyond sooner than you'd planned!

If a pole looked like it wasn't safe to climb, I didn't climb it; I'd put up a new one. In this job there's no reason to take chances.

I fell a time or two but I never was hurt. I've "burned the pole" and had my stomach full of splinters. People shouldn't tack signs on telephone poles 'cause it's dangerous; it's against the law, really. They'll nail those political pictures up at election time—or the circus or county fair posters—then leave them to weather off, with the nails still there. My spur hits the nail, the nail kicks out, and down I go! So, I learned to always tear all signs off the poles and pull out the nails. Why, I've seen poles with nails as thick as maggots on a dead cat!

When I first heard about the Good Friday tornado—April 11, 1965—I went out to Buffalo Road to see how much damage it had done to the telephone wires. I immediately got in touch with my superiors. The Company sent in line crews, cable men and repairmen from all over. We had them here from Ft. Wayne, Richmond, Lafayette and many more places.

That tornado was quite an experience. I had never been through one before, and I hope we never have one again. The devastation! Some of my friends lost life, homes, everything. The disaster hit the whole community with a mighty blow.

If a house was torn down—some were blown away, like the ones along Buffalo Road—course, they had no use for a phone. Those with shattered lines but no building damage, we got their hookups back immediately.

We couldn't do much on Buffalo Road till crews cleared the main roads and the power company got their work out of the way. Then we put up a cable and installed phones as quick as we could. It cost the company a lot of money, but that was one of the perils. A fund was set aside for such emergencies.

I was called to Rushville and Connersville to help with bad storm damage there. Whenever I'm called away like that, my job here is absorbed by someone else.

One time we had a call about a man who lived alone way out in the country. Nobody had seen him for days and he wasn't answering his phone. So I went out to check on him. He'd shot himself and had probably been dead for a week. To this day I can't go by that house but what in my mind I smell that horrible stench! It was real pitiful.

Everyone was so good to me. They would ask me to stay for a meal when I was installing their phone at dinner time, or they'd give me a cup of hot coffee. Well, a lot of them still do that.

I liked to come home for the noon meal that Mid had ready. We could talk about what had happened around town the night before or that morning. It broke up the day and maybe I'd have time for a fifteen-minute nap.

Most people wanted their phones installed way up high on the wall, and I don't know why, unless it was to be out of reach of young children. I've been in houses where I would almost have to stand on tiptoe to get to the transmitter to talk. When I started installing them, I put them where a lady could sit down and rest while she visited.

There was no charge to install a telephone, and the monthly fee was a dollar and a quarter. I was supposed to discourage people from having more than one phone in the house. I couldn't figure that out! Course, most could barely afford one phone.

On the old phones, the batteries went right inside the phone. Later on, when the desk phones become popular, I'd install a small box on the wall and run the batteries down into the basement or cellar.

We've had batteries to last as long as three or four years, depending on how much the phone was used. The battery was weakened only when someone was talking. I'd get a report that people couldn't hear a certain party very well, so I would go check out the batteries. Generally, they'd have little knots on them, all swelled up and corroded, so I'd replace the batteries and everyone was happy again!

The wires came out the top of little posts on the wall phones. People used to have metal combs, and the brush handles were metal. They found the top of the phone to be a good place to keep them handy and in easy reach. But they soon learned those metal things would touch against the posts and short the line out, and they'd have ol' Shelton on the line to come quick!

Oh, those desk phones! Women were so excited when the dial phones came in, and most bought a new waterfall desk to set it on. That was after the Depression, and times were getting better.

I installed one where there was a houseful of daughters. The girls asked for an extra long cord so they could carry it all around while talking. One day I had a repair order—their phone would ring in but they couldn't call out. I hurried to see what the trouble could be. Goodness, stuff was stacked—I mean *stacked*, piles of it—all over! They hustled around, scooting things here and there, to find the phone. Finally, one of them ran next door and called back. When we heard the phone ringing, we located it and I soon had it fixed.

I guess the worst annoyance in the telephone business is the long-winded person. There's one on every line. To get them to hang up in a hurry, you could take your receiver, pull it around and hold it in front of the mouthpiece. This caused a very loud squealing into their ears, which forced them to hang up!

When Agnes Haworth was bedfast from a broken hip, she didn't realize the receiver had slipped off the cradle. Myron Thompson, when calling her, soon realized what had happened. He gave shrill whistles directly into his mouthpiece until she heard it, and she then hung up.

The operator was permitted to cut in if someone from the outside wanted the line. If you needed your line, you could politely identify yourself and ask if you could please have the it for a minute and they could have it right back.

When I would go out to work on a line, sitting high on a pole, and someone was talking, I would wait a while, then go in on it, tell them, "This is Shelton Bishop. I want to work on your line." They'd always hang up right away. Some felt guilty that I had heard their conversation.

I have called people to test their lines, and immediately they'd know my voice and would say, "Well, Shelton, what are you doing out here?"

I don't mind the winter weather—I dress for it. Neither does summer heat bother me. There's a small amount of electric current in the telephone lines, and if I would get sweaty-wet working on them, I could get a good jolt!

One day I was out to Guy Black's farm to install a phone. Ebbon Beatty's family had just moved in. I walked in the back door. Later, I had to go out to the truck for some tools and I came back through the front door. As I pushed the door open, door and all fell down! I was upset with myself, thinking I'd broken it.

Ebbon started laughing, said, "I'd give anything to have a picture of the expression on your face, Shelton! I'd taken the door off when moving some wide furniture in, and I hadn't put it back in place!"

Mrs. Lulu Martz was the owner of the Arcadia Telephone Company when I came here. I have no idea what she had invested in it. She sold out in the late forties to Ralph Waltz, Orin Wiles, Newton Wiles, and Don Hope. In 1955, they saw it was going to take so much money to keep up with the modern trend, so they sold it to General Telephone Company. In 1956, all phones changed to dial.

Back then, there were a lot of family-owned telephone companies around. Aroma had an exchange in a home, and I think that house still stands, but no exchange. Atlanta had theirs in a home. The wife was operator and bookkeeper, and the husband took care of the outside line work. Most of those companies were later swallowed up by larger exchanges.

The hardest job for me was to go to remove a phone because of nonpayment. During the Depression, times were bad and I had to disconnect so many of them.

Sometimes a family would let their children play with the phone or be annoying when others talked. First, the operator would give a warning. Then, if the problem persisted, I'd have to go out and threaten to take their phone out.

A common occurrence was line-crossing. What I mean by "crossing" is when someone else was speaking on your line, and you knew they were on a completely different one—not coming through Central. This fouled up all the rings. Maybe they could call in, maybe not. They'd try to ring out and someone else would answer. Real distracting.

One day this happened and I took off early to find the trouble. I looked and looked. I think I climbed every pole out west of town, down across the old iron bridge, and on and on. Up there on the poles were two cross-arms of wires, with ten wires on each cross-arm. I had to climb about every pole and check each wire, and still I just could not find the trouble! I hunted for a week.

One evening, along about four o'clock, I started out that way again. I went down the hill toward the old bridge. Something caught my eye up there. Someone had taken a spool of real fine wire and thrown it up over those wires. I have no idea what possessed them to do a thing like that.

Once, the Tipton toll-line went out and I was chasing the trouble down. I never knew exactly what happened, but I figure a hawk had caught a chicken, flew over the lines, and, for some reason or other, let it drop. The chicken came down and hit one of those lines, bounced around and, as it bounced, wrapped the wires all together. I had to go up and pull the dead chicken out and untangle the wires.

At one time, we paid the Electric Company so much per year—per pole—to use their electric light poles for our lines.

We had an Arcola heating system up in the office, that made steam heat. The Arcola used those little pieces of hard coal. The man at the coal yards brought us fifteen hundred pounds of coal on a wagon. It was my job to carry all that up the stairs, a bushel full at a time—enough bushels to last a week.

The bank was just below the telephone office. I had a little telephone workshop in the back of it. One day Eulin Bardonner and Isabel Shorter were on the board. Eulin called me. She was just a boo-hooing—her nose and throat so stopped up from crying, I could hardly understand her. She was saying, "There's something awfully wrong. You better come quick!"

I ran up those steps. What a sight they were! The girls managed somehow to keep their work done on the board between sobs, but the tears kept rolling!

I checked out the odor. Well, Bob Correll, manager of the bank, had found an old bomb down there in some stuff that had been stored away for years. He went to my workshop for pliers to cut off the snout. It turned out to be a teargas bomb, and all those chemicals were going right upstairs to where the girls were!

I threw open the windows and doors and plugged in fans to blow it out. We ran them all afternoon and evening, but the next morning there was still evidence of it.

The problems and heartaches of everyone in our community touched the hearts of all those working at the telephone company. I caught the drift of it when I'd come and go. A lady called in saying, "Operator, the baby's fever broke and she's sleeping soundly now. I've been up day and night with her for so long. I'm going to try and get a nap. If anyone calls, tell them to ring me back in a couple hours."

One day I went out in the country to install a phone. After I knocked at the door, a little girl—I reckon not much over three—opened it. I said, "I'm the telephone man here to install your new telephone." She looked dismayed. "Oh mister, we just moved in. We're not ready for company. Everything's still a mess." I said, "Will you go tell your mother I'm here?" She went running and calling, "Mama! Mama! A man's here!"

Working in this business, you get to know the personalities of all the individuals. Men especially, when they want to use the phone, they want it *now*! Usually they have good reason to get irritable, but they'll take it out on the phone, sometimes even jerking the receiver out like a tooth from its socket.

We had one man who got so mad, he yanked the phone off the wall—yes, the whole box!—and threw it into the river right there next to his house. Well, when I got out there to repair it, someone of the family had fished it out and brought it back. I asked, not knowing what had happened, "Why is this off the wall?" The wife was standing there at the window, face beet-red from crying. She drew her lips in between her teeth as she stood fanning herself. "It just fell off . . ." was a child's worried answer. But I knew differently: It was full of sand and was still soaking wet.

I had to send the phone back to the factory to be rebuilt. I installed another one until theirs came back. No charge, but in a case like that, probably there should have been. And I always wished I'd known what caused the riff—was she talking on the phone when he came in and dinner wasn't ready? Well, I'll bet that didn't happen again!

One afternoon I stopped in at the office to see if there had been any calls for me. The operator was laughing when she told me about it: This farmer's wife was boiling mad—all but screaming, "If anyone sees my man in town, tell him the hogs got out! They're in my garden and yard and are running all over creation! And if he knows what's good for him, he'd better go to the hardware store and buy some nails and anything else he needs to fix that fence! And tell him to get himself right on home. I've been yellin' at him to fix that fence for weeks!"

At the last, before dial came in, more and more people were having telephones installed or getting two phones. There were two operators on the switchboard during busy hours. The different shifts of girls all worked together so well. They were happy with their jobs and so much fun to work with. Now we've lost all that personal touch. Many old people tell me that!

General Telephone bought the old company in 1955. Progress was taking over and there were many changes, but it had to be. I've been what you call an "I and R" man. That's "install-and-repair." This far from our district headquarters, we've been more or less on our own. We'd see something to do, we'd go ahead and do it. We still can't get away from the one-man plant. Although, generally speaking, there are more workers now and each has a specific job.

When General Telephone bought us out in 1955, all kinds of changes took place. I stayed on in the same capacity, but I had Cicero, Perkinsville, and Windfall to see to. Wherever they needed me, I went. Each man was assigned a certain job. Gone was the one-man operation.

Instead of the open lines on a pole, now we have buried cables. Most of the cables used to be lead-covered, and we had a cable car to use. I'd get into it and drive along, inspecting. See a crack or hole in the cable, I'd repair the damage.

Sleet doesn't bother anymore cause there's no open wires, but there are other problems. On buried cables, mice will get into it and chew through. Squirrels, muskrats and groundhogs gnaw them. I understand that now they have a treatment they put into the cable when it comes from the plant, so rodents don't bother so much.

We have what we call a "tone" that we put on the cable, then a receiver-like thing that is highly magnified. This tone goes to where the trouble is and it stops. Then I just go in there and open up the cable and repair it.

One of these days there will be no rotary dial; it will all be touch-tone. And, it is going to get more commercialized all the time. Every little thing the telephone company does, they'll charge you for it. We didn't.

It's been said there'll be a telephone in every automobile, as in every house. In time, I suppose there will be. I mentioned it to an old-timer the other day and he fumed, "How in the world could they drag a telephone wire all over?"

Telephone repairmen now have two-way radios in their trucks. That's why it is best to call in trouble through the company. They radio it right to us workers.

The modern builders cause us problems. There are some homes and business buildings so cheaply built that we don't even have to drill to get the phone wires through the walls—just push them in!

People move into a new house now before they have their gas and water hooked up. We have to get our telephone cable into it. Maybe the fellow in the next lot will start building a house. The ditch diggers are out to do their job. They cut cable after cable, time after time, and we have to go back and repair. People, out of service, get mad at the telephone company. I tell them if they can keep after the contractors to watch what they're doing, they won't have trouble with their telephone service. Every time you have a cut, there's potential trouble, even though we do repair real good. Water gets in and we can't ever get it dry.

Those old green insulators are getting to be quite a collector's item. There's a lot of green ones that aren't worth bringing home, but the real old ones, odd shapes, are valuable. Before that, there were the brown ones; they're priceless. Insulator books, of interest to collectors, are quite interesting.

When I first came here, we had stack after stack of telephones that had been taken out during the Depression. When times got better, as fast as people wanted a phone, I'd put new ones in.

The desk-type phone came along. I remember piling three hundred of the old wall phones in a heap and burning them. And right now they're worth at least a hundred dollars each! Look at the money I burned up!

I had five of the old, old magneto telephones when we lived in town in Arcadia. The day after we moved here, I went back to get things I'd left behind, and those phones were gone. Stolen, yes. Most old phones were two feet long, but those were real old—five feet tall and all fashioned on a long board. They would have been worth a fortune today.

Nowadays, since the local operators are all gone, the repairman is the only personal touch with the telephone company. I look back, remembering I wanted to be a veterinarian, but took the telephone job. I've never been sorry. I wasn't a person to jump from one job to another. When I came here, I made ninety-five dollars a month. It wasn't long after that I could have made quite a bit more at other jobs that were offered me, but I liked my work and stayed with it. I'm glad I did!

Everywhere I go, somebody is hollering at me. "Shelton! Shelton Bishop!" Even kids. It makes me feel so good to know I'm recognized. Men from the company will go out on the job with me. They'll say, "I think you must know everybody and his brother!" Well, I practically do, either through my work or

Mildred's piano teaching, singing lessons and her choirs, which have numbered in the hundreds!

The telephone future? This is 1975—there'll be many changes in another twenty to twenty-five years. Well, probably visual phones, something like TV. I think, in time, everything will be by radio—no telephone lines. It is expensive now, which is why we aren't already doing it. That's why it isn't too well-developed. Right now we can take two wires and put as many as forty-eight people on them at the same time. Thinking back, we've come a long, long way over a considerably short period of time. It will be interesting to see what develops in the future.

I really enjoy telephone work. Yes, I really do enjoy it! I like working for people, and people have been good to me all of the years I've worked here. There's just something about it I really love.

I think real joy comes, not from ease or riches or from the praise of men, but from doing something worthwhile!

Tri Town Topics, April 17, 24, May 10, 1975

Cleo Weber

Riding Along in a Sidecar

Cleo Weber was a widowed neighbor. After her husband's death, she moved into her beloved Grandpa and Grandma Williams' home. They are mentioned in this story.

BACK IN 1917, young men had a either a motorcycle, a horse and buggy, or a bicycle—or else they walked. There were only a few families with automobiles. Most lads couldn't afford one.

I remember the first time Bob came to our house riding his motorcycle—that's when he was courtin' me. We all rushed out to look it over. After a while, he had to hurry on. I remember how taken I was when he kicked the motorcycle into roaring life. Then, with a jaunty wave, he went barreling off down the road!

Right after Bob and I married, we moved to Huntington. Every month we'd travel eighty miles to Cicero to visit my grandparents, Grandma and Grandpa Williams. It took three hours. Bob drove the motorcycle; baby Helen, Grandma Weber, and I sat in the sidecar.

Roads were dirt or gravel—none were improved. They followed the rivers, the township or county lines. These dirt or gravel routes skirted around huge trees or boulders, and all had sharp turns and curves every half mile or so. And each one ran straight through towns.

We always started out real early. We could see the blue smoke curling up from each house we passed.

Bob's mother, Grandma Weber, just loved riding in that sidecar. She lived with us and was quite old. We called her Grandma Weber because she had grandchildren older than some of her children. She was forty-four when Bob, her ninth child, was born and forty-seven when she had her tenth. All were healthy. She wore a scarf or dust cap, winter and summer, and a nightcap when she went to bed. Her ears and head always hurt. She had been deaf for years.

Bob had a wide, double-sidecar motorcycle with leather seats. We, in the sidecar, sat with out feet stuck straight out in front. There was no windshield. Oh, the dust! We didn't mind. Got used to it, I guess.

I'd sit next to Bob and hold our baby, and Grandma was on the other side of me. Baby Helen just loved it! Her bonnet was tied securely under her chin. I protected her face with a thin scarf to keep out the wind and dust. Bob wore goggles, and Grandma and I had wool-knitted fascinators around our heads, even in the warmest weather.

During the week, Bob unhooked the sidecar, left it in the barn—everybody had a barn in town in those days—and drove the motorcycle to work.

Early on a Sunday morning, on our way to Cicero, we'd see a few windows light up here and there, but cabins were far apart and often a piece from the road. Long before we got to Perkinsville, we'd come to a little rise, and in the distance we could see the breakfast-time smoke spiraling above the trees, a few slender plumes rising to meet the morning sun. There, way up ahead, we'd see this old shanty with smoke coiling from the chimney. Purty soon we smelled the smoke. A man with milk pails in his hands paused to watch as we passed.

One house, in Perkinsville, was so close to the street that we'd catch the aroma of their coffee and ham a-cookin'. In the early morning freshness, I never smelled anything so good in my life! We always ate our breakfast before we left.

We'd pass through towns as the early church bells were ringing out. If all went well, we'd be at Grandma and Grandpa's in time to go to services with them.

Summertime—oh the sweet fragrances of clover in bloom or a freshly cut hayfield. I remember the pinks and whites of the blooming fruit orchards and the wild rosebushes and blackberry vines full of blossoms that vined between the fence rails. When berries were ripe, we'd stop to relax our legs and reach over and pick them to eat.

We watched cloud formations overhead. A clear day? Rain? Might the weather turn off cold?

Whenever we ran into a downpour, we'd stop near a house and go sit on the porch. If it was a storm, we were invited inside to talk with them and to have a cup of coffee until it blew over. One time we were caught in a sudden hail storm. We were thankful when we reached the shelter of that home! Everyone was friendly and enjoyed unexpected company.

There was a barn or two at every country house, with cattle and hogs in feedlots. Each had a garden nearby, a chicken house and chickens all around. Every farm had a big woods lot.

Springtime, we'd see all kinds of new baby animals out in fields: calves, pigs, lambs, colts. When they heard the commotion we made, they'd run to the protection of their mothers and start nursing.

On our return trip, late evenings, at every farm, baby chicks and mother hens were around their coops. Old layin' hens'd be scratchin' in the dirt. Roosters crowed on barnyard gates. Pigeons lined the combs of barns. Farm dogs ran out and barked us along.

In autumn, above the colorful tree foliage, wild geese and ducks flew overhead, going south. Goldenrod and purple wild asters bloomed along the roadsides. Pasture fields and fence rows were full of ragweed. I'd about sneeze my head off before we got to my grandparents' house! And then—*phew!*—we'd see a dead skunk where buzzards were picking the bones clean. Buzzards were always floating overhead in their search for food.

An interurban ran parallel to the road much of the way. One came along, going north or south, every half hour. As it rattled beside us, Grandma Weber would yell, "Race that car! Race that car!" Bob watched for a straight, level path before he raced. We got to traveling so fast the wind whistled past our ears! Even baby Helen, at that young age, enjoyed the excitement. Grandma Weber always loved to have a good time, right up until she died.

Grandpa Williams had a wheelbarrow, and Bob put some straw in it for a cushion and then he put Grandma in there. He took hold both handles and he wheeled her clear acrost the field and that shallow crick to see the beautiful field of corn he'd been bragging about. She just loved coming down to the farm, seeing how tall the corn grew in the bottom field. She was in her late seventies at that time and was still quite active. She could have walked, but Bob was always having fun!

Yes, rains made the roads treacherous to drive on. There was one soft spot as we went through the covered bridge west of Cicero—up that road to the top of the hill at the cemetery. The ruts were so bad I'd always have to get out and push while Bob revved the motor to get us through. Where the roads were all clay, mud packed in the front wheel up to the hub. We'd have to stop and pick that thick mud out before going on.

Dry summertime weather, the wheels went into dust up to their hubs. I'd hand Helen over for Grandma to hold, and I'd get out and push.

One spot near Marion—the size of a room—quicksand. Another push!

I don't remember getting caught in a snowstorm. We seldom traveled in the winter.

Early one Sunday morning, we came up over the hill there in Marion, Indiana. You know how that Courthouse yard is so full of

trees, even today? We saw four colored men a-hangin' there like rag dolls from a crooked tree—ropes around their necks, their tongues a-hangin' out. They said one of the three had raped a white woman on Saturday night. I don't know about the others. It was ghastly! I think of it even today, every time I come up over that hill in an automobile.

November 11, 1918, was a cool, sunny day. I was outside, up on a ladder, washing windows. Someone was shrilly blowing the factory whistles. All the church bells kept ringing—on and on. What was causing so much commotion?

Bob worked nights, so he was asleep upstairs. I woke him. He hurried into his clothes and rushed uptown. He no more than left, and I was changing the ladder to another window, when I saw Bob tearing down the street like a runaway colt—waving and puffing, full of great news: "The war has ended! The war has ended!" He was shouting for everyone to hear him all along the way. The war had finally ended—World War I. The Armistice had been signed and now everyone was out celebrating.

Bob's factory closed for a holiday. He was so excited. "Cleo," he said, "will your window washin' wait another day? Let's bundle up good and go to Cicero to see Grandpa and Grandma Williams." Even now, whenever I wash windows, I remember Armistice Day: November 11, 1917.

We rode through towns and saw children proudly parading down the neighborhood sidewalks, carrying little American flags and using their mama's pots and pans for drums. They were lustily singing their little hearts out, "My country tis of thee / Sweet land of liberty / Of thee I sing . . ."

My grandparents had already heard the good news by the time we got there. Grandpa hitched up his horse to the buggy, and we all crawled in and rode to Cicero and spent the day celebrating.

One time Grandpa and Grandma Williams rode the interurban up to see us. While I was fixing dinner, Bob took Grandma in the sidecar and drove her all around Huntington. That afternoon

Bob took Grandpa for a ride. When they got back, Grandpa shook his head and laughed, "Whee, what a ride! I had a notion to ask Bob if that's all she'd do, but I was afraid it wasn't!"

Grandpa just loved horse racing. He and John Leaming used t' go west through the covered bridge at Cicero, up the hill past the cemetery, then race to the crossroads. John lived north, Grandpa south. There they'd each turn to go on home.

Grandpa never raced if I was along though. It scared me. When I was a little tyke, a horse ran away with Mother and me in the buggy. Mother feared for my life, so she tossed me into the fence corner filled with thick grass and muddy water. Then she bailed out. Mama laughs, remembering it: "Cleo came up, hangin' onto her new bonnet and shakin' water from her dress and shoes, hollerin', "That naughty horse. Wait till I tell Papa on him!" That fear stuck with me all my life.

Always, when returning home, Bob drove the motorcycle right up on the sidewalk at the front steps to let us out. He had fun!

One afternoon Bob decided to teach me to drive it. We were going down River Road and come to an L turn. If I went right, I'd go into the river; straight ahead, into a field; so I turned left. I didn't realize I should slow down, and I went around the corner at full speed! The sidecar went straight up on its end in the air.

Bob kept yelling, "Slow down! Slow down!" In about a half mile, I got it slowed down in time to go around another bend in the road, and we made it. You see, when you turn it to the right, it takes a long sweep to get 'em around the corner. The sidecar is doin' the lead for you. Turn 'em to the left, then the motorcycle does the guiding.

At about every town, the big sport for young fellows was the motorcycle climbs. Bob drove in them until we were married. Several fellows—the reckless and daring—revved up their motors at a steep incline, then they'd have a race to the top. Some would lose traction half way up and turn over, dragging the driver down the hill with it. Others would shoot on up over the hill. Oh, that was exciting to watch!

I still get a thrill when I see a motorcycle. I'd like to ride a sidecar again, but at my age, eighty-nine, I don't suppose I ever will. I wonder, *Do they even make sidecars anymore?*

Tri Town Topics, November 7, 1974
Good Old Days, May 1981
Noblesville Daily Ledger, November 2, 1982

Pauline Mosbaugh Evans

Pauline's Poultry Paradise

Pauline an' Edgar Evans were our lovable neighbors. They made pets of all their animals. As we visited them, each pet came to life, like a character in a book. All the women in this story were her friends an' they exchanged yarns.

ALMOST EVER' FARM, big or small, had a hen house full of chickens back in the early 1900s, up into the '50s. Nowadays, the only ones in our neighborhood who still have chickens are me, Mary Earl, an' Lois Costomiris. Louie Sowers, Arcadia, she was like me, she just loved chickens!

It used to be you'd drive down the road an' there was a chicken house an' a flock at ever' farm. There's nothin' purtier'n a barnyard full of poultry—chickens, geese, ducks, guineas—out pickin' in green grass. Those beautiful sights have been gone for a long time. It's sad!

Much of the lore 'bout settin' hens is bein' lost. The secrets of hatchin' an' raisin' chickens are not bein' passed on from generation to generation like in the old days. But it was our way of life.

When women went to work in the factories durin' World War II, they got accustomed to that big pay check an' kept right on workin'. Then there was no time for chickens.

My raisin' chickens goes a way back. I was born in 1492—the same year Columbus discovered America. Well, I'm jist 'bout that old! I came along in 1907.

Ever' January an' February I'd get to thinkin' I'd have to order me some baby chicks. Edgar'd say, "It's baby chick time. Now you can go outside an' blow some of the winter stink off!" I jist loved raisin' all kinds. Me an' Edgar are past eighty—too old to be doin' it now.

That's the one part of the farm business where the woman was boss—raisin' chickens an' sellin' th'eggs. That was cash in *her* pocket! Paw would laugh an' say, "You women air in competition with each other as t'who makes the most money. Why wouldn't you do real good? Husbands furnish the feed an' pay fer the chicks—your money is clear!"

When I was a little tyke, I figured families had kids jist to gether their eggs. Standin' on tiptoe, I'd reach up into the row of straw-filled wooden boxes where the hens laid their eggs. Apple boxes or orange crates was nailed side-by-side up on the wall 'bout three feet from the floor for 'em to lay in. An' a three-inch-wide board was nailed across the front bottom side to hold in the nest-straw an' the eggs.

I had a pet hen that always laid the purtiest white eggs ever'-day in the paper box in the toilet. 'Long 'bout dinner time, I'd hear her triumphant cackle an' I'd go a-runnin' an' bring it in to show Mama.

When I'd see a nest full of eggs in the hen house, I insisted to Mama that one old hen had laid 'em all. "No, no," Mama corrected me, "hens lay one egg a day. *Only* one!"

I fed an' watered the chickens ever' day, an' gethered the eggs. That was my job. The other kids would drop 'em or rattle 'em around in the basket so they cracked. I was always real careful an' dependable, Mama said.

I liked doin' it, except ever' day there'd be one ol' egg with a big, thick gob of brown poop on it. *Ever'* day! I'd have to wash it off at the pump. When I complained to Mama, she told me about the neighbor walkin' under the trees at the Noblesville Courthouse. He took his hat off to scratch his head, an' a pigeon made his deposit on the man's bald spot!

For most of the farm families, the egg money was sometimes needed to tide them over between the twice-a-month milk check. The sale of hogs, beef cattle, corn or wheat went for the big farm expenses, but durin' bad times, Mama had to cough up her chicken an' egg money to pay the taxes.

Mama always raised her own baby chicks, an' ever' now an' then there'd be a stray one. She'd say, "Pauline can have this un for a pet."

There was us five Mosbaugh young uns in an' out of the house all day long. It was Everett, then me, an' Lloyd—ever-one called him Augie—then Mildred an' baby Max. Oh, so many flies. Our screen doors had strong springs to keep 'em shut tight. Lotsa times we'd have a peeled heel 'cause we couldn't git through the door fast 'nough.

The pet would foller behind me ever'where. It would get 'bout a third grown, then someone'd go through the door an' it'd snap shut—right on the chick. Kilt ever'one that way. I'd always bawl an' carry on.

From the time I was nine, ever' spring Grandma Mosbaugh'd put hens on eggs to hatch all the baby chicks she'd be needin'. Mama got her chickens that way, too—under settin' hens.

Grandma was short an' as wide as she was tall, an' she spoke very Dutchy. When she got all the hens set she wanted, she'd say, "Pauline, my ould hins air a-layin' aigs right wild. I sit two hins fer you. When they hatch an' yer chicks air raised, you kin sell 'em. That'll be yer spendin' money fer the year. Then you bring my hins back home."

Mama had wooden apple boxes ready for her broody hens—to set hers an' my eggs in. Late evenin', almost dark, Mama'd say, "Pauline, go git a armful of straw. I want to set a hen." Then she'd let me carry each broody hen to a dark, quiet spot where she had the boxes she'd gotten from the grocery store. I'd soothe the hen's feathers, talk to her quiet-like, set her down in the box, an' give her one egg at a time till she had fifteen eggs. She'd gently roll each one underneath her. Then came her settlin' motion—from one side to th'other, wigglin' her whole body. She spread her wings way out over the eggs an' gave a lazy look—she was broody.

For each hen, Mama had me hurryin' to the hen house several times a day to pick up eggs that was warm. I'd hear a hen cackle, bein' fussy about the egg she'd just laid. Then I'd listen for other cackles. I'd select the largest an' best-shaped ones—with thick shells, so they wouldn't break. I'd pencil-mark the date an' a continuous line to tell 'em apart. I'd take the fresh-laid ones out of the nest each day. Hens all crawl in with each other to lay.

Once a day the hen'd get off her nest for food an' water. She'd always cover her eggs with straw an' bits of feathers to keep 'em warm while she was away. A good hen'll quickly eat an' drink, maybe dust in the dirt, then she'll step back into the nest carefully. With her beak, she'll turn each egg an' settle down once more. This'll last three weeks.

Sure 'nough, in just twenty-one days I'd see the first little head lookin' out from under her, then another. When all of 'em was hatched, they'd be all 'round under her wings an' ever' place close by. I just couldn't wait to see if the eggs hatched, but ever' time I'd try to hold the hen aside, she'd give me a sharp peck on my hand that'd draw blood. You see, chicks don't all hatch the same day—it may take two or three days longer.

After they all hatched, she'd proudly take 'em for their first walk, cluckin' 'em all together—her little beady eyes'd be shinin' an' lookin' so happy! Then, I'd carefully take the chicks an' their mamas to little individual chicken coops. That was my job, to care for 'em. An' before long, my little bitties was packin' their craws with grain. That looked so cute!

We'd get 'bout ten hatched chicks to each hen. That was

twenty chicks that was all mine! Sometimes a hen'd hatch fifteen an' sometimes less.

It took all summer to raise a chicken. In the fall I'd take the two hens back to Grandma an' I'd sell my twenty chickens for 'bout thirty-five cents each. That come to seven dollars, my year's spendin' money. I'd be rich!

I cut gallon-sized tin cans in half with a butcher knife for their waterers. An' I set a rock in it so they wouldn't up-dump it. When water spilled, the wet straw had to be changed.

Chickens fascinate me when they drink, dippin' their beaks in the water an' then pointin' 'em straight upward as they swaller to let the water roll down. Grandma would smile, "Bitties'll look up an' say 'Thank you, Jesus!' ever' time they take a drink. We kin learn a lesson from 'em."

Paw made wooden feeders out of scrap lumber. That was so cute, a whole row of baby chicks lined up eatin' at a feeder, their little round bottoms a-stickin' in the air.

Mother used anything she could find for chicken coops. When you're poor, you make do. Same after me an' Edgar got married—durin' the Depression, we were poorer'n thunder. We took leaky washtubs, turned 'em upside down an' cut a little door in 'em, an' they made nice coops. I'd hafta put boards underneath, or the rats would bury up through. An' the weasels! They was more trouble'n anything.

Mama'd buy a new oilcloth for the kitchen table an' use the old one to put over the tops of the chicken boxes to keep out the rain.

Paw took several sacks of corn an' oats to town an' had it ground for mash for mine an' Mama's chickens. That's all we fed 'em at first. Might give 'em bread an' milk to start 'em out. But later on we had our own receipt for feed—so much corn, soybean meal, oats, an' salt. I also fed 'em cracked corn.

When they was 'bout grown, me an' Augie—when we was kids—took turns shellin' ears of corn by hand. Later, Paw traded for a corn sheller with a crank. After that, we didn't git raw, blistered hands ever' time we shelled corn.

Mama would read to me as she hunted a formula for a good mash. (By then, my folks were follerin' Purdue recommendations about new things on the farm.) "I got it right here in my receipt book." She fingered through the ragged yellowed pages—years of assorted information—mumblin' to herself: "Wallpaper paste . . . Weather signs . . . When to plant . . . When to wean calves so they don't bawl all the time. Here it is, the receipt fer chick starter an' layin' mash." She told me to write it down so I could refer to my own records when I was older.

She read from another page: "Remedy for cannibalism: Y'see chicks bloody all over, 'specially their heads an' hind-ends, they're eatin' each other. Put one teaspoon salt to a gallon o' drinkin' water an' keep all other water away from the chickens fer one-half of ever' day. Give 'em salt water in the mornin' an' clear water in the afternoon. Here's another: Give 'em tomatoes. I cold-pack tomatoes ever' year for that purpose, Pauline. After the tomatoes are well-mashed, put 'em in the waterin' vessel. If they're not finely crushed, the pieces get on the ground an' they're wasted."

Mary Earl told me the cure for the sprawly legged newborn chicks y'git once in a while. Feed it strong sugar water till it kin stand.

Coccidiosis was a dreaded chick disease. A parasite attacks the digestive system, an' you'll see bloody droppin's. Some women lost half their chickens 'fore they got it stopped. TB took a lot of flocks, too. We had a pill, turned drinkin' water purple. That helped.

Gaps. Sometimes little chicks would stand around gaspin' for their breath. It killed 'em fast. Louie Sowers' mother would push a timothy head down in their throats, then pull out whatever was blockin' their air. Louie would hold the chick while she did that, an' sometimes it died in her hands. She'd cry an' cry.

Roup. Other times chicks acted like a child with croup. Their eyes watered an' their nostrils got full of mucus. We had a salve we rubbed on their heads, an' we medicated their water to cure 'em.

Then there was limberneck. Those chicks looked just like the name—no strength in their necks, an' their heads'd drop down.

Edgar would buy five-hunnerd-pound barrels of semisolid buttermilk off the milkman. We'd feed the chicks a half gallon of it ever' day, poured over their feed, to ward off diseases. Oh, how they loved it!

When my chicks were half grown, I'd go to the garden an' pick big fat green tomato horn worms, cabbage worms, an' black potato bugs. They'd go scootin' to git 'em to eat!

In later years we'd buy the prepared chick starter an' growin' mash from the hatchery. Mama bleached the sacks out a snowy white to use for sewin'. When livestock an' poultry feed suppliers found women was makin' aprons an' curtains out of their feed sacks, the companies began turnin' out bags in all sorts of pretty flowered an' pastel prints. I went an' picked 'em out. That's one time a farm woman didn't trust her man to choose a design. Or even to get extries of some like she already had.

One neighbor said, "I'd been wantin' t'make a new dress. I had to wait the dangdest time to git four feed sacks all alike, then no more of that style come in. Now I won't get that new dress—I have to start all over." At one of our Home Economics Club meetin's, *all* the ladies wore a dress they'd made from feed sacks!

I always loved watchin' a mother hen proudly escortin' her little family all about the barnyard, huntin' bugs an' seeds for 'em. She'll cock a ear an' listen. When danger threatens, she'll call 'em all t'gether. Oh boy, she'd flop anyone, crawl all over you, if y'come too near an' try to pick up one of her babies. She'd know when they got tired, an' she'd stop an' hover 'em.

We'd 'bout die a-laughin', listenin' to the young roosters tryin' out their lungs before their voices was ready. Their squeaky little crows sounded like a boy with his voice changin'! They'd have the funniest expressions on their faces, too, like, *Was that me?*

When the chicks got their feathers an' little combs, I could tell the pullets from the roosters. Roosters always had bigger combs than the hens. The hens developed nice red combs later, when they was beginnin' to lay.

Hens hide eggs in impossible places: under the corn sheller, in the haymow, strawstack 'r out under the trumpet vine behind the toilet. Paw often found eggs where an old hen was stealin' her nest out; sometimes he'd even find a nest of baby chicks. He'd use his hat as a basket to bring 'em to the house. Mama hurried an' put chicks in a box close to the warm kitchen cookstove. When he found eggs, she kept 'em separate from the fresh ones, so as not to sell 'em.

Once, Grandma was workin' way out in the truck patch. I was a-playin' nearby when I found a nest of eggs in the corner of a railfence. I hurried to Grandma to show her. She studied a minute an' said, "If we leave 'em an' th'ould hin sits, a danged skunk'll rob her nest a few days 'fore they hatch. Skunks wait. Guess they like baby chicks without a-fightin' to git 'em. Pauline, you better take 'em to the house an' we'll see if they's fertile."

To tell a fertile egg from infertile one, she'd hold 'em up to the sun or a coal-oil light. The infertile eggs are clear an' don't give any indication of developin'.

"But, Grandma, what'll I carry 'em in?" I asked. "Jist make a nest by tuckin' up the corners of yer apern. That'll hold 'em."

Sometimes we'd find nests where the hen was prob'ly killed two, three, four days 'fore time for eggs to hatch. Hot summertime, they don't chill easy.

Guinea egg shells are so thick an' hard—a wonder the little things can make it through. Put 'em in a bucket of cool water fer a minute 'r two an' th'good ones'll bob around, so you'll know you have live birds inside. A duck or goose egg will bob way up an' down! Y'do this when y'find a nest the hen has abandoned. Then y'find a broody hen an' put all the eggs under her; she'll set on 'em till they hatch, then she'll care for 'em.

Mama always had me go throw the rotten eggs out. Like any kid'll do, I throwed 'em up against the barn to see 'em splatter. How that smelled—*phew*! Boy, was Paw mad—all that in plain view for anyone to see. an' I had the mess to clean up!

A neighbor lady found a nest of eggs an' gethered 'em up in her apron. A big storm blew up an' she took to the nearest shelter, the outhouse. The wind destroyed the privy. When she was rescued, she was completely covered with broken eggs. A good thing they wasn't rotten like the ones I throwed against the barn!

It's fun to watch chickens lay their eggs. Young pullets, they can't make it to the nests in time; they'll drop 'em anyplace, even out in the barnyard. An old hen sometimes takes hours. She'll set an' set, maybe half a day, till she's performed her duty.

Young chickens an' hens'll be up an' eatin' at the first light of day. Real old hens, so tired, will stay on the roost till much later, then go to roost early evenin'. Grandma told me that's the way it is with some old *women*.

I was readin' a novel one time, an' I knowed the author didn't know beans 'bout chickens, 'cause the mother sent the child out early ever' mornin' to collect all the eggs. Any farm kid, age five up, knows they're *gethered*—not collected!—ever' *evenin'*. Sure, some hens'll lay earlier than others, but not *first* thing of a mornin'!

When I got old 'nough to work out an' make my own money, Grandma still said, "I got these ould hins an' you kin sit aigs . . ." She humored me, 'cause I was older an' had accepted family responsibilities so young in life.

You set an old hen, if you didn't de-louse her first, lice'd sap all her blood 'fore the eggs could hatch. I'd go to the hen house to gether eggs in the hot summer; I'd be sweaty, an' them lice would be crawlin' all over me time I got to the kitchen. Even in my hair! Mama would scrub me down good with lye-soap an' hot water.

To de-louse, we dunked the old hens in a creosote dip—all but their heads. Later they started sellin' louse powder an' we'd shake

"The one part of the farm business where the woman was boss—raisin' chickens and sellin' th'eggs." For Pauline Mosbaugh Evans, raising chickens wasn't just a job, but a life-long passion.

that under their feathers to cover their skins good. We had to creosote-paint the roosts, too. Most women kept an old washtub in the hen house with wood ashes in it for the hens to waller in; that helped. They'd dust themselves in the dirt beneath an old plum tree in the chicken lot.

Lice can kill a baby chick. I watched Mama when she greased their little heads an' under their wings an' tails with a thin smear of bacon grease. Then I did my chicks. That smothered the lice. Mama told me a neighbor kilt ten of her chicks with too much grease.

Did you know chiggers killed a lot of chickens some years? I'd come in early of a mornin', after walkin' through dewy grass, an' I was covered with chiggers, too. How they itched! Poor chickens'd have a hard time scratchin'.

When I was twelve I got my first job workin' for Otis Zimmerman—cleanin' out brooder houses, makin' fifty cents a day. I wasn't very big, but I had learnt to work. Otis had several hunnerd chicks he'd bought from a hatchery. I shooed the chicks out an' shut the little front door, so's they couldn't get back in while I was carryin' the straw litter out through the big side door. I took up all the feeders, waterers, an' those big awkward square hovers an' set 'em outside. Then I shoveled that stuff onto a mudboat. I hauled it to the garden, truck patch or a field, an' I forked it all around. It makes wonderful fertilizer. Otis had a tame ol' horse I drove to pull the mudboat.

Inside all those brooder houses it was hot an', oh, that dusty smell of chicken litter. *Phew*! Took me all day, an' they had to be cleaned ever' week. I pert near went out of the chicken business doin' that!

I scattered clean straw all 'round inside. I brought ever'thin' back in, pumped water an' filled each of the waterers an' put mash in the feeders, then let the chicks in. They was so happy! Later on, Otis used heat lamps, so I didn't have to mess with big hovers. An' he started usin' peat moss for beddin', an' they didn't need cleanin' out as often.

Everett an' Augie was poutin' one evenin', wonderin' why Saturday was always the day for cleanin' Mama's brooder house an' hen house. They didn't get paid for doin' it, like I did. Paw come in the house an' seen 'em settin' there all bent over with their lips drawed up like they'd just bit into a green persimmon. "What's the matter with you two tit-suckers, anyway?" I knowed they didn't want to hear Paw's long drawed-out spiel, so they just looked over at me, then said, "Nuthin'."

Mama lost a lot of her chicks whenever a sudden shower blowed up. They didn't have enough sense to go in, or sometimes the old hen would stand in the door an' not let the chicks inside. They'd try to get underneath her, but that's a job when they get any size on 'em. A wet chick chills fast. I've brung a basketful in at a time, laid 'em out on newspapers, an' let 'em dry off an' come to life around the warm cookstove. *Phew!*—the smell of wet feathers!

Some chicks, of course, didn't make it. I've stuck handfuls of dead ones in the stove to burn 'em up. Oh no, we didn't give 'em to the dog to eat, cause that'd start him killin' our live chickens. Couldn't throw 'em over in the woods; they'd draw predators an' soon they'd be up raidin' the chicken house.

We didn't go away from home much when they was first turned out. See a storm a-comin', we couldn't make it very fast in a buggy or even our first automobile.

One day I was walkin' home from Otis' when a sudden shower blowed up. I ran as fast as my legs would carry me, afraid my old hens an' baby chicks wouldn't find shelter. Mama was holdin' each hen back an' pickin' up the chicks in her apron when I got home. Paw was helpin', snatchin' 'em up an' stuffin' 'em inside his shirt. They carried 'em to the house, an' stood at the winder together, watchin' greenish clouds boil overhead. Dad yelled at us kids to go to another room from the telephone 'cause lightnin' could come in on the telephone an' shock ya. Even kill ya!

One cool spring afternoon—it was a Saturday—Paw an'

Mama were out gettin' the baby chick's houses ready for when the old hens hatched their eggs. I guess I was five or six. Us four kids—me, Everett, Augie, an' Mildred—wanted to go out an' play, but the folks insisted we stay in an' watch baby Max. Much later, Mama came back in. Paw was on his way to the hog pen with a feed basket over his arm.

Mama shivered, "Criminy, it's cold!" She raked up the hot ashes in the cookstove an' filled it with cobs an' wood. She threw a handful of coffee into the pot an' stirred it down, then pushed it to the front to heat. Then she noticed ever'one was there but me.

"Where's Pauline?" she asked anxiously, glancin' around. No one knew. She was worried, annoyed. "When did you last see her?"

"We've been playin' hide an' seek, but we ain't seen hide nor hair of her," Augie told her. "She never, ever hides that good. She always gives herself away."

Mama ran out the back door, screamin' an' wavin' a dishtowel frantically. Paw knew somethin' awful was wrong, by the tone of her voice. "Where's Pauline?" Mama yelled, throwin' up her arms. Paw jumped over the railfence an' come in a mad run.

They looked in the first three or four most likely places with reluctant dread: horse trough, the platform at the pump, down in the privy, an' in the bull pen. Not seein' a sign of me, their anxiety grew. *Oh, dear! Oh, dear! If she's lost . . .*

In a distance, dogs was barkin' fierce-like. Gypsies! The word "Gypsy" invoked all kinds of frightenin' speculations. Paw went to the telephone on the wall an' cranked a long, continuous ring—the distress signal for an emergency. He told the operator that I was missin'. The operator passed the frightenin' news along the line: "It's John an' Goldie Mosbaugh's Pauline—she's nowhere to be found!"

Soon the neighbors, havin' heard the alarm, was comin' in buggies, wagons or on horseback. *Had anyone seen a band of Gypsies?* They was known to steal little girls, especially blond-headed ones. We heard they believed a baptized Christian would bring superior magic an' good luck to a whole tribe of 'em.

The talk shuttled back an' forth as they made preparations for an all-out search—who'll go south, north, east . . . The men put oil in their lanterns an' was cleanin' the globes, thinkin' it might be a long, disturbin' night. Mama didn't know which way to turn.

Just then I scootched out from under the cookstove, rubbin' my sleepy eyes. I looked all 'round at the whole roomful of people. Paw said my eyes was big as barrel rings.

"Glory be!" Mama cried. "Look! It's my child!" She went into chokin' hysterics, clingin' to her "lost" baby. Ever-one hugged me an' made a awful fuss for about a half hour, a-cryin', "Praise the Lord! Praise the Lord!" One lady rang up Central to tell her I'd been found.

"It's pert near time fer supper," Paw said. "Ma, bile some taters. It's time we all rejoice!" Paw went to the smokehouse an' come back with a hickory-cured ham to slice an' fry. "This supper's better'n a weddin' feast!" someone said.

The families finished their meal of appreciation an' was off into reminiscences of other lost children an' Gypsies, interrupted only long 'nough for refills of hot coffee an' for men t'refuel their pipes. The children were in other parts of the house, playin'.

CHICKENS WAS FOREVER findin' a way to git into the yard an' scratch out Mama's flowers. One hen always laid an egg in the corner of the porch. When I was datin' Edgar, I'd have to shoo chickens away with a broom 'fore he come over. He'd laugh, tellin' me 'bout the hillbillies who let their chickens roost on their porch railin'. "But ever' night," he said, laughin', "they'd turn 'em 'round with their tails outside."

A hen was tenacious in fightin' off a hawk or crow or snake or turkey buzzard or any predator that threatened her young. Mama kept her gun handy, an' when we heard the pitiful cries of a mother hen, Mama'd scan the skies an' look under bushes for the offender.

When a wild hawk would circle up there in the sky an' come wheelin' down behind the barn, Mama Hen would give the alarm to her little brood. Instinctively, they'd quickly obey. She'd try to get 'em under cover, an' if none was near, she'd gather 'em under her wings in a last desperate effort to save 'em. Mama'd shout an' shake her fist at the turkey buzzards that come soarin' overhead.

A persistent chicken hawk, crow or buzzard was usually caught by Paw's shotgun blast. I'd watch as it spun to the ground. Paw tied the feet with twine, then hung it on a pole in the chicken yard to warn other hawks of the danger. A hawk could carry a five-pound chicken away!

Louie Sowers always made a scarecrow. She'd nail two pieces of wood together to make a cross. Then she'd stuff a man's shirt, jacket an' overalls with straw—his arms were holdin' a wooden stick-gun. Put a hat on him, then nail it to a fencepost, an' it'd look like a man a-shootin'. They'd put scarecrows in cornfields, too, to keep the flocks of crows from stealin' the corn after it had been planted. Crows'll go down a row of corn an' clean it out.

A stray dog or cat come around, our old gander'd nip him good an' send him howlin' on his way. Louie, livin' there in town, was always bothered with stray, hungry cats comin' up the railroad. Puppies an' some grown dogs'll play an' tease a chicken till they kill it.

One afternoon there was a commotion from our orchard. "Run, Pauline!" Mama yelled. "I bet it's that hawk agin."

"Cheep! Cheep! Cheep!" We could hear the cry of a baby chick. We never did know where the little creature come from—maybe the hawk carried it from another farm an' dropped it when we scared it off. Mama got me a empty round Quaker Oats cardboard box, poked some holes in the lid for air t'git through, an' we put the chick in it behind the cookstove. Later I got a bigger box to put it in, with its bread, milk, an' water.

Mama was purty good with the rifle an' killed many a hawk. Paw was a good shot, too, but he was gen'r'ly out in the field when we needed him. Mama saved the fine, fluffy feathers off the hawk's breast to mix with duck or goose feathers for pillows.

Lois Costomiris had a hen hatch out fifteen chicks. That hen'd been a wonderful mother ever' year, but in this flock was one chick that wouldn't mind. He didn't listen when she cautioned the chicks about the dangers 'round 'em. She fussed an' jawed at him constantly. All the others obediently follered her, an' when they got tard, she gethered 'em beneath her. But not this un—he was out runnin' 'round, usually in tall weeds. She fretted an' worried. Somethin' would hide out there an' catch him! Finally, in desperation, she gave up. An' then, one day he was gone.

Another ever-present threat to put up with was those ol' chicken thieves—young fellows needin' to make car payments, or buy gas or smokin' tobacco. Late at night, when the chickens was 'bout ready to sell, Mama'd wake up an' start shakin' Paw. "What's that racket? Somebody must be at the chickens the way our dog's carryin' on." Paw'd hurry an' pull on his shoes, get his rifle, an' take off for the chicken house in his white nightshirt.

Not only would farm folks lose their chickens, they'd lose the pullets that would supply eggs for food an' expenses through the comin' year. They'd have to carry old hens over, an' they didn't lay as well.

Lee an' Louie Sowers an' their children went to a spellin' bee at Buffalo School one night. The next mornin' Louie went out an' all of her three hunnerd chicks were gone. One coop was right under their bedroom window! She was heartsick.

This clippin' was in the newspaper, in the Cicero news, in the "50 Years Ago" column. I've kept it in my Bible all this time:

> *William DeMoss, while he was shucking corn in his field near Cicero Crick, found three sacks of Plymouth Rock chickens*

hidden under a cornshock. Their feet were all tied together and they were alive, indicating they had been there only a short time. The owner can have his fowls by calling Mrs. DeMoss.

Someone had stole 'em, an' hid 'em there till dark. The theft had been reported, so the sheriff was contacted an' the rightful owner claimed 'em. The thieves made no response.

Snakes'd crawl right up into nests an' eat eggs—shell an' all. I'd be long gone if I'd a-reached in an' got a handful of snake! A weasel is another cunnin', sneaky thing. They can git in through the tiniest crack and, in one night, slit several chickens' throats an' suck the blood. They always suck blood—don't eat 'em. An' they's others that prey: rats, foxes, an' coons, even stray dogs an' cats.

Lizzie Venable had five hunnerd young chickens that was 'bout half grown. Lizzie, her husband, Ed, an' their grandson, Bud Costomiris, heard a awful commotion out in their chicken lot. It was a cold, gloomy afternoon, 'bout like today. They went to the door an' looked out. All those chickens was runnin' round an' round the chicken house, chasin' a rat! They finally run him down an' they pecked him to death!

One day a young couple drove in at Mary Earl's—she lives west of us here. They wanted eight old non-producin' hens: a month's supply for a ten-foot-long pet snake. His food consisted of one chicken twice a week.

"Ring its neck to kill it, but don't lose any of the blood," the lady told Mary. "I'll put 'em, feathers an' all, into a plastic sack, then into the freezer at home.

"What if I find a dead hen or rooster—I'll occasionally see one that had probably died of a heart attack or old age—would you want it?" Mary asked.

"Oh, yes, just stick it, feathers an' all, into a plastic bag an' put it in your freezer till the next time I come 'round." Then she paid Mary three times the market price for those hens. Mary's son,

David, shook his head as they drove away. "Just so they don't bring the snake with 'em the next time they come!" he said.

There was always a bit of rivalry round the neighborhood women—who had lost the fewest chickens by the time they was a month old; who'd have the first fry to pop in the skillet; who'd get the first egg from her pullets?

When me an' Edgar first married, we didn't have fifteen cents. We lost all the hogs from cholera, an intestinal disease that was goin' 'round. We lived on five hunnerd dollars the whole year, so we started eatin' chicks when they was a pound an' a half. Like eatin' a bird! Just as well et feathers an' all. When you don't have money, you don't buy meat. But, like kids, our chickens soon growed up.

Cookin' for a lot of hay hands, I had no way to keep the chickens cool if I dressed 'em the night before, so I'd clean several early in the mornin', then cool 'em down in a foot tub of cold water at the pump.

We et all we wanted. When the roosters got too big for fryin', we sold 'em. They averaged eight pounds. We'd keep 'bout a hunnerd pullets for layers.

It took eight cockerels to a hunnerd hens, so the eggs would be fertile. I was usually paid ten cents a dozen above market price. We put all the hatchery eggs in twelve-dozen-size egg crates.

The first pullet eggs of the year were small an' we'd git only half-price fer 'em. Sometimes we'd get double-yolk eggs. Max an' Mildred, little tykes, would cheer: "A rooster egg!"

I sold eggs to Mabel Anderson's hatchery in Noblesville. It meant extry work, but more pay. Each egg had to be candled an' weighed, an' the dirty ones had to be sandpapered—not washed. Washin' hurts fertility.

Mama knew by holdin' each one if it was big enough. She sold small eggs at the grocery. The unsuitable ones—the bloodstained, cracked or thin-shelled eggs—was set aside for our immediate kitchen use. We'd always break ever' egg with caution into a saucer before addin' it to a skillet or cake batter. Oh yes, I'd find a bad egg now an' then.

The twelve-dozen-egg crate would be hauled to market an' returned, filled with canned goods, boxes an' sacks of food; usually only a little money was ever exchanged. The wife always planned to come out way ahead.

Chickens are the only things that haven't gone up in price through the years. I used to dress 'em out, an' a washtub-full went to one person to put into her freezer. I'd get a dollar apiece an' twenty-five cents for dressin' each one. I always put the wet feathers in a cardboard box an' put feathers an' all on the trash pile, an' I burnt 'em. Some women just let all that mess clutter their barnyard. That looked awful!

Ernie Kennedy, he delivered Purina feed for Mabel Anderson Hatchery. He told 'bout a city-slicker couple that moved on a farm, prepared to make a million! The wife come in an' bought two hunnerd chicks from Mabel. Two weeks later she was back for two hunnerd more. "You sure are gonna raise a lot of chickens!" Mabel said. City lady shook her worried head an' said, "I don't know what I done wrong—if I planted 'em too deep or too far apart."

When a hen would go to settin', I'd put duck, guinea, an' hen eggs under her. I've had hens with three or four different kinds of babies, all colors an' sizes, trailin' her. She'll claim ever'one, just as if they was her own.

Duck, goose, guinea, an' turkey eggs take twenty-eight days to hatch. A week after they'd been under her, I'd sneak in chicken eggs, which take twenty-one days, so they'd hatch at the same time.

A guinea likes to hide her nest out in the weeds or brush. Somethin'll pert near always get 'em. Not only take the eggs, they'll kill the hen, too. So I'd set guinea eggs under a chicken in the hen house. Same way with banties.

A banty'll pert near always hide her nest out, an' hatch a flock of bitties real late fall. She's the best little mother you'll ever find—chatters away constantly to 'em. Even when they're grown, almost big as she is, she'll still jaw 'em with ever' step they take!

Mama came in one late October evenin', sayin' she'd found an old hen foolishly wantin' to raise a family out of season. Sure 'nough, there was thirteen or fourteen little ones trailin' her! Mama laughed an' said, "Pauline, we'll have to knit little booties for 'em for the winter!" Oh yes, they always weather the winter real well.

I enjoyed watchin' guineas. They step daintily, liftin' each foot high an' curlin' their toes delicately before settin' a foot down agin. A guinea hen: "Pot-rack, Pot-rack" or "Buck-wheat! Buck-wheat!" The cocks: "Chee-chee! Chee-chee!" soundin' like a squeaky wheel. They're the barnyard watchdogs. A stranger come 'round, they'll "Pot-rack! Pot-rack!" or "Chee-chee! Chee-chee!"—just as loud as can be.

They're always so busy hustlin' for food; they go rangin' in a back field, front woods, all over. They can fly better'n any other fowl. I've even seen 'em atop the comb of a high barn roof.

Farmers would keep guinea fowls an' peacocks in those days to warn off hawks. I liked to have at least one white guinea, so I could instantly tell where they all was. About dark, when the other poultry had gone to roost, the guineas would still be out playin', an' they're always up early.

I looked out the kitchen winder one day, an' a white guinea was chasin' a gray one 'round an' 'round the chicken house. After while I looked out an' th'gray one was chasin' th'white one 'round an' 'round the hen house!

One time I had baby ducklin's turned out on a paper in front of the kitchen fireplace. Edgar got a little cardboard enclosure thing to put around 'em. I set out feed an' water an' they et, then I put 'em back in the box. They slop water all over when they drink, an' they git so wet. They'll get a mouthful of feed, then hurry for a drink to wash it down, hurry back for another mouthful of food, then get another drink. They'd forget whether they et or drunk last, an' then they'd stop an' look—back an' forth. I might add, all that food an' water goes right on through 'em, too!

But there's nothin' as dumb as a turkey, unless it's me. They're so big an' awkward an' gawky. I read somewhere that a turkey is livin' proof that an animal can survive with no intelligence at all. An' to think Ben Franklin wanted to make it our national bird!

I had two hen turkeys; an' Shirley Higginbotham, my niece, she gave me a tom turkey. One hen turkey saw that tom turkey, lit in an' give him a awful floggin'. The other hen stood by watchin', as if thinkin', *That's just the thing to do!* They finally made up.

Turkeys don't even have sense enough to come in out of the rain. Ernie Kennedy said they'd lift their heads up in a rainstorm with their mouths open, an' they'd drown themselves. That's the truth! Ernie helped Mabel Anderson raise hunnerds of turkeys on her farm south of Noblesville.

When babies, a big group of turkeys'll crowd together under the hover, an' even in th'hottest summer, they'll bunch atop each other an' be smothered.

I raised turkeys right with the chickens. People used t'say turkeys had to be up on wire to prevent blackhead. I had no problem usin' medicated feed to start 'em. They'll look scrawny an' sickly, like a moltin' hen, until they was 'bout three-fourths grown, then they'd git real purty.

A turkey'll hide her nest out an' it's hard to find the eggs. I'd have to watch her to see where she goes.

Let a truck drive away an' they'd take out after it. Me or Edgar'd have to go down the road an' get 'em. Those turkeys'd foller Edgar ever' place. One evenin' he went to the woods an' wasn't payin' no 'tention. One old white turkey follered him. Edgar come up, no turkey. He had to go back to the woods an' git the dumb thing an' shoo it home.

Geese'll stand like sentinels, guardin' the barnyard. They'll give an unwelcome honkin' alarm at the sight of an intruder—day or night—be it a animal or human stranger. an' geese are the best parents of any fowl when hatchin' eggs. We had a waterin' pan an' they'd go an' wet their feathers underneath, an' they'd turn their eggs ever' day. The old gander'd be right there helpin' his mate all the time, settin' on the nest when she goes to eat or drink. They say geese mate for life an' if anything happens to one, th'other'll sometimes brood itself t'death. Both of 'em equally protect their young goslins.

Once you put geese out, they won't take near the work or feed as ducks. They eat grass an' weeds, an' a lot of it. Ernie also told me that a good big gander would flog a snake to death with his wings, an' wrench its head off with his strong bill, especially if the snake was tryin' t'rob eggs from under his mate. An' there's nothin' better than goose grease for a congested chest. Mama rubbed us good with it when we got a cold or croup.

If a chicken hen hatches goose or duck eggs, she'll go on like they're her own, an' the only difference is when they come to a body of water. The babies want to swim, an' the old hen just goes crazy with worry, a-tryin' to coax 'em back, thinkin' they'll drown, but she's ignored!

I put guinea eggs in with banty eggs a couple times. You know, those little mother banties can tell the difference? She won't claim the others when they're hatched, even though both look so much alike when they're little.

A duck will guard her ducklin's real well, too. I watch my big, beautiful, snowy-white Peking ducks go for a walk. Mama Duck, with her brilliant orange bill, leads, an' the others foller her in a straight line. Papa Drake, the self-satisfied male with the curled feather on his tail, brings up the rear, all the time talkin' to his family in a wheezy chatter.

There's such a difference in the sizes, shapes, an' colors of the poultry eggs. There's the huge speckled turkey ones an' the big white duck ones, then the eggs from hens, banties, an' guineas. Brown guinea eggs are more pointed an' narrow-ended—odd lookin'. The reason for this is that the guineas tend to nest on bare ground. The shape of their eggs, bein' narrow-ended, makes the egg roll in circles instead of straight, keepin' it close to the mother an' the nest.

There's a big variation of egg shell colors, too, accordin' to the breed of chicken: white, brown, blue-green, an' yes, even green! The green uns are supposed to be low cholesterol, accordin' to nutritionists—a lot of hog wash, I say! An' brown-shelled eggs are supposed to be more healthy, which I seriously doubt, but there's quite a big price contrast!

One drake we raised, Amos, got so mean. Amy Lane, our great-niece, stayed with us daytimes till she was in the first grade. Once, Amos slipped in the back door with Edgar. Amos chased Amy right through the house. Just scared her to death!

Amos got bigger an' bigger. We'd still put him in a box at night an' we turned him out in the mornin'. He follered us to the hen house, follered Edgar to the woods, an' he went up an' down through the garden rows behind us. He bit my ankles an' feet—his mouth clamped down just like pinchers. Got meaner'n thunder. Workin' in the garden, I'd lean over an' he'd bite me on the fleshy part of my bare arm an' draw blood. I'd give him a goin' over, an' he'd look at me like he was a-laughin'. Whenever Amy saw him comin', she'd run an' climb up on the picnic table. A car'd drive in, an' he'd bite the person that got out of it.

Mrs. Johnson, a big colored lady from Indianapolis, would always come up here to buy eggs. "Have you got a duck you'll sell me?" she ast once. "Yes, Amos," I said.

"Oh no, that's Amy's pet."

"He's too mean. I've got to get rid of him."

"Well then," she said, "I'll gladly buy Amos."

Mrs. Johnson was always crackin' jokes an' tellin' us stories: "Now, John," said his mother, "if anyone ast you what part of the chicken you want, what would you say?" He considered the possibilities, then answered, "I don't know." His mother told him, "You must say you want the piece that no one else wants." So John always remembered that, an' one night John was ast out to supper. The lady had fried chicken. She ast John which part of the chicken he wanted. "I guess I'll take some of the feathers."

When the young chickens had feathered out, they was ready to grace the Sunday table. Paw would say, "We havin' the Gospel Bird today?" Folks said a preacher could smell a chicken dinner a week away!

The children always had to eat at the second table when company was present. The adults took forever, then they'd talk an' talk—for hours, it seemed. Us kids had to be content with the chicken parts that was left: the flappers, scratchers an' backs.

One day, Lee Sowers decided to break up a huge boulder out behind his barn an' ended up losin' all Louie's unhatched eggs. Johnny Lorenze, he knew his stuff about dynamite; he set it ready to go, then lit the fuse. Ever'one ran to get as far away as possible. You don't monkey with dynamite! Well, the rock *exploded*!

"I'll tell you, that like to cleaned out our farm." Louie said later. "The calves bellered, then jumped over the barnyard fence an' ran away. The horses rared way up an' galloped around the barn an' took off! Chickens squawked an' ran for the nearest cover. Dogs howled an' sleeked under the back porch. The jolt set the telephone to janglin'. And, not one of my baby chicks hatched that I had in the incubator—killed them in the shell!"

I'm almost afraid to tell this story, for what people will think of the way we lived: We had this hen in the barn. She hatched five baby banties an' was still settin' on a bunch more pipped eggs. I told Edgar, "I'll go an' git those babies an' take 'em to the kitchen cause a rat or fox is liable to git 'em in the night." Next mornin' I went out there an' somethin' had et the hen an' all the eggs. Feathers scattered all over the place.

All I could do was raise the five banties in the kitchen. As they grew I kept gettin' a bigger box to put 'em in. Of an evenin' 'bout dark, they'd start frettin' an' hollerin'—just like kids do at bedtime. I'd gather 'em all up an' put 'em in my apron in my lap. I'd rock an' sing to 'em there by the fireplace. Then they'd settle down an' go to sleep, an' I'd ease 'em down into their box an' cover 'em with a big ol' towel. Next mornin', I'd put 'em outdoors in their fenced pen to eat grass all day, then bring 'em in at night.

They begun to think the kitchen was a chicken house, so I moved 'em to the back utility room, into a big cardboard box. I put two slidin' window screens on top so's they'd have plenty air, an' to keep 'em from flyin' out.

When they was almost grown, I turned 'em loose outside their pen in the daytime. They'd foller us all over. They liked to come an' set on the arm of the yard chair when I set down to rest in the shade of the big maple tree. 'Bout dark, I'd open the back door an' call, "Time to go nighty-night!" They'd come runnin' an' jump into my lap after I set down.

November come an' we put 'em out in the brooder house for the winter. Edgar watered an' fed 'em there.

Spring, ready to clean the brooder house for baby chicks, I ast Edgar, "What are we gonna do with those little banties?" They was the purtiest ones we'd ever raised—the size of a small pullet. Edgar said, "If we turn 'em out, maybe they'll foller the old hens 'round."

That evenin', when it come time to shut up the chickens, those banties was settin' on the back step. I opened the door an' said, "Well, hello!" They hopped in, craned their necks all 'round—no bedtime box. They follered me to the utility room an' they flew up on the washin' machine. Now what would I do? I took 'em to the hen house an' shut 'em up for the night.

Next mornin' we turned 'em out. That night they was on the back steps again! "They'll make nice friers," I told Edgar. "I reckon we're gonna have to eat 'em." We couldn't afford to feed 'em till they died.

I went out with my bucket of scaldin' water an' Edgar had his ax. I leaned over to ketch 'em, said, "Well, come on. I guess it's time to go to chicken heaven." Two came up an' jumped right into my hands. I thought, *Oh, lawsy!*

When it comes to killin' chickens, the housewife was a neck-wringer, an' husband was ax-wielder. Edgar chopped their heads off. We dressed all five. I held each one over the flame at the stove to singe off that fine hair, then I scraped 'em an' cut 'em up an' put 'em in cold water to cool.

I fried one a nice golden brown, for me an' Edgar's dinner. When I took my first bite, it just wouldn't go down. "That's the last time," I told Edgar. "Even if we have forty pets, they can all live till they die on their own." Never before was it like that. We'd had all kinds of pets—come time to kill 'em, it made no difference. I put the others in the freezer to sell to Mrs. Johnson the next time she came to buy eggs.

Through the years I've had all these city kids come—from one to seven youngsters at a time—for the livelong summer. Everett's kids an' grandkids from Michigan, Augie's, Mildred's, an' Max's. They was wild with delight soon's they stepped onto our farm, an' they all loved to play with my animals. Well, I guess I was as bad about pets as they were. Maybe I was that way 'cause I couldn't have children. I claimed brother Max as my baby, since I had so much of his care.

The city kids was forever runnin' after the old roosters, scoldin' 'em for jumpin' on the hen's backs an' pullin' the feathers on their heads. They'd come screamin' to me, "Auntie Pauline, that rooster's gonna kill all our hens!" I explained they were makin' love—they don't kiss. They didn't believe me.

Augie reminded me the other day about somethin' that happened when we was kids—a brother a-teasin' his sister. He laughed an' said, "You went a-fussin' to Mama after breakfast. 'Mama! Ever-time Augie eats a boiled egg, he looks in it for a baby chick!' " I was so mad. Almost made me sick!

I'd been seein' an old hen in the haymow a-settin' on eggs. One day she was in the driveway of the barn with a slew of babies all 'round her. How in the world did she get 'em down? I saw that many-a-time. She must have pushed 'em over the edge, down into the thick straw on the floor. Or did she fly down, then coax 'em to her?

One evenin' Bud Costomiris was throwin' down hay for his cattle, an' he saw an' old hen on a nest of eggs back between some bales. He showed them to his wife, Lois. Each day she took water an' feed up there to the hen. Come time to hatch, the hen, eggs, all was missin'. Just disappeared! She looked all 'round. An old coon was lumberin' over to a corner. He turned, saw her, an' put his paws over his eyes, as if he was ashamed of himself. Their teenage son Bill, hurried an' got his dad's rifle an' shot him. Bill showed it off to all the farmers 'round. One old hunter said he'd been tryin' to get that granddaddy coon ever' winter for years!

Louie Sowers kept eggs stored in her cool cellar. Since rats liked eggs too, she kept cats an' a rat terrier dog, an' she set traps. But the rats ignored 'em all. One night she spread rat poison on a slice of bread, then hid it where none of her animals would find it.

All at once—*whew!*—she was never so sick in her life! She was carryin' her milk bucket to the barn to start the milkin', an' dropped it. Louie keeled over an' rolled to the fence. Lee saw her an' come runnin'. He was so concerned. "Well, what's caused all this?" he asked. "I think I inhaled some of the rat poison." He got her to the house an' laid her on the couch. He kept askin', "Why don't you say somethin'? Can you hear? Answer me!" Louie thought he was afraid she was gonna die, but she was just too sick to talk.

Then me an' Louie got to talkin' 'bout people we'd hear of who ate rat poison on purpose to kill themselves—suicide. Or little kiddies who got into it accidentally, thinkin' it was peanut butter. They died, of course.

And Louie told me 'bout the time she counted out eggs into a basket, ready to go to the grocery. She set the basket, eggs an' all, in the middle of the kitchen table. She needed a few more to finish out a even dozen, so she went to the chicken house for them.

When she came back in, little Helen—just three—was settin' in the middle of them eggs, happy as could be, throwin' 'em all over the room!

There was nuthin' to do but clean the mess all up. Dried eggs is like glue. Louie had to bring in the washtub an' give Helen a bath. She tied her in her highchair with Lee's leather belt to keep her out of meanness. Then, one egg at a time, she picked the good ones out of the basket an' put 'em in a dishpan of cool water to wash 'em. Needless to say, she was real late gettin' to town, an' her grocery list was cut short.

I didn't have children, but most women did. They had to manage their kids an' do their chores at the same time, unless there was an older child to look after 'em in the house. Sometimes there was an ol' aunt or a grandparent livin' in the home. "When Kenneth was a baby," Louie told me, "I took a rope an' tied it 'round my waist an' to his carriage. I pulled him an' carried the feed in one hand an' water in the other."

I heard 'bout a boy who soaked bread in his dad's whiskey, an' fed it to the chickens. They got drunk an' staggered all 'round—singin', or tryin' to sing, an' cacklin'. They tried to pass through a gate, but they'd miss the openin' an' bump into the picket fence. I'm sure that boy got a trip to the woodshed that day.

Some chickens prefer the barn or other outbuildin's to the hen house. Wintertime, a chicken always knew where she could keep her feet warm on cold nights. There were fussin' an' fumin' husbands when chickens roosted on the rumps of horses. Farmers always brushed their horses good each mornin', before puttin' the harness on 'em to go to the field. They didn't like havin' that mess to clean off first.

And there were chickens that found their way to the warm backs of cows. At the sight of the droppin's, they were given a forceful ride through the air by the irate farmer, but they'd be back the next night. Some, not so smart, roosted out in the trees in zero weather an' froze their combs an' toes.

One lady had saved all the fluffy feathers from her geese an' ducks to stuff pillows an' featherbeds. She kept the big sack of 'em tied up tight, then she clothes-pinned it to the clothesline out in the hot sun each day so they'd dry thoroughly. She came home from her club meetin' one afternoon. Somehow the sack had fallen an' her puppies had torn it open an' scattered 'em all over ever'where! What a mess to clean up. All her hard work, an' no new pillows.

There's sayin's 'bout chickens: *Puttin' all your eggs in one basket . . . Don't count your chickens till they hatch . . . Chickens always come home to roost . . . If a rooster crows at night, somebody'll be sick.*

A rooster may crow, but it's the hen that delivers the goods! Roosters'll crow at the first sign of daylight: "Cock-a-doodle-doo!" That was sure to wake city folks that come to visit! Roosters are proud old fellers. They'll beat the air with their wings, then crow with a big lungful! I guess, when that ol' rooster out there dies, we'll have to get a alarm clock for our wake-up call ever mornin'.

Remember leafin' through poultry catalogues? There were beautiful colored pictures of rare breeds. I'd set on Paw's lap when I was small, pointin' out the ones I thought was the purtiest. I remember Paw sayin', "Now there's a bird that's got some right to holler at the sunrise—if they're as good as their pictures, that is."

We had our share of fighty roosters through the years. One would flog another for gettin' his hen; they'd fight till their combs was all bloody. One of 'em usually ended up in the pot; that'd put an' end to their feud.

One old fighty rooster, he had big legs an' straight spurs that looked like long locust thorns. He'd flap his wings an' crow—king of the barnyard! We'd never see him, as he'd hide behind the snowball bush or in the rhubarb bed.

One flogged me once. When my back was turned, he come a-runnin' an' clawed my legs, an' on up my back. The big ol' spurs—just like knife blades! I was a bloody mess an' screamin' my heart out. Mama got out the bottle of iodine, stuck a chicken feather in it, an' painted me all over. I screamed an' danced all 'round the kitchen: "It burns! Blow it! Blow it!"

It wasn't such a old rooster, but Mama caught it an' swung it madly round an' round by the head. Finally it come off. The body went flyin' through the air, then flopped down on the ground—blood all over. The dog an' cats raced to get the detached head. We kids cheered: "Chicken for dinner! He cain't hurt us no more!"

Sometimes roosters got mean 'cause the kids liked to tease 'em. Augie used t'run a big red rooster all 'round th'barnyard.

An old one caught Paw once when he come out of the privy, an' he started his floggin'. Us kids was a-dyin' laughin'—that rascal pickin on Paw!

Paw grabbed him by the tail an' tossed him halfway to the barn, yellin', "If that murderin' rooster ever tries that agin, I'll beat his head off with his own drumstick!" But that scoundrel didn't learn his lesson. Paw was comin' out of the privy the next mornin' when we heard him holler, "That guy's misbehaved on me fer th'last time!" Then he took a club to him. The rooster's broken neck swirled like a dipper dropped in a crock of milk. He flopped around in crazed circles, drippin' blood all over the dusty ground. He finally keeled over an' lay on his side a-kickin'.

Mama hurried an' het up a teakittle of water t'boilin', so's she could dress him. No, he wouldn't be cooked done in time for noon dinner. Mama said he'd probably be as tough as shoe leather. He'd have to cook all day. But nothin' was ever wasted on a farm. The unexpected supper of chicken an' dumplin's was a big treat durin' a weekday. Paw, enjoyin' it said, "I've got that big ol' black rooster where he won't hurt nobody no more!"

Another unexpected chicken meal was when one'd fall in the horse tank an' drown when it was tryin' to get a drink. The chickens always had their own water trough, but like kids, they'd try this. If the chicken was still warm, Mama hurried to cut off its head an' scalded it in a bucket of boilin' water. I pulled off the feathers.

When me an' Edgar lived close to the road, a chicken would invariably get through a fence an' be run over. The driver'd gen'r'ly bring it to the house. I'd check it all over an' if it wasn't damaged too much, I'd clean it for eatin'.

As hatchery chickens got moderately priced so we could afford 'em, we bought day-old chicks from the Mabel Anderson Hatchery. We brung 'em home in partitioned, perforated cardboard boxes that were prob'ly thirty inches square an' six inches high, marked LIVE BABY CHICKS. Four sections in each box, a hunnerd chicks in all. Holes were poked out to give 'em air. Kids'd collect the circles for play money. Oh, to watch those cute baby chicks pokin' their tiny bills through the holes . . .

Then we bought a twelve-foot by twelve-foot brooder house to put 'em in. I still remember the smell of the new wood inside that brooder house. I had always saved old license plates an' pieces of tin to patch rat holes in the old one. Now Edgar bought bales of peat moss for beddin'. It was much better'n straw, an' I didn't have to clean it as often.

Some folks used sawdust or shavin's from the lumber yard for beddin'. Chicks got splinters from 'em an' would choke to death. Crushed cobs was popular for a while. When chicks started dyin', Doc Young, the vet'nary who had his office at Mabel Anderson Hatchery, opened some of 'em up an' found they had choked to death on cuckleburrs they et in the crushed cobs.

After gettin' the chicks all settled in, I'd set on the sack of mash over in the corner an' watch the busy little bitties happily drinkin' an' eatin'.

Me an' Edgar liked to go to the hatchery an' look through the glass doors of the incubators. We could see, at close range, a baby chick pippin, breakin' the shell all 'round to git itself out—the struggle, then finally makin' it! The wet, naked body stretched an' looked 'round. It soon dried off, an' it was fluffily clothed!

They'll peep when they're still inside the shell, did you know that? You can hear 'em. They work for a while an' rest a while, an' then, all of a sudden, they make it out.

There come a time when most farm women had their own incubators to hatch their eggs in. I never did. Twice a day, the neighbor lady'd take a tray full of eggs out, set 'em on the kitchen table, then roll the eggs all 'round, jist like an ol' hen'll do. The incubator was kept a constant warm heat, supplied by a coal-oil lamp. The temperature had to be controlled perfectly. Too hot or too cold would kill 'em. The newer incubators used electric heat.

The husband usually saw to it that the brooder house was carefully warmed for the new hatchlin's. Some heated their brooder house with a little coal-burnin' stove set near the hover, or coal oil, then later, electricity.

Fire was a constant worry. Sometimes the coal-oil burner would blow up. So it was a relief when electric heat lamps could heat the house, although I never thought they was as good for the chickens. That thermostat-controlled heat—it'd be nice an' warm, then it'd shut off, cool down, an' then turn back on. Well, ever'thin' has its advantages an' disadvantages. The biggest worry with electricity was a storm—the lights'd go out. We'd have t'hurry with the lantern or flashlight an' put 'em in bushel baskets an' carry 'em to the warm kitchen until the power come back on.

The earlier you got your chicks in the spring, the earlier pullets'd start layin' in the fall, when the price of eggs is high. The scarcer the eggs, the higher the price.

A hen molts through the summer, sheds many of her feathers. Then, when the days get cooler, she starts layin' better an' puts on her pretty winter coat of new feathers.

When eggs was plentiful an' cheap, I'd salt 'em down in a wooden box to use when the hens wasn't layin'. I'd alternate a layer of clean, dry barn salt an' a layer of eggs till it was full, then I'd store 'em in the cool dark cellar. They'll keep for weeks that way. Mama did it like that, too.

Paw et so many eggs that Mama said if he opened his mouth

too wide, he'd crow. Sometimes, to make us kids laugh an' to tease Mama, he'd hold his head way back, break a egg, swaller the whole raw thing right down, then toss the shells in the coal bucket! Yes, he did!

Paw told us the story of a tramp in the chicken house a-stealin' eggs. "He'd crack 'em on top of his head," Paw said, "then, with his mouth in the air, drink 'em down. After he'd cracked one an' swallered it, he cracked another. 'Cheep! Cheep!' said a chick. 'You spoke too late, little feller!' said the tramp as the baby chick went on down!"

Paw would mimic animal noises to entertain us kids, then he did it for the grandkids. He'd crow like a rooster, gobble like the turkey, honk like a goose, quack like a duck, oink like a pig, moo like a cow, even whinny like a horse. He was so funny!

A chicken meal is a good company smell! There's a hunnerd different ways to cook 'em, I guess: eat 'em fried, boiled, or baked, or with dumplin's, noodles, or dressin'. Eat ground chicken in sandwiches, pressed chicken an' barbecued chicken. An' eggs! Have 'em fried, poached, scrambled, scalloped, or the picnic favorite—deviled! We dried the feathers for pillows, an' the dog et the guts. I guess the only thin' ever left was the squawk!

There was this lady—they was well-to-do farmers—she'd bring chicken an' dumplin's to all the church doin's. One time she was tellin' the women, "I saw this sickly hen stretched out under a elderberry bush; she couldn't git up, so I kilt her fer these dumplin's." I never et her cookin'—that day or anytime after that. A sick chicken—we'd doctor it good till it was well, or died, but we never et 'em!

A bunch of men was talkin' 'bout the best an' worst cooks at thrashin' dinners. One man told of a wife who had served 'em a old rooster for dinner. "Was old enough to vote," he said. Another piped up, "Old enough to be president, you mean!" They were all in agreement; they couldn't abide half-done or burnt chicken or fish.

One of the fellows asked, "Do you know why the farmer's wife chased the chickens out of the barnyard? They were usin' *fowl* language."

Grandma had a puppy that got to suckin' eggs. Oh, they're hard to break, but Grandma said she'd teach him a thing or two—to leave her eggs alone! Done it many a time. She cut out a portion of egg shell an' mixed a lot of red an' black pepper in with the raw egg, then she set it in his dog pan an' stood back an' watched. He lapped it up—shell an' all, an' even licked his lips! Why no, it didn't break him!

Grandpa got his fill of hearin' Grandma rant an' rave ever' single day 'bout that pup, so one mornin' Grandpa took the pup to the back of the farm an' shot him dead. When the grandkids found out, they 'bout had a conniption! Well, who'd a taken him? Even town folks raised chickens an' had their own eggs. That pup'd have found 'em! Grandpa said, "I ain't makin' no enemies over a pup!"

Y'couldn't git much for a old rooster at the store or huckster. Mebbe three or four cents a pound. The fat, sunburned, bald-backed, big ol' bare-assed hens I sold to the huckster. Women knew they'd cook up tender with lots o' rich broth to make the best dumplin's, noodles, or dressin'.

The poultry buyer, with crates stacked high in his truck, made his rounds in late fall to buy the year-old hens to take to an Indianapolis market. This certain stingy ol' guy offered one lady twenty-five cents for each of her plump one-year-old hens. She was so insulted an' told him, "I will not give away my hens to a daylight chicken thief!" She then let all her penned-up chickens out to eat grass. Her kids carried canned chicken sandwiches to school that winter—to the envy of their peanut-butter-sandwich classmates.

There was good money in capons. Capons got big—the size of a turkey almost—an' was very tender. The vet'nary come an' operated on the young roosters. He'd raise one wing an' cut a little slit through the skin by a rib. He had an instrument he'd go in with to snip out the two testicles, an' he'd throw 'em to the cats an' dog that was standin' there. We'd release the "capon" in the clean chicken house. They was kept separate from the pullets, so they could be fed heavily until Christmastime. Later on, they started usin' a pellet implant, supposedly to get the same results, but that was soon outlawed by the government.

Usually we could count on havin' half roosters an' half pullets in a flock. When I got older with arther-itis, cleanin' the roosters to sell became quite a task, so I started sellin' the young fryers to poultry men.

I can't remember when me an' Edgar started buyin' "sexed" chicks—all pullets or all roosters. The pullets cost more, but I didn't want the roosters to fool with.

You put Leghorns in the hen house an' they're a sight best layers—big white eggs an' a lot of 'em—but they won't bring two cents sellin' as old hens—too light in weight.

I've raised all makes of chickens: Rhode Island Reds, Plymouth Rocks, Barred Rocks, White Rocks, Brown Leghorns, White Leghorns, Silver-Laced Wyandottes, Buff Orpingtons . . .

When I was a kid—late fall, cold, just before the weather turned off real bad—Mama decided to sell the year-old hens an' put the young pullets in the hen house. I remember hatin' this job; it was freezin' cold out there. We couldn't wear gloves 'cause the chicken legs would slip on through our hands an' they'd git away. My fingers, as cold as a frog's behind, were numb. I kept shakin' 'em, but we'd have to wait 'round till Paw caught each one with his hands or a wire hook, then hand 'em over. Mama could carry six at a time—three in each hand. Paw would carry five in each hand if someone else caught 'em. Their agonizin' squawks would ring out through the clear frosty night air. Us younger kids held one in each hand. Sometimes one or two would git to floppin', an' the frightened kid'd let it escape. Then Paw'd yell, "I told you to hang on tight! We ain't got all night to do this job!"

Me an' Edgar always had a lot of company; I was known for the delicious meals I put on th'table! Mama, too. Durin' the Depression, city folks come out for a good farm meal—always just droppin' in, no call ahead. More'n once, when I still lived at home, I heard Mama complain: "Those people, green as a gourd. Don't they know I've got all this work to do? They think I kin jist drop whatever I'm a-doin' an' put on a big spread!" Well, she always did.

I can still hear Mama call to me on Saturday mornin' when I lived at home: "Pauline, go kill a ol' hen, one that ain't a-layin'—a settin' hen—for Sunday dinner." A hen that had stopped layin' ended up in the pot. Old roosters would go to the guillotine.

Nothin' tasted better on the Sunday dinner table than Mama's fried chicken, mashed potatoes, new peas from her garden, cole slaw, sliced tomatoes, an' fresh apple pie. The egg bag never made it to the table; Mama an' I divided it; it was excitin' to find a hard-shelled egg an' a handful of little yellow ones. Paw laid claim to the gizzard, liver an' the breast. Mama liked the backs an' wings. The drumsticks went to the younger kids, an' the thighs to the older ones. Mama took the gristle off the leg bone, an' baby Max was content an' happy to chew on it, a-settin' there in his highchair.

Eastertime, the dime stores sold colored baby chicks an' ducks—blue, purple, an' green ones. Soon, these pretty little babies outgrew their cuteness an' the families was lookin' for a farmer to adopt 'em. In time, they outlawed this, prob'ly 'cause they was mistreated by children who no longer wanted to care for 'em.

Years passed—some of 'em good, some of 'em not so good—at me an' Edgar's farm west of Cicero. All in all, I thoroughly enjoyed my poultry paradise an' their country choruses! Many, many folks came out from town to look 'em over—in the barnyard, chicken house or my kitchen. When she'd seen 'em all, one lady asked,

"Anything else in your nursery?" So I showed her my baby goat; he liked to be rocked, too!

It's good now to talk of "The Good Old Days." Durin' one of these bull sessions, somebody mentioned Sunday dinners, an' one ol' feller slapped his knee an' said, "Those were the times fried chicken tasted so good that if I put it on top of my head, my tongue'd slap my brains out tryin' t'git to it!"

Tri Town Topics, March 15, 22, 29, 1979
Tri Town Topics, March 29, 1973 (Louie Sowers' story)
Cicero, Indiana: 1834–1984

The Good Old Days

When I hear some people praise
What they call "the good old days,"
And they tell me what they miss,
I remember things like this:

Coal oil lamps, a wheat-straw broom,
Outdoor wooden powder room,
Cast-iron stoves and wood for fuel,
Walk a mile or more to school.

Pitch the hay and scrub the floors,
Fill the lantern, do the chores,
Carry water from the spring,
Swarms of flies on everything.

Milk the cows and slop the hogs,
Chink the cracks between the logs,
Mend the harness, shoe the mare,
Clean the barn, no time to spare.

Horse cars, gas lights, button shoes,
Muddy streets and avenues,
Whiskers, corsets, derby hats,
Rubber collars and cravats.

Up before the sun's warm rays . . .
Yessir! Those were "the good old days"!

—*Author unknown*

Fred Heinzman

Southpaw Pitcher

Whenever the name Fred Heinzman came up in conversations about baseball players, folks remembered: "Southpaw pitcher! This is gonna be a hot game tonight!"

I'VE ALWAYS ENJOYED A GOOD GAME OF BASEBALL, and that's saying a lot, since I'm ninety-two years old!

Back in the early 1900s, bib-overalled baseball teams were found on Sunday afternoons and holidays—especially on the Fourth of July. Those were hotly contested games, played at schools and church picnics. Occasionally there were suited teams. I didn't have a suit until much later.

From the first grade on up to the eighth, that was what was on my mind—baseball. As soon as school let out for recess and noon, us boys were out that door and down the steps like a bunch of penned-up dogs. We hurried and chose up sides. I was picked first, since I could throw a mean curve ball and was good at stealing in home.

The two little runts were last to be called. They couldn't hit the side of a barn if it was standing two feet from 'em. They were always striking out or they'd walk. We didn't make fun though—

kinda felt sorry for them. They hung in there. By the eighth grade, they'd shot up around all of us others and were real good at playing basketball. That's when I realized something important: It's easy to give up, but you have to work for things that are important and worthwhile.

Men and boys talked baseball over dinner tables and back fences, during horses' rest stops, on porches, at the farmers' elevator—they were all experts of the game.

The last day of school at Baton Rouge, we had big pitch-in dinners. You just never saw so much food! Then we had a short "last-day-of-school" program that the kids participated in. Whole families and friends came, even those who had no children or had some that were already grown. All this time, I was dying to get out there and play ball!

The north side of that brick school—all eight grades were in one room—was the baseball diamond. We were hard on the grass and shoe leather.

Noah Sowerwine was the township trustee and J. F. Haines was the county superintendent. They made it to all the dinners. Both went out and played baseball with us in the afternoon. All their dignity was forgotten as they participated. They'd whoop and yell, wave their hats and bawl at the umpire—all in fun, of course.

One time Mr. Sowerwine got up to bat. He made a big hit and busted his pants out clear up the back—his underwear showed through. He was in a terrible fix. We all bent over laughing, then looked around to see if any women had seen what happened. One came to his rescue!

Back as far as I can remember, I was ball-throwin'. Whether I was herdin' cattle or out doin' the chores, I was bouncing it against the barn or playin' ketch with a brother. I throwed rocks—aiming at birds, fence posts, or the clothesline and telephone wires to hear 'em zing! I got purty good.

We had homemade baseballs at first. We used grocery-store

string we'd zealously saved. At stores, everything was wrapped in brown paper and tied with cord. We rolled that around a rubber ball—wrapping continuously until it was large enough. Then we encased it in pieces of leather. We laced that together so it wouldn't come unraveled. A sudden shower—the thing got wet, and we'd lay the ball in the sun to dry. If we hit it into the weeds, we hunted till we found it.

Our first bat was the handle of an ol' stub of a broom with the business-end sawed off. When we were older, we whittled one by hand from straight-grained hickory. I can't remember when we first had a store-bought bat. I suppose one of us saved enough money from doing farm jobs for neighbors. We had an old mitt. I wonder now, where did it come from?

All of our family lived with old Uncle Johnny. There was our mother, Mary, and our father, Henry, then Louise, Walter, Leonard, Harry, John, Katherine, Mariester, and me—Fred. We were an active bunch! None of the girls cared much about ball-playin', except Mariester—she was the tomboy of the girls.

Every noon after dinner, us Heinzman boys went out in the barnyard and played ball. I always got to throw. In a little a while, after Dad's short nap and while the horses rested, he'd yell, "Time t' git back t' the field!"

We had a ball team of neighborhood kids over at Stringtown Pike—Ote Roberts, Tal Kepner, Lenny Eck—I can't remember who else right off. We played a team at Noblesville for our first game. They were too good for us, so we played amongst ourselves.

Then Dad moved our family to a farm he bought in Jackson County where land was cheaper. I got to playing ball down there. Mr. Coleman taught me how to throw curve balls and other tricks. I was left-handed and I could throw hard. He was impressed with me.

But back home, Uncle Johnny was so homesick for us. And Dad didn't like the poor soil down there. Uncle was talking of his concern to neighbor Mike Kaiser. Mike had a suggestion: "Johnny, why don't you deed your farm to Henry with the understanding you'd have a home there with them for the rest of your life." Uncle agreed—that was a good idea. We'd been in Jackson County a couple years by the time we moved back.

Uncle Johnny led a quiet, solitary life. He had his own room which was full of old furniture, pictures, books, and relics of a past no one else cared about. He was a man of few words. He spoke mostly in German—his English was usually too Dutchy to understand. He was worth listening to though. If you didn't, you would pay the price—out back in the woodshed with the razor strop. He emphasized, "You must understand, here and now boys, that when I give an order, it is to be carried out. Is that clear?"

North of our house was a good-size truck patch. Uncle Johnny raised two rows of Long Green tobacco for his own smokin', and the remainder of that big patch was in potatoes. He worked out there all summer.

Us boys began throwin' rocks at his tobacco. Oh, we got in plenty of trouble. We were purty careful of windows though—Ma saw to that!

Mike Kaiser chuckled as he told about one of his visits when Johnny was enraged with his nephews. Uncle said, "I'd hear a *whoosh*! Down would go a tobacco leaf. Then another *whoosh*! I yelled, 'Who done that, dadburn it. Who done that?'" Mike said he laughed, but it wasn't funny to Johnny. Then Mike told us about being there when our strawstack burned down. "We musta been smokin'," he said. "But your mother yelled out to your Dad in her Dutchy voice, 'Keel 'em, Henry! Keel 'em, but don't hurt 'em!'"

Our folks didn't approve of Sunday ball-playin', so we always ran off to the back pasture or meadow. They, or anyone traveling along the road, couldn't see us. We scouted around until we found a level place across a ravine to play.

One day I was walking past John Zelt's. He yelled, "Come up here, Fred. Here's somethin' I want to show you. Ed Kepner sent me this letter. He needs help down in Kansas on his ranch. He has lots of cattle, horses and grain. Be interested in a job?" Oh boy, would I! Every boy dreamed of goin' west and ridin' a horse to round up cattle.

Well, I went down there and liked it. Neighborhood boys'd set up ball games behind the schoolhouse. Orie Kepner said the high-school fellas wanted him to get a good team together to play them. They needed exercise and experience before playing scheduled schools. I was the pitcher. Beat 'em purty easy, too. I stayed two summers—over a year and a half altogether.

The manager of the Missouri Pacific Railroad team saw me play. He asked, "Would you consider coming to pitch for us?" I said, "Yeah, sure I will!" Ed, my boss, when I told him about the offer, he grumbled, "Naw. Too much work around here to do." I reminded him, "Last week you said we was gettin' all caught up, and you promised that I could have more time off now, after working long hours every day all those weeks. I've already promised to go pitch. . . ." He warned me, "If you go, I'll have to fire you."

Well, I went. I played and we won, but I was out of a job. A neighbor boy and his sister wanted me to come over a while and work for their family. So I went.

One day we took off for the Stockman's Carnival, down at Garden City. They had cowboys and the ropin'—a regular rodeo. Cowboys in there from Montana, Wyoming, and all over, a-bull-doggin' those steers and a-ridin'. I was havin' the time of my life!

They had the usual carnival booths there, too. One they had was with the fuzzy-headed dolls. Knock three down, get fifty cents. No one was havin' any luck. If you remember, the way they were placed—were they screwed down tight? Well, it was almost impossible to beat that game. I walked up, took the ball that was provided, drew back my arm and *wham*! went the first one. I struck all three down, and the fella handed me the fifty cents. He said, "Where in the world did you get that arm? Not just doin' ranch work, I'm sure!"

I got caught up at that place. It was time to move on. I was gettin' homesick anyhow. So, I started back to Indiana on foot with all my belongings and some spending money in a grip.

At home, whenever there was a ball game, I pitched. I got a job working for seventy-five cents a day on a farm, when the weather was fit. Then I got an offer to go to Fairbury, Illinois, to work on a farm there for twenty-eight dollars a month and room and board—rain or shine. Whoopie!

My boss there, Mr. Hargersheimer, belonged to the Baptist Church. I attended services with him; I always went to church back home. They had a Sunday School league. I was their pitcher at games every Tuesday afternoon. I thought I was the cat's pajamas, gettin' off work to play ball! The local newspaper had write-ups of all the games.

Saturday nights we went to the picture show. They beamed it outside, up on a building's brick wall. There were vaudeville acts between pictures. This feller came out a-talkin', sayin' something about Heinzman, southpaw pitcher. All at once, my ears perked up. He said, "It was like the silence of a empty church as he drew back and fired away. 'Stee-rike!' called the umpire as Heinzman's fast ball split the plate. 'Three strikes and you're out!' " The man went on and on. I hadn't realized, until then, I was such a big topic!

When our grain was all thrashed out, I needed to look for another job. A bunch of men told me they already had a contract to go up in the northwest for that harvest. So I hitchhiked out to Minnesota where they was cuttin' wheat, barley and oats.

When I got into that town I asked a feller, "How do I get a job?" He said, "Oh, put on a pair of overalls—I had on hack-about work pants and a shirt—and stand in the street corner. Purty soon someone will come along needin' help." So I did. Got a job right off. Must a been 1915. Three of us were hired on at the same place. We caught a ride with two other fellas in a little ol' Ford Roadster—five of us in that little ol' open-air jobby.

After working weeks on end, we were given time off. The five of us decided to go way down towards Ft. Dodge—a hundred miles across country—in that ol' car. Just a trail down through there—six-inch-deep tracks. We was a-goin' along—all us boys a-singin'. One of 'em was drunk; I was glad he wasn't drivin'. Didn't have to steer 'cause the wheels stayed in the ruts. The driver threw up his arms, like the rest of us, while he was singin'. No worries about passin' anybody—not a soul came along. We had a great time!

Towards the last of the season, there was a big street fair, and a game was scheduled. They lacked a pitcher. A feller questioned me about my playin'. I threw him some hard, fast curves. He was impressed and said, "By golly, you'll do!"

We played a few innings of the first game, and it started to rain. I was glad. If a fella plays all the time, he's toughened to it. But I wasn't, even though I'd been working hard on the ranch.

When that work was finished, I came back to Indiana and went to work unloading cement at Burdick Tire and Rubber, at Noblesville. I was playing ball again.

After one of the games, Mr. Krepser—he ran the Brass Works up at Kokomo—he came to me and said, "I'm gettin' a team together. What would it take to have you to go to work for me and pitch with our ball team?"

"I get twenty-five dollars a week. If I could get forty . . ."

He jumped at the chance. "I'll give you that! I'll give you fifty dollars!" I went and played till the season was over. Then I was off to the army. That was before World War I.

In training at Ft. Harrison, I played in waist-high ragweed. I got hay fever so bad—my nose run, eyes watered and I sneezed constantly. I couldn't do that and play ball at the same time.

We were all transferred to Camp Shelby, Mississippi. They gave us Saturday afternoons and Sundays off. Some would druther go to New Orleans, Jackson, or Biloxi on pass. Others, like me, wanted to play ball with a team.

Someone said, "That Heinzman—you oughtta try him out.

He's as good a pitcher as you'll find anywhere." From then on I pitched them all.

They were playin' a series of games to see who was the all-over-best of the whole camp. The 113th Signal Co. thought they were superior. So we played a series—two out of three. We won and got the title: THE UNDISPUTED BASEBALL CHAMPIONS OF CAMP SHELBY 139TH M.G. BN. (Machine Gun)

Next, our outfit was shipped out. As we landed in England, an Englishman, riding on a big old white horse, handed each of us a letter from King George. When the Armistice was signed, November 11, 11:00 A.M., 1918, I was on the train, headed up front. So I missed all the action and, somewhere along the way, I lost King George's letter.

By next spring, I was home. Bill Hare—he had the Chevy dealership in Noblesville—he was getting up a semiprofessional team. His two brothers, Frank and Albert, were players. Bill pulled out good performers from Indianapolis, Frankfort, and Lebanon—all over. Emmet Fertig was the publicity man and scorekeeper.

Then one day, the manager of the Indianapolis Indians came up and wanted me to sign a contract. I did. I was to go to Texas the next spring. I waited to hear back from him. I never heard . . . and never heard. When they got home from spring training, I contacted him.

"I'll send you down to Florida to the Florida State League" he said.

"Naw, I don't want to go," I answered.

Ernie Burke, manager of the Florida team, sent me a letter. He said, "I'll be mighty disappointed if you refuse to come. There are a lot of Noblesville people living down here now and they are anxious to have you."

Well, I sure wanted to go, but my three brothers—Harry, John, and Walter—were away in college. Our house, settin' so close to the railroad tracks, caught fire from flying sparks and burned down. I can still smell those pine boards burning. Dad wasn't able to farm much and he needed me at home to help. So I had to refuse the offer.

Nostalgic memories linger, now that I'm ninety-two:

At a game one day, a little girl, watching from the side, started laughing so hard. "Look Papa—that boy up there at home plate—he's playin' in the dirt. His mama will be so mad if he gets it on himself!" You players will remember dusting your sweaty hands in dirt before taking the bat.

There were often diamond disputes—someone would angrily stomp from the field or sometimes there'd even be fights.

Remember the eight-gallon water-filled milk can with a dipper? Sweaty players lustily drank from the same dipper, but there were no germs in those days!

At scheduled games—spectators in buggies, Model T's, Chevies, and an occasional Buick—ringed the playing field. Folks cheered wildly—had to, to be heard above the loud honking of horns.

There were no lights yet in the fields, so games were played during the daytime.

You've heard the expression, *I'd rather play ball than eat*? Well, that fit me to a T. I can hear old Doc Tucker yet: "Southpaw pitcher! This is gonna be a hot game tonight!"

Tri Town Topics, October 2, 9, 15, 1975
Good Old Days, Spring Summer Special
Noblesville Daily Ledger, October 18, 1983

Floyd Shelton

My Ol' Kain-tucky Home

The Floyd Sheltons, from Kentucky, moved into our community. Immediately everyone regarded them highly. His humor and speech were so different—quite a contrast from Hoosier. And this is how he told his story.

I WAS FETCHED UP in them hoots an' hollers of Kain-tucky with all them ridge-runner mountain people.

We farmed with mules down thar. They ain't as hard to break as a horse—once you git the bridle on 'em. I druther work a mule any day, than a horse. Their feet take to the ridges better. A mule can be so con-trary, downright o'nery. Coaxin' did no good. Knock him down to show him who's boss, an' he'll git up an' go on real good. Now, a horse, he'll be so plum put out, take him half a day to git over't.

Pappy worked fer one man, then I did, an' altogether we put in twenty-three years at the same place. Thet man went 'round the fall of the year and he'd buy up all these little mules—maybe have anywheres from fifty to a hunnerd at a time—an' fetched 'em home. Then he'd go out buyin' more. Bring 'em in an' we'd take care of 'em till they's two-year-olds. I 'spect he'd let five hunnerd mules out a year to farmers. They'd break 'em to work fer two year, then he'd take 'em back to the feller who'd put 'em on the market, an' he'd sell 'em—already broke, ready to work. The farmer'd pick up two more fer another two year.

We grew our allotment of t'baccer—'bout three acre. Back in '30 an' '31, it was dry—dry as a Sunday sermon. Ever'thin' jist burnt up. We had three acres t'baccer, sold thet fer fifteen dollars, which we got half of an' t'other guy got half. We had to run a grocery bill all thet time. Good thin' we didn't need much—jist coal oil, sugar, salt, an' coffee.

We notched all the hogs' ears or else we put rings in them, so's we could tell they's our'n. Then we turned 'em out on them knobs. Late summer, they filled up on acorns fer several weeks, till the corn was hard 'nough to start feedin' it. Then we rounded the hogs up an' put 'em in a rail pen 'r a pole pen an' fed 'em corn till they's ready to sell. Sometimes we'd stretch up a line 'r two o' bob-war to hold 'em in jist 'fore goin' t' market, so's they wouldn't run their fat off.

Down thar ever'one knew his own hogs, as good as he knew his kids. They didn't ever have over one 'r two sows at a time, and thar litters. They didn't wander away. You give 'em a little dishwater slop—tater peelins an' other kitchen scraps—an' mix in some ground corn; give 'em thet once or twice a day an' they'd stick 'round. Wasn't 'nough grass to tare out to.

Pappy was askin' one feller how his sow did. "Well," he laughed, "iffen she'da had one more, she'da had twins."

We could take a beef, and in eight months it'd be big an' fat. Lespedeza was good hay; it'd grow almost on a rock. But mostly they et corn fodder, then feed out on punkins. An ol' cow'll eat punkins 'fore she'll eat corn. I guess the word is pump-kins, but we allus called 'em punkins.

A feller ast me 'bout thet th'other day. I said, "Yeah, we raised punkins on them hills. First, y'open the barn door wide. Then go up on them knobs, cut the punkins from the vines, give 'em a little shove, an' they'll roll right down into the barn!" Suppose he believed me? An' I said, "A feller fell out of a cornfield once down thar." He laughed.

Cows'll go wild over thet moonshine slop—get knee-wobblin' drunk on them corn squeezins! Sure they do. Why you'd have t'pen 'em clear away from it. Still they'd break into it sometimes. They'd eat thet thar stuff an' begin a-weavin' back an' forth. Thet's the truth. Drunk cows! They'd fight to git 'round them mash boxes thet're four foot wide, six t' eight foot long, an' four foot deep. They'd battle to git to it—runnin' over each other! They'd drink it as fur down as they could reach an' then they'd be so danged drunk y'could hardly git 'em outta thar. Lots of folks liked the milk from those cows—called it "white whiskey!" Hogs liked moonshine too, but they couldn't reach it.

Moonshine was also called wildcat, rotgut, white mule, an' white lightnin'.

Hear the name Kain-tucky, folks automatically associate it with moonshinin' an' bootleggin'. Know how bootleggin' got its name? Men'd hide their liquor bottle in their boots. Pappy used t' say thar was a whiskey still on ever' creek an' holler down thar.

We planted lotsa our land with a hoe. Couldn't git a mule or horse on it; it was so rocky an' steep. Shucked the corn out a acre wide. Started at th'top, throwed each ear down to the bottom of th'ridge, come right on down shuckin' till we got to the foot of the knob an' we was done. Then we picked it up an' throwed it in a little wagon Pappy had. The mules pulled it to the barn.

You couldn't hardly judge a acre of corn down thar. Sometimes it was only four or five rows wide. All we got was jist enough to feed our hogs out, a cow, an' a coupla mules. Fifty bushel a corn'd last a ordinary farmer all winter.

Thar was a feller up in Indiana thet worked fer a loan company up thar. They loaned money to a Kain-tucky boy to buy a car—he was livin' up thar at the time. The boy took off to Kain-tucky but didn't settle his bill 'fore he left. The loan man went down in them hills, said he felt skittish. "So I looked up the sheriff an' ast him to go 'long with me to find th'boy."

Sheriff said, "Well now, Mister, let me give you a little advice. Them guys are as hard to pin down as smoke from a bottle. They're allus a thorn in a sheriff's short ribs. Jist better turn 'round an' go back home. You go up in them hills an' you'll never see Indiana agin."

Th'Indiana feller said, "I was plenty skeered, I'm here to tell ya! I was as nervous as a hay fever dude with diarrhea. Well, thet settled thet. I went on back home!"

Another one of them Kain-tucky fellers went to th'army 'fore World War II. The colonel thar at thet army camp had been a big shot in the NRA [National Rifle Association]. Fer years he helped put on a huge rifle match in Ohio.

Thar was over four hunnerd recruits out on the rifle range thet day. The Kain-tucky kid laid his head across the rifle an' he'd shoot—sightin' with his left eye.

He was ast to learn to shoot the *kee-rect* way—with his rifle on his right shoulder. Finally, the lieutenant realized th'private couldn't git th'hang of it thet way, so he told him to put the rifle on his left shoulder, like he was used t' doin', if thet was easiest.

The colonel come along an' watched. Well, the private was a-doin' it all wrong. The colonel scolded the kid, "Learn to do it th'right way, Private!"

The lieutenant pleaded, "But Colonel, if thet's the way he can shoot, an' he's accurate, let him shoot his way. He's had years o' practice down in the hills!"

Th'colonel ignored th'lieutenant and went right ahead explainin': "Two clicks on the sight will move it four inches—a hunnerd yards. What's the windage rule, Private? Now, tell me, how do you sight at thet bull's-eye?"

The private pondered a minute, an' said, "After the first round, I knowed I had to go two squirrel's eyes to the right."

The ol' colonel reddened, thinkin' the kid was bein' a smartass. Then, seein' he was serious, he motioned him on. He watched as th'private hit a bull's-eye ever' time! The colonel walked away, shakin' his head, suppressin' his laughter.

Down home we had a ol' yeller cat thet went all over, nosin' in ever'thin'. Mammy, my mother, had a big ol' churn she used fer makin' butter thet she sold in town. Between the churnin's she kept the cream in th'churn behind the livin'-room stove, till it soured good. She added cream to it each day. We had twelve-foot ceilin's; th'stovepipe went up through thar an' the floor upstairs and on out the roof.

Summertime we took the stove an' the pipe down, an' Mammy laid a flat board over th'pipe hole upstairs. She kep' the churn settin' the same place year-round. She tied a clean white cloth over the top to keep the flies an' dust out.

One evenin' Mammy took off the cloth, lookin' in to see if the cream had clabbered. Well, here come thet son-of-a-buck cat—*ker-plop!*—into Mammy's thick cream from thet hole upstairs! An' when thet cat come up outta thar, he brung all thet thick yeller cream with him. He didn't leave 'nough in thar to put in yer coffee, an' Mammy was splashed all over!

Cat, blinded by th'cream, went crazy—skeered to death! He slapped cream all over th'daybed, all 'round the walls, 'round an' 'round he went, huntin' the door to git out. When he finally found it, he shot right on through, leavin' a big hole in the screen.

All th'family set thar laughin' their fool heads off! Not Mammy. She was frothin' at the mouth, mad enough to fight a buzz saw! Thar went her butter money fer a week. She shot out a arm an' pointed to us, shakin' with rage. "I think we've had quite enough of thet lunacy! I-god, I wish you could see yerselves," she wailed. "It's a fine how-d'ya-do when y'all kin set thar haw-hawin', an' thet devilish cat ruint my buttercream. Now, you jayhawks, if thet's so consarned amusin', git rags an' buckets an' hot water an' dig in!"

I laughed so hard I was limp as a neck-wrung rooster, an' Pappy was still buckled over, holdin' hisself. We knew thet cleanin' up the house was wimmin's work, but thar was no arguin' with Mammy. Even Pappy set to work, helpin' all us boys, an' still we kep' on laughin'.

Down thar in Kain-tucky where I was brung up, they don't say, "We raised twenty bushel corn to a acre." We'd say, "We raised twenty gallon to a acre." An' they don't drink water—thet's fer worshin' feet.

Normal year, we'd git 'bout three gallon o' whiskey outta a bushel o' corn. Thet's the only means some of them people had a-makin' a livin' with such poor, rocky soil. Thet was way back in them thar hills, a-course.

Helen's dad—Helen's my woman —he worked fer her uncle. He'd moonshine, an' they'd put him in the jug; but not fer long 'fore somebody got him out.

Her mammy had a Santy Claus 'bout a foot high—head broke off. She stuck the moonshine money down in thar an' it'd be full a lotta the time. They didn't bank. Not enough greenbacks.

The still I was helpin' with, a good run, could git a hunnerd gallon a day.

We didn't have no water up on them knobs. Had to haul it fer whiskey-makin' like we watered our stock—in barrels in a wagon pulled by two mules.

The cricks'd dry up in summer, but at home we had water at th'pump. Don't take much fer a Saturday-night bath in a round tin tub!

Once I was workin' fer a man. Oh, it was foggy. We'd done run off one batch an' I was cleaning the still in th'barn, gittin' ready to set another'n. The boss, he come runnin' down thar, excited. He jerked his thumb in thet direction, said, "Floyd, I think thet was th'law went by in thet thar car. You better clear out!"

'Bout the time he got me told, thar the man was. Stood out like a tall man at a funeral—right big bruiser. Make two o' me. He was allus as mean as a badger with his tail in a trap. He'd fight anythin' thet argied with him, so mostly nobody did. More'n one said they'd like to shoot his belt buckle out through his backbone. They claimed he done nothin' but drink an' play with any maid thet had th'right sort of gleam in her eye.

I spotted him. Thet law man grabbed open the side door, an' I shot out the other'n like wind before a storm. He took after me an' I s'pect he run me a mile. I was 'bout gone. My stomach cartwheelin', I jumped over a log, hopin' t'hide. Didn't have 'nough wind left in me to let a healthy poop. I could tell he was tard, too. He took out his gun an' shot. Man, then I wasn't a bit tard! I took off like a turpentined dog. He yelled, "Why, you son-of-a-bitch you!" If he'd a caught me, he'd a put me in the clink.

"Pappy, they got my boss." I said when I got home. "We're gonna have t'go up to Bardstown an' see Charlie 'bout gittin' Nolan outta th'slammer."

Charlie always furnished the money to git the little guys out, the moonshiners. They'd hurry an' git y'out 'cause they was 'fraid you'd tell whar the big money was comin' from.

Charlie said, "Yeah, you take this money an' go an' git Nolan out." I measured him with a long stare, said, "You ain't a-sendin' me! He's already run me all over them hollers. You go git him!"

Thet shite-poke Charlie, he was gittin' rich an' all we was doin' was barely makin' a livin'. He loved the juice. His only ambition in life was to outwit the revenuers. He spent the live-long day a-settin' on his end-gate.

Pappy used t' be a heavy drinker an' was often on the wrong side o' th'law. Ever' time he got all likkered up, sleepin' off the bottle flux, he'd swear, "Honest to God, I'll never touch a drop agin, honest to God." Next week, moseyin' 'round with the whiskey makers—they's a-boozin' up—he'd come home drunk as a skunk, smashed.

People wonder why makin' moonshine whiskey was 'ginst th'law. Well, some bad eggs was sellin' sorry stuff. What they'd do, they'd give th'buyer a drink o' good whiskey, an' then whut he bought, it'd pie-zen a body—tarantula juice! I tasted some once an' thet stuff took all the hide offa the roof a my mouth an' burnt me all the way down. I could exactly tell where thet stuff lit in my craw.

'Course, thar was those who sold th'good stuff to git thar customers back. But some would jack up th'price for't. One feller tasted some, said, "Why, I kin git better likker by holdin' a bottle under a mare's tail till she pees."

The farmers run whiskey off inta kegs. Men'd come an' buy a thousan' gallon at a time. Could git a dollar an' quarter a gallon.

When th'little ol' airplanes come out, a pilot'd fly 'round them knobs a-huntin' th'moonshine stills. They didn't make many trips, an' moonshiners didn't shoot nary a plane down, but they come pert near't. They would've picked 'em off if they'd kept flyin' over.

Thar was electricity in towns but not in the hills. Fer us mountain people, they come out with a little generator you put up on a pole, an' the windmill run it. I think I was the first guy bought a radio down thar—drunk when I done it. Ever'body wished they had one, but the price was out a reach. Well, buyin' thet radio, thet was th'wrong thin' I done! Ever'body in the neighborhood, eight or ten houses in thar, whole families'd pile in ever' night—walk a mile and a half'r two—ever' night! Come listen t'Amos an' Andy, Lum an' Abner, all them, laughin' till they cried! Stay till awful late, settin' 'round in thar like flies 'round a keg a molasses.

'Tween programs, they'd talk 'bout their coon dogs an' swap 'shiner stories. The women talked 'bout th'ailments of ever'one they knew, but th'men didn't pass 'round no jug. Oh yeah, they all liked their likker, but Mammy put a stop to it when they come to listen to the radio. She put her foot down—"No drunks!" So they'd smoke an' chew. Pappy chewed. Mammy didn't smoke like many of the mountain wimmin.

We got sick an' tard of thet bunch allus thar. Those fellers was poor and rougher'n a cob, but they wasn't poor in th'things thet make a man. You're in trouble, they'd come a-runnin'. They ain't strong on brains, but they ain't short on guts—all heart above the waist, an' guts below't.

I recall the evenin' in 1927 when news came through th'cracklin' static thet Lucky Lindy had landed in Paris after his Lone Eagle flight acrost th'Atlantic. Oh boy, imagine thet!

Pappy was a widder when he married Mammy. I had two half-sisters an' four half-brothers, but they was 'bout grown time I come along. Thar was me, then John, Lawrence, an' Mary. We had a little house, but got by.

'Fore the radio, we'd all have doin's ever' Saturday night. Walk a mile, mile an' a half or two. Neighbors an' kinfolk git t'gether at th'store or school. Folks brung baskets o' food, sugar tits fer the babies, an' lanterns to spell the dark. I kin still see 'em a-goin' home—their hand-held lanterns swingin' from side to side; the parents creepin' along, overseein' their young; boys an' girls runnin' an' whoopin' an' cuttin' up; sweethearts with their arms 'round each other, lollygaggin'; an' old folks hobblin' 'long, barely makin' it over them rocky places.

I not only helped make moonshine, I'd git all tanked up at times, too. But Mammy said I'd better never git on a bender an' disturb the neighbors. Oh, I 'member yearnin' to be old 'nough t'be like them big uppity fellers, pull out th'cork with my teeth an' take a deep swig, then hand th'jug over to th'next un. An' I'd cuss thet mule-skinner language, an' git myself in the pokey like they's allus talkin' 'bout. A poor boy's daydreams. I never let Mammy hear it.

One ol' feller showed me how champions drunk whiskey. Hunkered down on his heels, he put a finger through th'handle of th'jug, swung out his elbow, so's elbow raised jist high 'nough to send the proper 'mount a likker to his mouth. 'Fore I knowed it, I was one a them boys passin' 'round the booze.

They was this one dude, as dumb as a ox an' big as a two-year-ol' bull. Had to watch whut y'said to him. He'd git sore as a stepped-on snake. Fight? You never seen th'likes o' him to fight! An' by-grab, I ain't takin' thet a-layin' down! Once I landed a haymaker on his jaw, causin' him t'topple all th'way down thet mountain. He come up outta thar—hot as a broken blister—n'blacked both my eyes.

The next mornin' Mammy took one look at me an' said, "I-god, I wish you could see yerself—eyes like two piss holes in the snow!" Mammy understood men, an' she understood likker. She dealt with both 'em all her life. I was a-grinnin'. I'd had a fight aginst a big feller.

She was patchin' me up, an' a-lecturin'. I've heered 'em a hunnerd times if I've heered 'em once. "I cain't abide a man who cain't hold his likker an' then tarns mean-spirited. He makes others suffer fer 'is weaknesses."

She'd regale me with stories: One kinfolk gambled, drank an' womanized his pay. His whole family suffered. But he was a pleasant fellow—drunk or sober. Another old un, his face as long as a dried possum hide, an' skinny—as poor as a hind-tit calf. He allus carried a gun, an' was 'bout as dangerous as kickin' a loaded polecat. Drunk, he said it made him see double and feel single. Another kinfolk was a loudmouth when sober, let alone th'booze to oil his jaws. An' mean-faced, lookin' like he was raised on sour milk. Another'n, th'more he drunk, th'wilder'n louder th'stories.

Thar was a bunch of us young bucks—wild as corn-crib rats. One of 'em couldn't smell a cork but whut he'd git on a cryin' jag, then he'd git the trots. We'd fool round all night. Next mornin', standin' out by th'barn, we made wagers who could piss the furthest.

One feller, he'd lived in Indiana fer a long spell after movin' up thar from another part of Kain-tucky. He come down in them mountains on a whiskey-buyin'. He begun recountin' this story to me: "I didn't know nobody. I jist kep' goin' up an' round them hills. I'd look down in thar, kep' a-lookin' down in thar, an' I finally seen a beehive, but it was a house."

Well, I'd lived in them parts fer so long I knowed all th'lizards by their front names. I ast him how it was. He said, "Dangdest place. I had t' stay thar overnight so's I'd not git in trouble with the law." Sheriffs're always suspicious of strange cars in an' outta towns—them whiskey buyers.

Then he went on, "As I found my way up to th'door, a voice called, 'Y'all come on in,' which I did. The man had a scarecrow frame an' greeted me with a handshake. His face was red as a lobster from both sun an' whiskey, I s'pect. He set down on a backless chair. His boots was so frazzled, he couldn't scratch a match without burnin' his foot. He unlaced 'em, best he could around knots, an' pounded 'em upside down. Dirt an' twigs fell to th'floor. A smotherin', yeasty odor drifted from his socks, which had holes th'size o' silver dollars. He didn't have on 'nough clothes to pad a crutch. I tol' him whut I'd come fer. I studied him—looked to me as harmless as a bee in butter. He rubbed a bony finger up an' down th'side of his nose, a-thinkin'.

"The barefoot buxom wife come waddlin' in, hips a-swayin'. She was puffin' an' pantin' as she come from out back of th'house—prob'ly the privy. The floor squeaked under her weight, dishes an' pans rattlin' with ever' step she took. Her dress was stained over her stomach. Like most Kain-tucky wimmin, she smoked a pipe. She flopped down in her rocker. It was jist like air goin' outta a balloon! 'Whar y'all from?' she ast, smoothin' her dress under her legs. She was so fat her sides hung over th'sides of her rockin' chair an' sorta squeezed out under th'arm rests an' spokes. My, my, ugly as lye soap! So bucktoothed she could eat a apple through a picket fence.

"I turned to see a round, purty baby—prob'ly a year old. Her loaded didey looked an' smelled like it was a week overdue fer a changin'. *Phew!* Baby saw me an' give a little crow of delight. Her fat little legs bowed like a wishbone. She tottered to her mammy, climbed up an' started nosin' 'round fer her supper, an' got it. At th'mammy's large saggin' breast rested a contented baby—her pudgy hands patted 'em. How sweet.

"Mammy was comfortably rockin' her babe back an' forth, lookin' as pleased as a stray dog in a hen house. Purty soon Baby was 'bout asleep. Not much lap thar to set on an' she kep' a-slidin'. Mammy'd pull her back up. All at once she fell off—smack dab on th'floor! She let out a awful wail, a-sqwallin' an' a-kickin' like a cow with a sore tit. Mammy reached over an' picked her up. 'Now-now-now-now-now. You ain't hurt none!' Then she offered her th'other tit.

"Nothin' 'round much in them two rooms but old furniture, an' a strange mix of odors—dirty clothes an' bodies, wet didies an' wood smoke from th'stove. The wind kep' blowin' up through the cracks in the floorboards, which was uneven an' splintery and as old an' drafty as a spinster's nighty.

"The man stirred up th'fire in th'stove, then set back'ards astride another chair, with his arms folded and his chin restin' on 'em on the top rail. He was chewin' a wad of t'baccer. Juice had run down his front, when he was outdoors, I s'pose. In th'house he'd hit the spittoon with true markmanship. The mister asked, 'Y'want a chaw?' He pulled a greenback twist from his pocket an' handed it t'me. I thanked him kindly.

"I told him my mission—on the prowl fer some good whiskey. 'Better come an' have a look whilst it's still light,' he said as he got up to go.

"We talked whiskey prices. He offered me a drink o' his whiskey, which I accepted. Good stuff, too! Sometime later we went back inside. Both of 'em recalled many moonshinin' stories—it was an enjoyable evenin'.

Baby started fussin' terrible. Mister finally said, 'Better hit the shucks. Long day t'morry.' His missus stood up an' yawned an' stretched. As she walked past, he patted her bottom, said, 'Jist look at thet. 'Nough thar fer ten men an' it's *all* mine!' She give a hearty laugh.

"I hadn't et since real early breakfast an' had no vittles with

me. None was offered. Y'see, it was gittin' kinda late when I found the place.

"The lady threw a ol' blanket on the floor over in th'corner fer my pallet, an' a extrie kivver. She turned the lamp low then put a hand half over the lamp chimney an' blowed out th'light. The baby slept 'tween 'em.

"Their bed creaked with ever' movement. Then, listen to this—you won't believe it. Next I heerd the comfortable sounds of *love makin'*! Here with a stranger in th'same room! She seemed happy to accept her wifely duties, no matter who's 'round. Then a real wall-rattler performance an' finally his contented snorin'.

"The two-room shack was 'bout three feet offa th'ground. All night long, hogs was under thar a-fightin', rootin', or snorin'. I eventually dropped off t'sleep. Then suddenly I woke up. Durn hound dog was layin' agin' me—scratch, scratch, scratchin'! Fleas, yeah! All night I could feel 'em all over my body a-bitin'. Blanket was probably full of 'em, an' bed bugs too! I considered goin' out to my car t'sleep. I changed my mind on thet thar thought. I'd probably carry a sight o' bugs home with me, an' I didn't want thet!

"I went to th'door whisperin', 'Here, boy! Here, boy!' an' coaxed the dog outside. Then the howls—folks don't know a hound dog wail less they've lived with it. The mister kep' yellin' out the winder fer him t'shet up. Fer all th'sleep I got, I might as well have stayed up with th'hoot owls. Ever' time I closed my eyes, I started itchin' an' thet dog kep' howlin'.

"Next mornin' I was as empty as a widder's purse. Hadn't et since breakfast yisterday. The woman was out in th'kitchen makin' biscuits. All she had on was a ol' pair o' black bloomers an' a dingy white petticoat and it was tore down. Her skin was white as a fish belly. She had th'fat little girl thar a-nursin' as she rested on her mammy's hip. The baby, she was jist a-goin' after it, an' milk was streamin' down from th'other tit—right into the biscuit batter. An' she kep' stirrin' it all in thar. An' me so hungry! 'Bout took my appetite away.

"While th'biscuits was a-bakin', she went to git a bowl o' molasses outta a five-gallon tin lard can over under th'winder. Someone who'd been thar t' buy whiskey'd brung it to 'em. Th'durn cat was a settin' in th'winder an' somehow he fell in thet can o' sorghum! The woman jist pulled him outta thar by his neck, rubbed all thet molasses off with her hands—clear down to his feet, like this, on down into th'can o' molasses—then throwed th'cat out th'open winder. She dipped out a bowl of molasses fer us t'eat on our biscuits, cat hair an' all. An' me a-dyin' o' hunger!

"I was lookin' out th'winder at th'beautiful mountains all around. The mister called to me: 'Coffee's bilin'. Ankle in an' put yer feet under th'table.'

"The biscuits looked right purty when she took 'em outta th'oven. I et 'em an' they was good! No molasses, thanks. Th'coffee was strong enough to stand alone—black an' hot.

"Much of the time I was thar, th'missus was settin' down in th'old rocker, her bare feet hooked in th'round wood rungs, she a-nursin' th'baby. Milk run down under her arm from her other tit onto th'old wooden floor. Th'fat, spotted cat stood thar lappin' it up. Thet mammy had 'nough milk to wet-nurse a dozen babies!

"Sometimes th'little tyke didn't act hungry. She'd tease away at th'nipple, then all at once she took a big bite. Mammy slapped her mouth hard. 'Now you nuss thet tit or I'll give it to our mister over thar!'

"Well, I did git real good whiskey. Thet man was purty clean in his operations. Too bad I didn't drive on over t' th'next knob. Folks said I'd a found a nice family thar, a good bed to sleep in, an' I'da et good, too. An' good whiskey!

"I struck a real good deal—both of us was happy. All th'folks urged me to go back down thar an' buy more. 'Not on yer life,' I said. 'Once was 'nough!'

"Well, thet was quite an experience—I left Kain-tucky on a Revenuer's bullet!" th'man said, laughing.

Some of them mountain babies, they jist never could git 'em

broke a-nursin'. Stand up thar at th'mammy's side to suck. Age five an' they's still draggin' on th'tit. Ended up sneakin' behind th'door if someone comed. Weaned when they went to school, I reckon.

Me an' Helen went back to our school reunion a few years ago. This here lady was thar, a giggly bundle. She was still happier'n a pig in a mud puddle. Dressed real nice an' with her man. Him an' her both lookin' right smart in their brand new duds. Him in his dark blue bib overalls an' her in a printed cotton house dress.

She hobbled in with a crutch under one arm. Her foot was all bandaged up. They set down 'side me an' Helen. The lady dug into her pocket, brung out a kitchen match an' snapped it to a flame with the edge of her thumbnail to light her corncob pipe.

When I ast her what happened to her foot, her fat belly shook with laughter. Said she'd won a power mower in a drawin' in town. One day she was runnin' it 'round their yard. Th'danged thing choked up an' kilt th'motor. She tipped it up an' reached in with her foot so she could jolt th'blade lose. Th'motor sprung to life, an' her big toe somehow got cut off. As large as she was, her husband an' several men had a time gittin' her into th'car to take her to th'hospital in town.

Then she continued: "One of th'men said, 'Run back thar an' git her toe. I heerd tell of 'em sewin' 'em back on.' Another feller took off after't, but was soon back. 'Too late,' he chuckled, 'durn hound dog done et it!' "

Down thar now, you'll see beautiful brick homes an' fine churches—all built back into th'mountains. Folks'll drive miles to their work, usually in breweries, where th'wages is high. Once in a while you'll see a house abandoned—th'winders broke an' a tree growin' through th'porch, weeds higher'n yer head, an' th'people gone.

Mostly, folks down thar have come up in th'world, after all these years. I'm supposin' some of 'em still make moonshine—jist fer themselves, jist fer th'fun of it. I never did go into th'moonshine business. Thet gunshot skeered me out fer good! Lotsa folks like me come up to Indiana an' worked at th'Firestone factory in Noblesville. We made big wages compared to whut we'd been used t' in Kain-tucky. I never was book-read.

Mammy was right, when she saw I was makin' sheep's eyes at purty girls, she said, "Fer ever' man thar is jist th'one right girl in this whole world. Someday you'll meet her, and when you do, you'll know right then an' thar she's th'wife fer you." Well, it was Helen. She soon had me walkin' the fence. She was cute as a bug's ear—purty as a speckled pup. I fell fer her faster'n apples rollin' out a basket.

Me and Helen married an' lived here in Indiana. We had six young uns: Kenny, Mary Ellen, Gary, Doris Ann, Bobby, and John—nice family.

We've lived away from Kain-tucky fer years now, but I do like t'go back home, t'git t'gether with kinsfolk an' old neighbors—what's still thar—an' listen to all them moonshine tales!

Tri Town Topics: November 30 and December 7, 14, 1978

Ruth Morris and Hildreth Foulke

A Long Journey — 1910

A Conversation Around the Kitchen Table

Many, young men especially, yearned to "pull up stakes" and go to greener pastures. Reality is never as good as the fantasy, as you'll see in Ruth's and Hildreth's story.

RUTH: "Now, that's what makes you scratch your head, how we'll get it all on this train!" I remember hearing my father say that when he was preparing to make our move to Carrington, North Dakota. It would be a long journey from our home right in the center of Indiana—in Noblesville. Carrington was the county seat of Foster County.

Papa, Alvin Reese, had talked to Henry Miller in Arcadia, who told him he'd read of this great place up there. He said, "The soil is rich, black, deep and fertile. Its productivity is valuable for settlement. You could make a real good living." It didn't take long for Papa and Uncle Calvin Hiatt, with their families, to decide to go. We didn't homestead—just rented a section of 640 acres.

"What? Moving to North Dakota?" Papa got surly reactions from neighbors and family. "You'll lose your shirt." I'm sure Mama quite agreed with them, but whatever a husband decided to do, a wife had no say; she just went along with his wishes.

One old neighbor was adamant: "I'll bet you dollars to doughnuts you'll be back home in Indiana in a year." Well, he lost that bet, but we didn't stay too much longer.

One family member—I won't say her name—she fussed. "I never, in all my born days, knew of anything so downright crazy as wanting to give up a good farm and go off to some forsaken place at the other end of the world because of an advertisement in a newspaper or the hearsay of someone who hasn't even been there. If it is so all-fired great, why haven't they gone and made a million?"

Most other men, of course, said they wanted to venture out, but couldn't get the wife to agree—always putting the blame on the little woman. But it was plain to see, Papa was itching to be off and he would have his way no matter what!

I've heard it said: *Men like to up and move on, and women want to nest and stay*. A woman needs her family, friends and community. She doesn't want to raise her children so far out she can't see smoke except from another county.

One man, who was making the move, said, "It's gettin' so settled through here in Indiana, I have to go to the toilet to take a leak. I want to move where there is plenty of fresh air!"

It took two long days for the men to load all our belongings into two boxcars. The things set beside the railroad tracks in Noblesville. It was like a big puzzle to find the best place for a team of horses, several milk cows, crates of Plymouth Rock hens, hogs, hay, sacks of grain, the cream separator, household goods and furniture. Wagon wheels were removed and laid flat to make more room. Farm machinery and all kinds of hand tools—rakes, hoes, garden plow—those things were placed in and around the wagon bed. Father made sure it was packed tightly. Otherwise, when the locomotive bumped the cars to connect them together, everything might go tumbling.

Late one afternoon they hooked up the cars. By the crack of dawn the next day, we were on our way—the beginning of a long journey for a little girl—me, Ruth Reese, age seven. I was born January 1, 1901. The trip took two days and a night.

Papa and my brother, Charlie, slept in the emigrate cars to quiet the restless horses and cows. It was an endless and difficult task to feed and water the livestock. They milked the cows once a day, instead of twice a day like back home. Cows don't give their milk down when they are nervous. Dad and Charlie milked, then poured it into troughs to feed the pigs and chickens. People laughed when they saw freshly laid eggs in the hen crates. Traveling slowed egg production, too.

My mother, Ella, my sister, Lorena, and me; and Uncle Calvin and Aunt Fanny Hiatt and their daughter, Mabel, and five sons: George, Noel, Worth, Clifford, and Malcolm—all went together in the passenger car. There were thirteen of us altogether, counting Dad and Charlie.

There was no diner on the train. Well, now, there might have been one, but we probably couldn't have afforded to eat in it. Mother and Aunt Fanny packed sandwiches, cookies and fresh fruit in straw suitcases and shoe boxes.

When the train windows were opened, clouds of cinders and ash blew in. We got them in our eyes and all over ourselves, but when the windows were closed, it was stifling hot. Mother could never stand a dirty child. She was busy all the time, wiping away cinder dust from one kid, then another.

Once, between towns, the train whistle blew three sharp blasts in rapid succession. It lurched slowly along, quietly beeping, before it jerked to a complete stop. Kids and adults pressed their faces against the soot-covered windows to see what was causing the commotion. Hurriedly, the conductor threaded his way up the aisle to the front, calling out, "Stand back, folks. Don't crowd!"

After a while he came back laughing, and reported his information to the curious passengers: "Some dang-fool cow is on the track. The engineer saw her headed toward us from up on a hill. He gave the three blasts, hoping to head her off in another direction, but she came on anyway. If he couldn't have stopped the train, we'd have had beefsteak for supper! Now she keeps runnin' along the rails in front of the train. The engineer is beeping the whistle to frighten her, so she'll veer to the side ditch."

This could have been a dull trip, but episodes like that along the way made it exciting!

At railroad crossings between towns, we'd see horses and wagons on both sides, waiting for us to pass. The friendly farmers always gave us big waves, and we returned them. We kids played guessing games, like who'd see the first white horse, a big barn, a country schoolhouse . . .

We made so many trips to the water cooler, necessitating many trips to the toilet. We washed our hands real often and didn't have to be reminded! All of us had so much excess energy. Back and forth. Back and forth. Finally Mother scolded, "You're making a nuisance of yourselves. I don't care if all the other kids are traipsing up and down the aisle, you're not going to make a spectacle of yourselves. Now, sit down and be quiet!"

Clickety-clack, clickety-clack. The wheels sang a cheerful song as they clipped off the miles. Clifford's head swayed back and forth with the train's movement. He always fell sound asleep after the train took off from each town. It didn't affect us others that way.

A funny thing happened at Hankerson, South Dakota. The conductor called, "Hankerson! Hankerson!" to alert those who were to get off there. It wasn't our stop. Us kids were sitting in seats across the aisle from Mother and Aunt Fanny. We each stood up—we were so hungry—to get a fried-ham sandwich. Clifford, nine, had been snoozing. He woke up. Still half-asleep, he fell in line with the passengers who were getting off. Aunt Fanny held up Clifford's sandwich to give to him.

"Clifford? Clifford! Where's Clifford?" We searched the line of passengers—everyone was getting frantic. The conductor called: "All aboard! All aboard!" The train started moving slowly, then faster and faster. Still no Clifford.

Aunt Fanny described her lost child to the conductor. He remembered seeing him file out with the others who were leaving. Uncle Calvin had to get off at the nearest station and wait until the next train brought his son. From then on, Clifford was called "Hank" after that town, Hankerson!

I don't remember too much about the train trip, but some of the events have been told so often through the years, I can almost repeat them word for word.

After our arrival on Saturday, all of us stayed in the hotel until the stock car came into town. The men would then unload the horses and wagons to take us out to the farm.

Mother and Aunt Fanny decided we'd go to church on Sunday. There were three denominations: Congregational, Catholic and Dunkard. The women chose Dunkard. During services, they started washing feet. I fussed, "My feet's already clean!" Mother poked me in the ribs. Why, I'd never seen them wash feet in *church*! Families supplied their own song books. We sang from memory.

I remember the distressed look on Mama's face when she overheard a lady talking: "It's a wild, vast, empty country out here. You can ride for a hundred miles without seeing a house or a fence or any other sign of human endeavor." Mother's face showed concern. She just shook her head. Back home, neighbors were within halooing distance of one another.

Father's train, with the livestock and implements, had arrived ahead of us, so he was there to greet everyone. He saw to the loading of our baggage in his wagon. He motioned to Mama and helped her to the high seat in front, then he hoisted each of his two daughters up. We happily settled down among the valises, bags, bundles and wraps. Charlie stayed behind to look after the livestock and all else that had to be moved later.

Dad's beautifully matched bay team jingled its shining harness as we were on our way out to the ranch. Driving horses and their harnesses were a source of pride for my father. The smell of horse flesh and leather was a welcome change from the train's smoke and cinders. I noticed horses' barnyard buns at the side of the road, just like at home. We rocked along to the plodding rhythm of the horses' smooth gait. The wagon jolted on. I kept looking back to see if Uncle Calvin's were following us in their wagon.

Papa told us there'd never been trees on the prairie like back home, where every farm had a huge woods lot and every yard was full of them. In Indiana towns, trees framed each street like huge umbrellas protecting those walking beneath them.

On the way to our new home, not a sign of a farm or a homestead. Mother kept shaking her head and clicking her tongue. "I just can't imagine how barren this country is! No shade for the men to rest under on a hot haying day, nor trees to shield the sun for my two little girls to play in the cool grass." Papa tried to comfort her. He could see she was getting real discouraged, even before they reached their home. He said, "They'll just have to go to the shadows made by the house and barn." Mama continued complaining, "In winter, no trees for windbreaks. Nothing will stop the icy, raw blasts!"

After the long, smoky, noisy train ride, how invigorating the fresh air was! I gazed at the beautiful countryside. I felt the swaying of the wagon and heard my parents' quiet talk. It lulled me to sleep.

After a thirteen-mile drive, we turned off the road. I woke up when the horses started following the bumpy lane—a quarter of a mile to our new home. Dad yelled "Whoa!" to stop his team when we arrived. He jumped down, wrapped the lines around the whip socket, and we all piled out.

Dad already had a house for us to live in, but construction on Uncle Calvin's cabin had just begun, so, at first, all thirteen of us lived in our big, four-room wood-frame building—two rooms down and two rooms up. When we entered, the whole empty house echoed the sounds of all our footsteps. To accommodate everyone, the men strung blankets from wires upstairs and divided it off into four bedrooms.

There was a thrill about first arranging our belongings in the new place. As the women unpacked, the empty dry-goods boxes served as cupboards and bookshelves. They placed tidies on the backs of all the chairs and splashers behind the washpan and water bucket. Upstairs, they made up the beds, finishing them off with the prettiest quilts. They scrubbed, cleaned and shined the entire place. The dust and cobwebs were soon gone and the rooms began to bear more of a resemblance to the ones we had left behind. In no time at all, the women were cooking, and we were eating and sleeping quite comfortably. This was *home*!

HILDRETH: My folks, Gertrude and Omer Williams, went out there a year and half later than Ruth's. It was Ray Williams, Dad's cousin, who coaxed Dad to try his luck. A man by the name of Hiatt rode in the railroad car with our horses, cattle, chickens and Pony Joe. He had a little stove, and he fried bacon, ham and potatoes. Mom had prepared bread and other provisions ahead for him. Cows furnished milk, and chickens laid eggs. The other men, women and kids went by passenger car. We took our food on the train, too.

I was three, too little to remember much. Sister Martha was just a baby. We were sixteen months apart. I'm six years younger than you, Ruth. I was born July 12, 1907.

Dad had rented a farm. We didn't move in with Ruth's folks. Until our little home was ready, we lived in a community house. Mom complained, "It was awful! Just a shell. So many strangers and no privacy or accommodations."

The first year, our crops were good—beautiful wheat. The second year, it was so nice and pretty, then those hot winds came through. "Sneak winds" is what they were called. A stranger came by and said, "By morning you won't have any wheat left." And we didn't. It was gone. We couldn't believe it.

Ruth: I remember standing at the kitchen window looking out over 320 acres of wheat. I said, "Isn't that pretty?" The wind was blowing it like ocean waves. Dad said, "I'm afraid it's the wrong kind of wind. Sneak winds."

That night all the wheat wilted, fell flat to the ground. Dad put in seven crops and harvested three. No wonder he died young—fifty-six. In 1920. Nephritis. Mother lived to be eighty-two. My sister, Lorena, is four years older than me, and she's still living. I'm ninety-two! Charlie was forty-six when he died in 1940. He was in World War I, got that awful flu and never saw a well day after that.

Hildreth: One time a dust storm came through. Dad was at the barn and didn't dare try to get to the house. Out in that, you couldn't see where you were going; it was just like a blizzard. It frightened Mom. She stood Martha and me on chairs by a window, and we both looked out toward the barn to see if we could get a glimpse of Dad. The storm seemed to last an eternity, but it was probably only an hour or two. Mama fussed about so much dust. We could hardly breathe. It was all over everything, even though the doors and windows were tightly closed.

Ruth: We brought my black and white dog along. We wouldn't have thought of leaving him behind. Back home, we lived near a fire station. Every time there was a fire, our dog howled and howled when he heard the siren. Well, now, the coyotes started yelling, and our dog turned on his siren. I got so tickled—laughed and laughed. Mother cried, "That makes me so homesick!"

I remember one dog we had back in Indiana. He was so destructive; he sucked eggs, killed chickens, dug holes in the yard and garden, and clawed big grooves in the door to get inside or out. No matter how hard they tried, the folks couldn't break him of his bad habits. One day, they'd had enough. Dad loaded him up, and we took him several miles from home, making every imaginable turn so he'd lose his way if he tried to return home. They dumped him in a wooded area near farm buildings, where Dad knew he'd find the house and be well-fed. We kids cried and carried on something fierce—poor dog!

On our return trip we stopped to do the Saturday shopping and to eat dinner with relatives. We said our good-byes that evening and started the long journey home. And who do you suppose came running and barking to greet us? That dog! Us kids—the whole family—we were so glad to see him. He lived with us until he died years later.

HILDRETH: We took our dog, Scotty. When dad got ready to milk, he'd send Scotty to get a certain cow way out from the buildings. Dad had trained him that way as a pup. Sometimes Scotty would bring the wrong one up. We thought he did it for devilment. Dad would scold him, say, "Now Scotty, you go get Old Jersey." And off he went, tail a-waggin'. He'd bring back Old Jersey—both of them on the run, the cow's full bag a-swingin'.

When Dad milked, he'd set the milk bucket, full of milk, down. He'd say, "Now Scotty, don't bother this." And he wouldn't! When a cow has a new calf, you can't drink her milk for three days. Nature provides that first nutritious colostrum milk to give the calf a good start, but it isn't for human consumption. He'd set that down, and Scotty'd lap it up. Yes, he knew the difference. Dad said it was good for dog and cats.

RUTH: My first year of school in North Dakota, we walked two miles to the little one-room Rosebud School. Miss Martin was the teacher. She had come all the way from Indianapolis, and she roomed and boarded with us. My classmates were almost all Norwegians and Swedes.

I went to school even when it was fifty-four degrees below zero! We'd never ever had it that cold in Indiana. No one back home believed it when Mother sent letters. Dad put a thick bed of loose straw on the bobsled for us kids to hover in when taking us to school. Mother heated big stones and wrapped them in heavy cloths to put to our feet. Dad threw a horse blanket over Lorena and me, then wrapped himself in a huge buffalo robe. Dad was forever freezing his nose and cheeks.

The teacher met each student at the door. She had a tub of snow, and any child who had frostbite on his fingers or feet put them in the snow to draw out the frost. Then she dried them good and rubbed coal oil all over the affected areas—that was healing.

Mother had a cookstove to prepare our meals on. Then we had a round stove in the living room, and the smokepipe went through the upstairs room. In winter, we got right next to it, where it was warm, to undress and dress.

The closest church was thirteen miles away. All we had to get us there were our work horses, but we couldn't use them to drive that far. They needed to rest all day on Sunday so they could work weekdays. So my brother, Charlie, ordered some Sunday School papers. He conducted Bible classes in our little schoolhouse. Lots of children came. I still have his ledger. The offering was thirty-four cents one Sunday. He used that to buy more supplies.

Mother and us girls got to town once in two years, since we had only our work horses to use. Mama had to stay behind to take care of the livestock. I'm surprised she didn't go plumb loco, having only her little family around her in such a desolate place. Somebody asked, "Well, what did you do for food?" I said, "My father made the trip. He bought flour in hundred-pound sacks, sugar in fifty-pound cotton cloth bags, salt in ten-pound pokes and coffee in five-pound containers. Of course the men went hunting and we had our own meat, lard, milk and eggs.

Mother made our bloomers, panty waists, and petticoats out of the empty cotton sacks. Oh, they were so nice and soft! She trimmed them in lace and embroidery. She also used sacks for towels, curtains and our nightclothes.

Finally Dad gave that farm up and we moved closer to town. We raised wheat, oats and also millet for hay. Mother was happier.

Uncle Calvin's house was seven or eight miles from us. They got fed up with conditions out there and went back to Indiana before long.

I can't remember how many cows we took with us. How did Dad keep the stock contained when they were unloaded at our farm? No fences. The second place we lived, they had to be driven a mile and a half to the only pasture field. I rode bareback on my horse and drove them to and from. The gate, where I let the cows in and out, was made of barbed wire. I had to get down and open and shut it; that was hard to manage—me being so little. I was always scared of getting scratched bad. I told Dad, "If I had a saddle, it would be so much nicer."

So Dad borrowed a saddle. He put it on my horse and lifted me up. Oh, I was proud! And, you know, that horse promptly bucked me off—right into the haystack! He stepped on my leg but I wasn't hurt. I cried, "Dad, I want you to take that saddle right back!" And he did.

Charlie graduated from Carrington High School, then he went on to Jamestown to business college. Later he taught and lived at a one-room school several miles from home. He drove his horse and buggy back and forth every two weeks. Mother sent provisions to last him between trips.

The first winter, he got snowbound for about a month. When he saw the blizzard coming, he hurriedly sent all the students home. After many days, he ran out of food. An Indian brought in supplies for him and hay for the horse. Charlie always had a kind feeling for Indians after that.

Oh, those terrible cyclones! Back home people called them cyclones, too, but most referred to them as tornadoes or twisters. We were all scared to death when we saw one coming and so glad we had a safe underground storm cellar to go to. Our house was always spared. One cyclone moved our barn six inches off the foundation! The smokehouse set right next to the house. It went, but not the hams and bacon.

Each Saturday I walked to Carrington to collect from Mother's milk customers. Late one morning, as I arrived in town, I saw all the posters advertising a circus. Walking on further I saw it was setting up. That afternoon I took Mother's milk money and went to see my first circus! Mr. and Mrs. Slurth, our neighbors, saw me and they asked, "Ruth, what are you doing here?" I said, "I'm watching the circus!"

"Do your parents know it?" I answered, "No."

"Well, when it's over, we'll take you home." I ought to have known better. I imagine I got a good scolding. I never, ever got a spanking though.

Gophers were destroying crops—hundreds of gopher mounds all over. They are a striped ground squirrel of the prairies and are so destructive. The state was paying a bounty, half a cent a tail. There was a little knoll out in one field, and the badgers and gophers were thick. Horses—so vital on a farm and expensive—would step in a badger hole or trip over a gopher mound and break a leg. Then it'd have to be shot.

Badgers were also a problem. A full-grown badger will weigh up to twenty-five pounds. They have short legs, are broad and sturdily muscled, and are a grizzled-gray color. Their long fur fluffed and rippled in the breezes—oh, they were so pretty! They don't make mounds like gophers, just dig out holes under the sod. They are hard to detect at a distance.

Badger pelts were in demand. They used some of the soft part of the pelt to make fine hand muffs and coat collars for Eastern ladies. Mostly the bristles were used in making shaving brushes. Charlie was always imitating one ol' neighbor: "Ain't nothin' makes better shavin' brushes than badger fur, and I reckon they're usin' some fer makin' pitchur-paintin' brushes, and ain't nary a lucky piece no better t'tote 'round in yer pocket with ya'n a badger tooth. Indians figgered they kep bad spir'ts 'way."

That neighbor always railed on and on about all his horses that had to be shot because they stumbled into a badger hole and broke a leg. I'd giggle when Charlie mimicked him after he'd gone. Then, like Charlie, I'd do my own imitation. Mama scolded us both for making fun of that poor guy!

I was anxious to make some money. I waited with my snare at a hole. I'd snare the little thing to choke it, then I'd whack off its head and tail with the kitchen knife. Boy, I went running home so excited and yelled, "I got six tails!" Dad gave me six cents. I thought I was a millionaire!

One man said he'd lost two horses in the two years he'd been here; they broke their legs in badger holes. Charlie didn't want anything to happen to our team, so he decided he'd catch the badger he'd seen around the farm. I wanted to tag along. Dad said, "You keep plenty of distance between yourself and that animal, Ruth. Badgers're plain mean, and one of 'em could tear a little girl like you apart in two shakes!"

It's true that if conditions were such that it became unavoidable, the badger would attack a man without hesitation, but it's a nocturnal animal, preferring to do its hunting by night, so they're rarely seen by man, even at a distance.

Charlie had the awfullest time getting that badger. He knew it was in the hole, so he waited and waited. I didn't like to stay quiet, so he sent me on to the house before long. I don't remember how he ever outsmarted it—a badger den has a front and a back door. When Charlie brought it in, he was smiles all over! It was so beautiful—brownish with an almost white stripe down its back. Charlie tanned the hide and made a rug from it.

Every evening I went to the barn and gathered eggs from the horse mangers. When Dad found time, he built a chicken house onto the barn. He sealed it tight to keep out weasels. A weasel can get through the tiniest crack, and he'll slit the throats of several chickens in one night. It just sucks the blood—doesn't eat its prey. One winter we got a terrible blizzard, and, since there was no ventilation in there, Mama lost a lot of her chickens. She felt real bad. We needed the eggs for food and for buying supplies.

One time Mother sent me out to feed the chickens. A real pretty prairie hen came up. Clustered around her were six little ones, all eating corn. I was so thrilled. I went flying into the house to tell everyone!

Dad bought coal in town for our two stoves—to heat and cook with—and hauled it home in his big wagon, pulled by our team. There were no trees to have wood for fuel, like back in Indiana. It was a cold house. Dad piled manure around the foundation. Manure generates heat and cuts drafts.

One winter it snowed so much—such a blizzard. Dad stretched a clothesline wire from the house to the barn. He held onto it, so he wouldn't get lost going back and forth. He said a person could easily get snow-blinded, lose the way, and freeze to death in that kind of weather.

It snowed and drifted clear up over the clothesline. The toilet was on the other side and Dad, when cutting a path to it, made steps to get up and down over the clothesline. He made the trip to the privy only once a day to empty the slop jar. We used that in the house when it was so cold in winter and during heavy rains or storms.

Mother made Lorena take me to the toilet whenever I had to go. She'd race on ahead, running as fast as she could, then she'd look back, yelling, "Hurry up! Hurry up!" I always needed help unbuttoning and buttoning that trapdoor in the back of my long underwear in the winter and my pantywaist in the summer. And all the time I sat there, Lorena fussed, "Hurry up! Hurry up!"

Oh, those high snowbanks! I fussed, "There's nothing for me to do. I wish I could go outdoors and play." So Dad dug a cave in a huge drift, with an opening to the south for the sun to shine in. Mother gave me a rag rug, and I took it and my doll and other playthings out to my own little igloo. It was warm in the sun and so much fun to be in there. Me, a little Eskimo girl, like the one Mother read to me out of one of my books.

When Dad had to go to town in all that snow, he'd cut through and go cattey-corner right over the yard fence.

Snowdrifts made interesting patterns everywhere. Back home, Mother had shown us the winter trees, their bare limbs beautifully decorated with a marshmallow-like frosting of inch-deep iciness. Squirrels ran along the limbs, bouncing off lumps of snow that fell and landed softly on the drifts below. But here we didn't have trees. Nothing but snow heaped high.

Seemed the wind blew endlessly! One time it was so strong the little privy shook. I was terribly scared, so I hurried out, not finishing my mission. Another time I shut the door, picked up a catalog, then saw a black and yellow spider dance on his web in the corner above it. They always scared me.

One bright winter day, I said to Dad, "I just have to go sledding!" So he built me a sled. I climbed up in the haymow, carrying it. I'd crawl out the window and—*zoom*—slide down a big, long snowdrift. Then I'd go all the way around again, pulling my sled back up.

When Dad came out to do his evening chores, he said, "Aren't you getting tired?" I said, "This is a lot of fun!" No, Lorena didn't go with me. We didn't play much together, her being older and not interested in what I wanted to do. She'd be in the house with Mother. She'd knit, crochet, or embroider.

Hildreth: I remember a big snowstorm when Dad dug one tunnel to the barn so he could feed and water the livestock, and another tunnel to the pump to bring in water. The horses got out and they walked on drifts higher than the barn!

We had a hired hand working for us—a Swede. He'd get Martha and me, bounce each one of us on a knee, and he'd sing "Pumplelance." I had no idea what the word meant.

Ray and Louise Williamson's baby was born up there. They probably had a midwife deliver it, since no doctors were near.

Edith Williamson, in her late twenties, got appendicitis. She and her parents were visiting from Indiana once. It was wintertime—we were so isolated. Dad had made a big horse-drawn sled—a wooden-box affair—and he put it on runners. He placed boards across for everyone to sit on while riding through the snow. He drove right across sections in it, hurrying to bring the doctor.

Mom sterilized all Doc's instruments with boiling water from the teakettle. The doctor did the surgery right on the kitchen table under coal-oil lights, and it was successful!

RUTH: We lived between two Indian reservations. One was north, almost to Canada. In the fall, the Indians all traveled down to winter in South Dakota on the Missouri River. They'd steal you blind! One time I saw them coming. Mother and Dad were both out in the field, bringing in the fall crop. I was so terrified. I raced to the barn and hid in the manger. I learned later that was the worst place to go, because Indians would hunt for eggs in mangers—they always wanted eggs. Dad and Mom got to the house just as they came in. They gave them some eggs and other supplies.

An Indian came to the door one day. They always bought milk and butter from Mother. This Indian asked, "Is that your little papoosie?" Dad smiled and said, "Yes." I grabbed hold of Dad's legs, afraid the Indian would steal me. I cried, "I is not. I is Dad's little girl!" On his way out, that Indian stole my overshoes that were sitting by the door. No one saw him do it. Slickest people you ever saw!

The second year we were there, Grandpa and Grandma Hiatt came up from Indiana to visit us. Grandpa brought Lorena and me a pencil for Christmas. Mine was green with white polka dots on it. You know, I still have that pencil. Here, I'll show you. I've never even sharpened it.

Uncle Doll Reese, Dad's brother, was always coming up for Mother to do for him. He was the wild one of the family. He played cards, gambled, drank, and spent nights in bed with the wrong kinds of women.

We weren't allowed to have cards. Once he came when Mother was gone, and he taught me how to play Old Sol. Mother came back and I'd forgotten to hide the deck. She said, "I'll put a stop to those dirty old things right now!" And she did; threw them into the stove. Later, Uncle asked, "Where's my cards?" I said, "They disappeared!"

Grandpa and Grandma were such devout Quakers. My cousins, Myron and Malcolm Hiatt, and I were always together. One night, after we got ready for bed, Myron and I had to kneel—it seemed like hours—while Grandpa read out of his Bible and prayed. Oh, how tired my legs got! If we wiggled, he yelled at us.

I reached down and pinched Myron on his foot. He let out a yell! Grandpa looked up in the middle of his prayer and demanded, "Which of thee done that?" I looked at Myron and Myron looked at me—both trying to keep a straight face. Grandpa said, "Thee knows thee should keep quiet when thy elders are talkin' or prayin'. I think thee both better get to bed!"

Grandma was such a tither. She strictly adhered to the rule of giving one-tenth of your money to the Lord. One day I went with Grandma out to the huckster. The man counted out the eggs, then paid her. She stood there counting, putting money in one pocket and money in the other. I asked, "Why're you doin' that, Grandmother?" She said, "That's the Lord's money; one-tenth goes to Him."

When she finished she said, "Now Ruth, thee can have some candy. Huckster man said there is seven cents left after I bought the groceries." I pointed, "There's money in that pocket." She said kindly, "I told thee, Ruth, that's the Lord's money. Thee must not spend it for candy."

Hildreth: Everyone went into town for the July Fourth parade and celebrations. In front of The Mercantile, standing there talking and watching, my mother and Ruth's mother were visiting. Mom said, "I'm fed up with this country. I'm going to leave. It's desolate! Level as a racehorse track and no trees!" Poor thing; she was always so homesick.

Mom got so tired of cranberries. That was the only fresh fruit we could get in the wintertime.

We had reunions: Slurths, Picketts, Hiatts, Williams, Williamsons, and the Bert White family—all of us got together. How wonderful to get with the folks from back home! Hawksnest was the only place we ever went where trees grew. There was a little pond and trees around. Wonderful! Out at our farm, we had a well to supply water for use at the house and barn, but no trees.

Mom wrote a letter home, said: "This land, where we hold the reunions, won't grow trees bigger'n buggy whips. It's no place for us! Not even a well and pump near that clump of trees."

To make extra money, Dad went to thrash in several different sections, a long ways from home. Mom was left with all the chores to do. Once, Dad didn't come home . . . and he didn't come home. He explained the delay later, said he would start home and go for miles, thinking he was about there, and every time, he'd wind up back at the thrashing machine! He was going in circles. That's so common in flat country with no landmarks—nothing but wheat fields—no homesteads and no roads. He remembered someone had once told him, "Just let your horses get you home; you don't need to drive them." Yes, they did know the way, and we were all so happy to see him.

There was a cook car and a bunk car that went along with the thrashing rings. One time a cyclone picked them up and dropped them in another field. George Hiatt was one of the cooks. He had a coal-oil stove in the cook's car. The cyclone picked it up and set it a ways out, but no damage was done to it, and, thankfully, no field fires!

Ruth: What was amazing to me was the jack rabbits. They turned white in the wintertime, like the snow. They were no good to eat, though. Tough—not tender like our Indiana cottontails—but we got so hungry for meat, we had to eat them sometimes. Mother soaked the bunnies all day and night in salt and vinegar water, if I remember right, to tenderize them, then she put them on to cook slowly, with spices, for a long time.

In winter we had our own pork, but we never butchered a beef. We always had a big summer garden. Mother canned and canned. Dad's potatoes won prizes at the fair.

One day we all kept smelling smoke. Mr. Lowery, our mailman, came running his horses, driving his route, yelling, "Minnesota's on fire! Prairie fire! They need help!" Dad ran and jumped on his horse and was gone—just that quick!

A thousand acres burnt. I don't remember how long Dad was gone or how far away the fire was or what had caused it. Some claimed it was lightning or maybe a careless smoker. Or was it sparks from the steam engine?

When crops failed, we had to find other ways to make money. Fortunately, a courthouse in Carrington had just been built. Dad served on the first jury that met in it. His pay furnished us with extra income.

A banker by the name of Landing, he had a field of flax. It was all in bloom—real blue, and oh, so pretty waving in the breezes. I ran home from school and said, "Daddy, let's raise some of that blue stuff!" I don't remember how they harvested it—the only field I ever saw.

Mother planted soup beans in the truck patch. When they were good and dry, ready to harvest, we gathered them into gunnysacks. Each evening, when I came home from school and changed into my everyday dress, I beat on the tied-up sacks with the broom to break open the pods to help shell them out. Our school teacher came home; she lived with us. I didn't see her. I raised the broom way back to get a good aim. Wham! I slammed it right into her face! She didn't fuss at me though. She knew it was an accident.

One time, Dad came home with a couple bushels of apples. They were unheard-of up there. Mother wrote to Aunt Mary in Indiana: "I made apple pies, applesauce cakes, and I canned apples. I covered the peelings with water, cooked them, poured the juice off and made jelly. Then I ran the peelings through the colander and made apple butter."

Hildreth: They used those gray or brownish pottery crocks to preserve their food in. Remember how heavy they were? Mom poured hot red sealing wax around the tin lids to seal them tight, so the food wouldn't spoil.

Mom made sauerkraut in a crock. She covered it with a dinner plate, then a heavy rock. She tied a white cloth around to cover it all. It kept real well. That sure tasted good in the winter, especially when we had pork.

Ruth: We were in North Dakota seven years. We came back 'cause Dad went broke. He sent Mother, Lorena, and me ahead of him to Indiana. He stayed that winter by himself to sell the stock, hay, and grain, so he'd have enough money to get home. We moved on 9th Street, into the first brick house built in Noblesville, and it's still here. Charlie was away teaching.

Hildreth: We were there only two years. They all went up there with high hopes and left discouraged and defeated. Our Dakota disaster was wheat. I don't know what ruined the other crops. Was it grasshoppers? Hail? Drought?

When we'd talk about those years after moving back, I recall Dad's remark: "The houses were so far apart we had to use a shotgun to communicate! They all told me, every last one of them, a fellow couldn't raise an umbrella up there. Well, I was determined to prove them wrong. I learned that hopes die and man moves on, but the land stays." I guess the problem is this: Reality is never as good as the fantasy!

RUTH: Years later, we went back to North Dakota for a visit. They must have had better weather conditions after we left, 'cause there were telephone poles and fences, nicer farm and ranch buildings. People seemed to be prospering. We were happy for them, and we prospered back home in Indiana.

Hildreth's and Ruth's "Long Journey" was written for Noblesville's First Friends Church's history, of which both were members. Ruth passed away soon after the interview. Hildreth celebrated her ninety-first birthday July 12, 1998. She and her husband, Russell Foulke, observed their sixty-ninth wedding anniversary March 28, 1998.

Lois Costomiris

Grandma Duck, the Barnyard Matriarch

Farm families have a lot of pets, but some are more precious to them than others, as you'll see in this story.

GRANDMA DUCK was no ordinary duck. She was personified. A stately lady—pert and proud.

Grandma Duck came into our possession in an unusual way. Walter Beechler, his wife, Inie, and their two young children, Inita and Billy, relocated here from Blufton, Indiana. This family moved to a farm west of Cicero, onto a busy highway, along with their herd of beef and milking cattle, pens of hogs, a hen house full of layers, and a flock of ten or so white Peking ducks. They made pets of all their animals.

The Beechlers knew the days of their ducks' lives were numbered. They kept scooching under or through barnyard fences onto the busy gravel road in front of their house. Several times a day the kids were out driving them back. It would be cruel to keep the ducks penned up in a chicken house.

What's to be done?

Early one morning, I stood at the sink doing up the breakfast dishes. This was a peaceful, enjoyable time of day—looking out my kitchen window at our cattle, chickens, ducks, guineas, our dog, barn cats, and our white mare, Pet.

All at once I saw and heard such a commotion: ducks quacking, feathers flying, old Duke a-barkin'. It brought me and our three young daughters—Wanda, Becky, and Toni—out to investigate. A man, a woman, and two children were talking to my husband, Bud, as they shook ducks from wooden chicken crates and gunnysacks. This is how we made first acquaintance with the new neighbors.

Inie explained: "Billy and Inita wanted to find a good home for their pet ducks, so we started driving all around these backroads. We saw ducks eating grass in your big front woods, and we decided our ducks would be safe with them, being so far off the road as you are."

I noticed that Billy and Inita were devoting more time to one big duck than the others, stroking her soft white feathers and tearfully telling her good-bye. Grandma Duck, The Queen! She was special. There was one request: she was not to end up on a company dinner table!

"Come and visit your duck family anytime you get homesick for them," we yelled as they pulled away. We waved good-byes to the Beechlers as they drove down our lane. Bud went to the tool shed, I came into the house, and our daughters drove the accumulation of ducks—theirs and ours—out behind the barn, so they'd all get acquainted.

Grandma Duck was the Barnyard Matriarch! She immediately took over her rein!

For the next several years, she and her duck kingdom of twenty-five or so furnished us with many a laugh. It was like watching unusual, individual characters acting out a barnyard stage play. The Queen's smile spoke assurance as she dominated her flock. She tossed her derriere about when she led her whole family throughout the chicken lot, down the lane, or into the woods.

If something got her nettled, she had a gruff way of issuing ultimatums that seemed to settle matters once and for all. But a sad thing happened to Grandma. One day, she found herself being bossed around by a vain and cocky drake. She indifferently turned away from him, but he was always there—so cocksure of himself. Her feathers ruffled every time he approached.

Late spring, she and her daughter Princess took to their nests. Princess possessed her mother's grace and charm and was happy to be setting on her nest of eggs for the first time.

Every evening Lord Drake, showing his newly acquired authority, pridefully escorted each lady out of the shed for a long walk and a drink of water, then guided them back to their nests. The girls didn't need a fellow's help, he should have known that, but they mildly tolerated him.

Grandma was doggedly patient.

Princess was quietly amiable.

About dark one evening, just before the hatching date, there was a black, rolling cloud from the west. The rumble of thunder worked closer and closer. The three came early from their evening walk. Hurrying for shelter, avoiding dust-devils, their heads bobbed forward with each step. The wind whipped them back and forth as they went for safety in the tool shed and on their nests.

The storm hit with all its force!

In the days when farm women set hen eggs in an incubator, more than anything, they dreaded a storm. Experience had taught them that huge thunderclaps made the eggs infertile.

The hatching date passed. There were no ducklings. Patiently the two ladies stayed on.

One evening, still a good hour before dark, during one of their daily walks, I went to the shed, pushed back the puffy feathers-and-straw covering and looked at the warm eggs. They were dark and very shiny. I knew, by the disagreeable odor, there would never be a hatching. Grandma Duck already knew this and so did Princess. They stayed off their nests longer periods of time.

Each morning, Mesdames Ducks left their nests to wander into the woods. One by one, Lord Drake, in his insufferable way, paraded them right back. Grandma didn't like being ordered around, especially by a drake. Her pride was fractured. She was hoppin' mad and gave him a talking-to in her loud quack-quacking voice. She jawed at him every step of the way, bruising the air with her outrage. Her fury came from both sides of her bill at once, but it did no good.

Drake continued walking along beside them. A monotone of wheezy words came from his breezy beak. His white feathered swagger portrayed him the domineering chief of this duck kingdom. Grandma continued to complain heatedly until she was half crazy. Her feathers bristled out as she cried with her whole heart. She seemed to say, "I tried. I did my duty!"

It did no good. Lord Drake apparently knew he was tangling with an Indiana tornado, but he would not let her have her way.

After each trip back, Grandma obediently made an attempt to settle back on the eggs again. She was frenzied and nervous, and jabbed angrily at some shelled corn nearby—but she wasn't hungry.

Barnyard royals — Grandma Duck and Princess.

All the while Princess seemed to bide her time with the thought: *Surely these annoying episodes will soon blow themselves out. I don't know why Mama lets that old fool bother her so!* She pattered along gingerly with Lord Drake, taking his admonishments gracefully. She was always congenial. When they returned, she settled back onto her nest cheerfully and carefully.

But just as soon as Drake had gone, Princess perked up and stretched her long neck way out and around. Seeing he was out of sight, she then crab-walked from her nest to the hay baler, squeezed through a crack in the big sliding doors, then went out to the back lot for a swim in the hogwaller.

Perhaps it was bribery, but it worked. At least she let him think she carried out his orders and had served her self-proclaimed master.

One day, after being returned to her nest several times, Grandma got up, gathered all her dignity, and stared straight at Lord Drake. With a look of smiling finality—"I told you so!" was written all over her face—she furiously scratched all the eggs out of the nest, cracking and breaking them. She stood looking at the mess and smelling the overpowering odor.

She then defiantly walked outside, stretched her long neck and screamed. She flapped her wings with elation, hard enough so that she could skim along the ground—with the tips of her webbed feet barely touching it. Released from imprisonment, Grandma Duck flew way out to the woods to be with all her feathered barnyard friends.

This time she did not return!

Grandma Duck again reined supreme!

Tri Town Topics, July 30, 1970

Lois Costomiris

A Christmas Wish

This account was given to me by Thelma Dobson and Mabel Knapp. I entered it in a Christmas story contest at the TRI TOWN TOPICS *in 1970—the beginning of my writing career.*

THELMA SIGHED WISTFULLY. "In the morning I'll have my own baby. A girl."

"Law me," said Mabel with a smug grin, "maybe you'll get a doll like the one I'm getting."

"No. This year Santy will bring me a real live baby, not just a doll," Thelma told her. Thelma, seven and a half, and six months older than her Aunt Mabel, had a determined mind.

Even though it was now the joyous Christmas season, a cloud of gloom hung heavy over the Pheanis household as they went about their daily chores. The Pheanis's daughter, Orpha, had lost her husband, Neville, to diabetes, the sugar disease, a month before. In 1908, there was no known cure for the affliction. Nev died at age thirty-two.

Orpha, with her daughter, Thelma, had come back home to live after her husband's death. It would have been a struggle for her to continue living in their rented house. For several weeks Orpha couldn't seem to stop crying. Her family had been a big comfort to her through it all. Now she was uneasy that her sorrow would blanket the family's Christmas fun, and most of all, her daughter's.

The Pheanis couple, John and Emma, had three of their eight children still living at home: Mabel, and her two older brothers, Glen and Mark, ten and twelve respectively.

Orpha had a common-school education and was working at Modes & Turner Glass Factory over on Main Street.

Mabel and Thelma, so close in age, played together as sisters. Thelma called her grandparents "Maw" and "Paw," same as Mabel did.

The day before Christmas was always spent preparing for the holiday. The two girls and two brothers made bright-colored paper chains from the brilliant pages of Sears Roebuck or Montgomery Ward catalogues. They cut the pages into small strips and joined each one together with paste from a can lid of flour paste, then they fashioned the rings into tree chains.

"Go back and watch that skillet of popcorn, Glen," instructed Thelma. "Mark has a needle and thread ready to string them."

Cranberries rolled from the paper bag on the table, waiting to be threaded into a rope.

"Thelma," Glen remarked, "that popcorn will get strung a heap faster if you'll work as fast as you talk!"

When they were all finished stringing, they wound the chains and ropes around the tall tree. Maw stood up on a kitchen chair to tack the red, twisted crepe-paper strips into place, so they'd criss-cross the room. She brought flat cardboard pieces, which opened out into glorious red tissue-paper bells, and hung them in the doorways. She cut out a huge pasteboard star for the top of the tree, then she covered it with tinfoil she'd saved throughout the year. She went up the ladder and said, "Mark, hand it to me now."

The night before, Paw and the boys had gone to the woods and picked out the tree, one that reached to the ten-foot ceiling. He'd made a stand with two short pieces of two-by-fours. When the tree was placed solidly in place, Maw brought out a new roll of cotton batting to put around the base to make it look like snow.

"Maw, will you let us clip on the candle holders this year?" asked Mabel. "We'll be careful and not pull the tree over on us."

"You girls aren't tall enough," said Glen, knowing he'd get a fuss out of Thelma.

"The boys better clip them on," instructed Maw, "but Orpha must light the candles; we always do that Christmas morning." A bucket of water stood near the tree in case it caught fire from the candles.

To Thelma, the day before Christmas was always the longest one in the year. In 1908 it seemed to be endless. "I wish every day was Christmas, don't you, Mabel?"

"Mark, what do you want for Christmas?" asked Thelma. But before he had a chance to answer, she added, "I want a real live baby, and that's all I want! Mabel asked Santy for a dolly with real hair and eyes that open and shut, and that's all she wants."

"Lawsy be, Thelmie," admonished Mark, "you know Santy doesn't bring babies! The stork brings 'em or the doctor fetches 'em in his black bag. And, if you been bad, you'll get switches in your stocking!"

"Maw, Mark's startin' his teasin' again!" Thelma complained. "You and Glen best be learning your Christmas pieces for school and church."

Glen, eating from the bowl of popped corn, added, "Thelmie, Santy don't bring babies! It's winter, so a bird can't drop it on a cabbage leaf for the sun to hatch it out, like it did you!"

"Or find it in a holler stump!" added Mark. "Too cold for storks to be out in this weather! Mark and me been talking and we're going to make it easy on Santy. He has a choice of bringing us either ice skates, a gun or traps. Now, girl, don't just set your head for one thing!"

Thelma was determined. "Well, I don't care. I just want one thing—a live baby. I'm going to have lots of children. Maw and Paw have eight: Delphia, Charles, Orpha, Sadie, Omer, Mark,

Glen, and Mabel. Maw told me that regardless of how many children she had, there wasn't none to give away."

Thelma had overheard the old folks talking. Aunt Amanda and Uncle Henry didn't have any little ones. They wanted Mabel, knowing she'd be a lot of work for sister Emma with all her other children. That couple had money and were so happy—always kissing. They'd be loving parents, but Maw couldn't consider giving Mabel away.

In the early 1900s, grown-ups spoke in guarded language in the presence of youngsters. It was never mentioned that a woman was carrying a child, except indirectly. Children were kept in the dark concerning all things in the adult world.

Late that afternoon the snow began to fall—dropping into a velvet silence—covering the house and yard and the curve of the hill beyond. The white frame house stood in front of a big pasture lot; the barn was just beyond. The Pheanises lived at the edge of town, back along the railroad tracks. A garden plot and a huge truck patch kept food on their table all summer. Jars of vegetables and fruits lined the cellar shelves for use in the winter.

Standing at the kitchen window of the big house, Mabel rubbed away the steam to see out. Large flakes hit with force, then melted a little and slid down to join the others.

Orpha came in the door from work, shaking away the snow, then she rubbed it from her boots on the wiping-rug. "Whew, it's cold and bad out there!" she remarked. "What's that? Smells just like Christmas! Boys, I don't like the looks of that cloud—a deep snow is coming. Why don't you hurry on out and do up your chores early this evening."

"Come and see the tree first," the boys motioned. "It's a beaut!"

"Oh, yes, it *is* a beaut—so pretty!" Orpha pulled off her knitted hat. She had thick, dark-auburn hair. The long braids wrapped around her head like a crown. She spread her arms to her little daughter, and Thelma ran into them. They walked over to the stove to get warm. Orpha saw where the good odors were coming from—pine needles were scattered up on top of it, perfuming the whole house.

Bent in the wind, the two brothers legged it to the barn, pulling their knitted toboggan hats down to meet their coat collars. Glen hung over the fence at the pigpen to pour slop into the wooden trough. As soon as the two brood sows saw him, they waddled over in a hurry, rooting each other out of the way. Mark measured out oats for the horses and pitched hay into their mangers. He broke a skiff of ice in the tank. By morning it would be thick enough to chop with an ax.

The flock of chickens scattered as Glen opened the door to the hen house. Over his shoulder, Mark carried a sack of ground oats mixed with corn. He poured it into the feeders while Glen threw handfuls of grain around in the fresh straw. They watched them scrambling to get it. "Here, chickie! Here, chickie!"

Glen gathered the eggs. As he went back through the door, a squawking rooster flew over the top of his head into the outside world. "Dad-gum you!" he yelled and then picked up a handful of snow and threw it at the rooster as he skittered into a protective corner.

Darkness was falling rapidly now. Paw was always expected home just about dusk. The boys still had to milk the old cow, carry in the buckets of soft coal, fill the woodbox back of the cookstove, and pump water for the reservoir.

"Remember, Glen," said Mark, "it's your turn to milk Clara Belle tonight. Paw said she has a sore tit, and she'll kick the shit out of ya if y'don't be careful!" Of course, that wasn't exactly what Paw said, but the boys enjoyed using oaths when talking to each other. They never talked like that in the presence of women or their father though.

Paw—John Pheanis—at fifty-five, was a large man, thrifty and industrious, with graying brown hair, a mustache and a long beard. When he was nineteen, a horse had kicked him in the head, tearing away an eye. He was fitted with a glass one that perfectly matched his own, but his hearing on that side was impaired permanently.

Early of a morning, six days a week, he drove his spirited team, Pete and Bill, to the huckster wagon for Dan Black's and Vincent Case's stores on his patterned route through the Jackson township countryside. He went to the store with his team and the huckster wagon to replenish the shelves in it. He folded down the tailgate in back and climbed in with boxes of supplies, stocking every imaginable item that a housewife needed between his trips: sewing needs, patent medicines, groceries, a wheel of cheese, spices, even coal oil.

All children knew Huckster Day; their favorite huckster, old John Pheanis, gave each one a free stick of candy.

The familiar crunching of the wheels in the snow alerted the family that the head of the household was returning.

"Paw's home!" someone called as Paw stomped the snow from his felt boots on the back porch, then came into the kitchen and closed the door behind him. Standing on the cotton rag rug in front of the cookstove, he pulled off his mittens and lay them in the warming oven to dry. He took out his red handkerchief and blew his nose vigorously.

"That wind is right sharp," he said to his wife. "Clouds are heavy over there in the east—good direction for a deep one. A real blizzard, probably."

"Oh my," Maw said in the voice she always used when she worried about her loved ones. She knew this was the time of the year in Indiana when foul weather could bring drifting snow and sullen sleet, and hold the community in its bitter grip—and here at Christsmastime! "How long do you think it'll keep this up?" she asked.

Paw pulled his coattail up and backed to the fire to warm himself. "Hit'll die down during the night, likely. It looks purty deep out there already. Hit's liable to be a good two foot 'fore it's through. I'll git the lantern an' light it. The team is waitin' to be unhitched; they'll enjoy the warm, dry stalls and plenty to eat."

"I best get the lamps lit too," Orpha was saying.

"Omer's still planning to come and spend the night? I hope they git here 'fore this weather really sets in," John said, thinking about them driving the fifteen miles over frozen, deep-rutted roads from Strawtown. "When's supper?"

"Soon. Let's get done early tonight," Maw replied. She was in her starched, blue calico wrapper, which was almost covered by the big dark apron that tied in a neat bow in the back. She wore a biscuit of hair on the nape of her neck. You couldn't hope for a lady to look better—tidy and in good flesh. She had few interests outside the home: she attended Cicero Christian Church with her family and she raised a prize flock of Plymouth Rock chickens.

Maw and Orpha prepared the evening meal, skirting the two little girls as they played on the floor. Mabel and Thelma had gone around for a week with fixed smiles on their faces. It's Christmas, you know!

Glen sloshed water across the floor as he lifted the full bucket to the washstand. "Glen!" yelled Thelma, "watch what you're doing!"

Then Thelma looked up with a question on her face. "Mama is a widdah. Paw said so to that lady down at the store. What's a widdah, Mama? Mama, I want a real baby for Christmas. I bet you wish Papa would come back for Christmas, don't you?"

Silence. A long stabbing silence. It made the perpetual ache in Orpha's heart sharper, and she rushed toward the dark pantry to have a good cry. The two lines between her eyes had cut deeper since her husband's death.

"Maw, is Mama crying? She tries to hide her tears from me, but I know by her red nose and eyes. She'll feel better when Santy brings me a new baby," Thelma reasoned.

Maw tucked her lower lip under her teeth. Her eyes began to fill with tears. She brushed them away with her apron, then shook her head in thought. *Husband dead at thirty-two, leaving all this life and these beloved people behind. The child, poor little beggar, is still too young to understand. Is there any sadness greater than the first Christmas after the death of a loved one? Even though we've told her time and again Santa doesn't bring babies, Thelma is determined.* Maw wiped her eyes but they just filled up again.

Orpha pushed through the pantry door and closed it behind her, sobbing convulsively. After a time, partially cleansed, she found some relief.

"Girls, run into the other room and play till supper's ready," suggested Maw. Then she cut thick slices of smoked ham and trimmed off the rind. It was soon sizzling in the black iron skillet. She poked it with a fork to turn each piece over, so it'd brown on the other side. She raised a lid and peppered a skillet-full of sliced potatoes. Such tantalizing supper smells!

Sauerkraut simmered with chunks of salt pork in a stew pan. It had been fingered out of the five-gallon crock in the cellar. Mabel and Thelma had gone earlier with Orpha to get it and had begged for the cold, tart cabbage hearts that were embedded therein. Their mouths puckered and jaws ached at the first bite, then they smacked their lips with delight.

Paw Pheanis had come in now from the barn and hung his oxford-gray wool cap and mackinaw behind the door. Before washing up, he went to the sitting room to stir up the Florence Hot Blast circulator with the poker. He picked up the coal bucket and let fresh fuel fall on the red-hot coals.

He turned, listening. "It's them. Omer's. I hear their storm buggy headin' in!" At this, all the Pheanis family rushed to the door and waited anxiously as the trio made their way. The wind surged in with them.

"Come on!" Paw called. "The wimmin's 'bout got supper ready."

"Snowflakes, big as goose feathers and a-flyin' dead level into our faces, made it purty hard to find our way!" Omer explained, half out of breath as he bent to put Little Opal on the floor. "Dogged if we ain't gonna git a big un tonight!"

Della, Omer's wife, was at his side, greeting everyone. Little Opal had pink, puffy chipmunk cheeks and a short, sweetly shaped nose with a sprinkling of freckles. She twisted shyly on one foot and hung her head. Thelma said lovingly, "Take your finger out of your mouth, Sweetie. That's no way to greet all of us!" She and Mabel bent down to unbutton Little Opal's coat and take off her bonnet, then Thelma picked her up and saddled her on a hip.

After a while, Little Opal disengaged herself and went running to Mabel's outstretched arms. Mabel said, "You're growing like a weed and your hair looks like milkweed. How old are you now?"

"Three year, come April," she said and held up three fingers. She looked over at the big cranberry-and-popcorn-bedecked Christmas tree that stood in the corner, then pointed, smiling, and said, "Prit-tee! Prit-tee!"

As the two girls fussed over the little one, Thelma asked, "Little Opal, what's Santy bringing you?" Not waiting for an answer she continued, "He's bringing me a baby—a real live baby!"

Little Opal chirped, "Me baby, too!"

Thelma corrected her. "No, Little Opal. You're too little to care for a real baby. He can bring you a baby doll."

The three women went out to the kitchen. As she rolled up her sleeves, Della said, "It smells so good out here! Anything I can do to help, Maw? Just look at all the pies you've baked. I'll bet you've worked like a slave all week!"

"Della, take this bowl and mix up a batch of biscuits for supper. Here's the breadboard." Maw skimmed the cream off a pan of milk and put it in a pitcher. She set the milk near Della for her to use in the biscuit batter. Opal came running, spreading out her arms for her mother to take her.

Della looked down at the little apple-cheeked girl and said, "Don't bother Mother now; she's busy makin' biscuits for supper."

Little Opal coaxed, "Can I helps y'bake bik-its, too?" The

child, always singing, was crooning, "... not a preacher was stirrin', not even a mouse ..."

Orpha said, "She's a happy little thing, isn't she, Della? Little Opal, here's a bowl and some newspaper. Tear it into little pieces, like this. Take your spoon and stir up your own biscuits." Then Orpha sat down with a pan of cracked walnuts and started picking out the nutmeats.

Maw Pheanis, hair mussed and cheeks pink as roses from the oven's heat, was in her element. The kitchen was the center of her household; in it she was queen! The place fairly seethed and bubbled with humanity of all ages as she worked. She could cook in the nest of them.

"Boys, I need you a minute! Mark," Maw directed, "fetch me the dried apples from the back room so's I can put them to soak. And Glen, go to the cellar and get a jar of mustard pickles and a pan of apples."

Maw pulled a string from the mouth of Aunt Jemima, from her red-bandanna-covered coconut head, hanging up on the cabinet. "Here, take this and tie that Christmas bell up—it came loose and keeps falling to the floor."

Orpha stood, shaking the errant nutshells from her apron into the coal bucket. "The walnuts are ready now; I'll bake the cake after supper. Omer and Dad, move back so I can set the table."

She placed the earthenware plates and the silverware on the red-and-white-checked oilclothed table. In the center was a spoon holder full of teaspoons, a mold of freshly churned butter, sorghum, apple butter, and quince honey. A few leftovers remained on the table from the meal before. She poured tall glasses of buttermilk.

The cupboard door was ajar. Pumpkin and mincemeat pies lined the shelves for the holiday. A fat goose and oysters for dressing were stored in the cool pantry off the kitchen.

Omer came and sat at the table after washing his hands and combing his hair. Glen pumped rainwater into the washpan from the pitcher pump in the corner of the kitchen, then he warmed it with boiling water from the teakettle. As he scrubbed up, Thelma reminded him, "Don't be chintzy with the soap. You know the saying: Poor but clean. And don't forget to take a comb to your hair."

"Thelma," Glen snapped back, "I don't need you telling me what to do!" Then he took the cake of Hardwater Castile Soap and lathered his hands good. Mark gave him a shove, dipping his own hands into the pan. Glen yelled, "Maw! Mark's hoggin' the washpan!"

"I'll wash your face in snow!" Mark threatened. Then they wrestled with the towel on the back of the door until the roller clanked to the floor.

Paw wheeled, "Stop it over there!" He got up and went to the sink, pumped water, plunged his face in it and scrubbed. With wet hands, he patted his hair, then ran a comb through it.

The three women dished up supper. The family gathered around the table. Maw said grace: "Bless this food . . ."

As dishes of victuals were passed around, there were animated conversations. Mark questioned his mother, "Why don't we thank God for our food after we eat instead of before, like when we say our prayers at night?"

"And," reasoned Glen, "why don't we eat our dessert at the beginning of each meal?"

"Maw," said Thelma, "Glen's only picking at his food. Eat your carrots . . ."

Before she could finish, Glen interrupted, "The Lord didn't make carrots fit to eat. If he woulda, I'd eat 'em. Here, you eat my carrots." He pushed his plate toward Thelma.

Little Opal was chanting, ". . . not a preacher was stirrin', not even a mouse . . ."

"You're in luck, Omer, picking out a biscuit-cookin' woman like Della!" Paw bragged as he poured brown ham gravy over his biscuit. "Fall to and help yourselves."

"Mama," questioned Thelma, "won't we have to get a babybed

and highchair for my baby? Mabel, you can help me feed my baby and put her to bed . . ."

Before Thelma could finish, Mabel interrupted, " 'Member, Thelma, you'll pro'bly get a dolly like mine. We could ask Santy for a dollybed and highchair, and we can play 'Mother' all the time."

Glancing at the table, Thelma asked, "Did you know you can quiet a baby by putting honey on your finger and letting her suck it?"

Glen was annoyed, "Oh shoot, Thelma, all you ever talk about is baby, baby, baby."

Little Opal, finishing her meal, was singing, ". . . not a preacher was stirrin', not even a mouse . . ." Della lifted her out of the highchair. Little Opal continued, "I fell outta bed 'ast night, and it scared me half to death!" Her little pug nose wrinkled when she smiled. "They tell me I'm as cute as a button!" Everyone laughed.

Glen teased, "I thought they said you were as ugly as a mud fence!"

"Oh, Unka Glen." When Opal was delighted, she was as likely as not to stand on her tiptoes and clap her hands. If people laughed at her, she laughed with them.

Della playfully spanked her daughter, saying, "Run along and look at the prit-tee Christmas tree."

Mark, reaching for a second piece of pumpkin pie, was remembering, "Sunday, at church, Thelma asked the preacher, 'Do babies come from under a cabbage leaf or find them in a holler log, or does a doctor or a stork bring them? Mark and Glen told me Santy can't bring my baby 'cause he can't slide down our chimney.' Then she asked him, 'Preacher, can you bring babies?' I was so embarrassed when Preacher looked at me for an explanation!"

Orpha, who'd been quiet throughout the meal, hurriedly changed the subject, "Remember, Paw, the time the saloon keeper sold Omer liquor?"

Paw looked serious. "I remember. Omer was so giggly all evening. He's always pleasant, but not that way. I said, 'Omer, you come with me!' I was hoppin' mad. We wasted no time gittin' to that beer joint. I could tell by the look in their eyes what'd been going on. I said, 'By gad, I don't intend for my son to be a booze-hound. If I ketch you in here drinkin' agin, Omer, I'll call the law. You—I looked the owner right in the eye—deserve a bullet in your hind end!"

Omer laughed, "By the time Paw got through with him, he looked like a rag that had been used to wipe up the floor. There were no good-byes. I hightailed it for home, knowing what was waiting for me with Paw in the woodshed. By then he had cooled down, but he did give me one of his well-known lectures!"

Mark and Glen looked knowingly at each other. Mark laughed and added, "Yeah, Paw always preaches. Been better havin' a good lickin' with a razor strop and gettin' it over with than the dressin'-down that seemed to take forever!"

"I recollect," Paw hurried onto something else, so as not to get back on the baby discourse again, "when I was a young fellow comin' from doing the barn chores late in the evening, Christmastime, I was sure I could see the same star the Wise Men followed so long ago. I imagined how Bethlehem looked on that first Christmas night and could almost see the shepherds on the hillside."

Maw was reminiscing, too. "We always had school and church programs like we have today. They'd retell the story of the Christ child with small children dressed up in their parent's or borrowed bathrobes, holding homemade shepherd's crooks, reciting carefully memorized lines around the Nativity scene. We'd sing all the familiar Christmas hymns."

After the happy, satisfying meal, the kids scattered into the other room. The women cleared the table, washed the dishes, and swept up the floor. Paw lit a stogie and opened out the newspaper to read it.

Omer rolled a little chicken-bill cigarette and lit it. He leaned back in his chair and blew a smoke ring. Little Opal watched it float toward the ceiling. She laughed and pointed and, jumping to her feet, she ran to catch it. He blew another.

Looking at the front page, Paw whittled out the affairs of the nation: "It's 'bout time our politicians got a little starch in their backbones," he complained as he slapped the paper on the table. "Well now, let's see what Taft will do since he's been elected. Politicians—they're all crooked. Gittin' so a feller can't cure a bellyache without a government say-so."

Omer snapped his gallouses with his thumb, let his belt out two notches and smiled with satisfaction. He gave a playful yank to his wife's apron strings, and an affectionate pat as she bent over to cover the condiments on the table with a cloth. "Dellie," he teased, "a few more sunups and yer apron strings won't tie." Della giggled.

Paw grinned lopsidedly at the two. "They say there's nothing so strong as a pretty woman's apron strings t'tie a man down!"

Orpha came from the back bedroom with a handful of white cotton rags to put up Thelma's hair. She took pride in her daughter. Thelma envied Mabel her naturally curly blond ringlets; she didn't have to sleep on rags every night in order to have long curls. When she was younger, Thelma'd ask her mother, "Why don't you comb my hair curly like Mabel's? I always eat all my crusts so it'll be curly."

Maw brushed Mabel's hair every morning. She'd slightly dampen each section and comb it around her finger. She'd ease her finger out and the fattest sausage curl would come bouncing down. But Mabel's hair tangled, and she didn't like to stand while her mother brushed out all those rats. She wished her hair was straight and combed easily like Thelma's and that she could wear rags to bed. Naturally curly hair was desired, but the real envy was those girls whose long braids could be sat upon!

Mabel wanted her hair and her clothes to look just so—at

home or school. She was never mussed-up, never dirty, never fell and skinned herself. Thelma always had scabby knees, scratched legs, and the hems torn out of her dresses.

Paw put down his newspaper, got out of his chair, went to the other room and kicked up the fire. A shower of sparks popped out and the chimney started roaring. He sat down in his easy chair, relit his cigar and drew on it slowly. He heard the women in the kitchen working on tomorrow's meal. The odors were tantalizing. He took out his watch from the breast pocket of his bib overalls and looked at the time. Mabel and Thelma ran to sit on his lap.

Little Opal stood by quietly. Her tattered blankie and favorite rag doll dangled lopsidedly from one arm. She was singing, ". . . not a preacher was stirring, not even a mouse . . ." She ran and jumped onto her father's lap, then slid down to his right foot, saying, "Trot me, Papa!"

"Trot a horse to Boston to get a loaf of bread; trot the horsie back again, the ol' horse's dead," he babbled to her.

Thelma and Mabel listened, in turn, to the tick of Paw's dollar pocket-watch, shiny with age. "Listen. Hear it go tick-tick-tick?" Paw asked as he chewed on the end of his cigar. Thelma lay back and folded her arms under her head. Teasingly Paw took one of Mabel's blond ringlets in his fingers and drew it out straight. Long wood-shaving curl, color of new pine. It was warm and silky, almost like something alive. When he let it go, it sprang back softly into the curl. The whole Pheanis family, except Sadie, had curly hair.

He gave a playful yank to one of the white frayed rags in Thelma's hair. The girls smacked wet kisses on his bearded face and smelled the faint odor of tobacco on his breath. They moved his face from side to side, scrutinizing his eyes—which is glass? One or the other would whisper in his bad ear, "Now, what did I say?" He couldn't answer.

He put his finger in Mabel's armpit, then Thelma's. "Let me count your ribs!" he teased as he poked down each rib. "One, two, three—now sit still and quit your giggling till I count them all! Sit still, I said!" But three was as far as he ever got.

Paw announced, "Ol' Santy will be lookin' in the windows to see if you girls are going to bed early tonight."

Mabel spoke up first. "I know, and I already asked him to bring me a dolly—one with real hair and eyes that open and shut, like the ones they have in the store window uptown. Mine will have the blue dress and bonnet and Thelma's will be yellow, our favorite colors. He always brings us both the same things. If I could only have one of those, I'd never ask Santy for another thing as long as I live—a dolly with real hair and moving eyes!"

"No, Mabel," Thelma corrected her. " 'Member? Santy will bring me a real baby! My own baby! A girl."

Those somber words struck her grandfather's heart like a barb. A sense of loss swept over him. Pityingly, he gave her a warm hug as he dropped his voice to a confidential whisper. "There are times, girls, we don't get exactly what we ask for. Some things are impossible. However, Santy knows best. Everyone's been tellin' you that for a month."

"But, Paw!" Thelma was disturbed. Her chin quivered. "I am going to get a baby!"

"Now, don't go gittin' all in a knot." He gave each girl a bear hug and slipped them to the floor. "The place for you girls is bed. Go now. Scat! Jack Frost'll paint lovely pictures on all the windows by morning, making it almost impossible to see if Santy left any tracks."

As they were going to their room, they stopped to watch as Mark and Glen played a game of dominoes. Thelma reminded them, "Paw said we'd have to go to bed early if we want Santy to come. I can hardly wait to see my new baby in the morning!"

Mark griped, "Oh, shoot! All you want is a real live baby? How do you think you'll take care of it?"

"Well, I can!"

"How can you? It takes ninny-pies to feed a new baby."

"Mark, I'm gonna tell Maw!"

"Tattle tale, tattle tale, settin' on a snake's tail. When the snake begins to rattle, you begin to tattle!" Mark continued his clowning.

In their unheated bedroom, the girls unbuttoned the back of each other's long, dark calico dresses. Shivering, they squatted and unbuttoned their black high-top shoes. It was the kind of night when the touch of anything sent goose pimples all over you. Behind the door was a row of hooks on which the girls hung their outing flannel gowns each morning. They took them down. The soft folds of the girls' gowns descended over their heads and fell around their slim bodies.

They slipped off their long stockings, then remembering, they ran and each hung one from the tall organ in the sitting room. Mark called, "Did you hang up the holey one, Thelmie?" Back in their room, each girl took turns using the slop jar.

Just then, they heard Little Opal fussing, "I want to sleep with Thelmie and Mabie!" She came running into their bedroom, naked as a newly hatched bird, carrying her nighty. "I haffa do number one, too." Mabel patted her plump, dimpled backside. "Oh, you're so cute! I'll hold you on the pot, then I'll put your gown on you." The two girls smiled, looking at Little Opal's chubby girl-front. "Isn't that the cutest little thing!"

Mabel, Little Opal, and Thelma swung themselves up onto the featherbed. "Now, time for beddy-bye!" Mabel squeezed the child's feet, then each toe, "This little piggy went to market; this little piggie stayed home; this little piggie had roast beef; this little piggie had none; this little piggie cried 'Wee, wee, wee' all the way home."

The three pulled the covers up to their chins. "Good night. Sleep tight. Don't let the bed bugs bite!"

They were no more than settled when Little Opal started whimpering. "What's the matter, Sugar Babe?" Thelma asked.

"I want Mama!"

"You said you wanted to sleep with us all night, didn't you?"

"I chains my mind," she said as she jumped to the floor and went running from the room.

Thelma took a deep breath and exhaled slowly. "In the morning I'll have my own baby. A girl." She wiggled her toes, watching the bed covers move up and down slightly above them. My own baby! And, in her mind's eye, she passed her new and wonderful little tot from lap to lap. She'd gather it up again, diaper it, then seat herself easily in the big rocker. Then she'd fold the blankets carefully around the babe and let the infant nurse from her flat little breast.

The sound of the lonesome train whistle and the sight of sparks and fire shooting out of the stack from the west window thrilled her. She snuggled down deeper under the patchwork covers. For months she had planned for her baby. The glass jar had pennies she'd saved for baby's bank.

She had it all planned. Next summer she and Mabel would

Thelma Curtis Dobson had her father's coloring and her mother's determination. The set of her chin shows that determination that was a big part of Thelma's personality, even at a young age.

take the infant out in the yard under the maple tree and spread an old quilt down for baby to roll on. They would braid necklaces and bracelets out of the little white and pink clovers that covered the lawn, or bring her the dandelion seed puffs and tell her to "blow hard," knowing she'd reach for them happily as they scattered in the wind.

She would be teething by summer, Thelma thought, looking at the ceiling. *Babies get cross when they cut teeth. I'll buy her some Job's tears to hang around her neck to chew on, and rub teething lotion on her swollen gums so she won't fuss so much. But if she cries and cries, I'll make her a sugar tit to suck on. When she gets older I'll give her a lump of brown sugar out of the stone jar. Maw says whenever a baby smiles in her sleep, she's playing with the angels.*

I'll watch my baby laugh and babble and pat the tray of her wooden high chair and beg for the sugared doughnut holes when Maw fries the big yeast ones in her black iron kettle. When all the family and friends gather around, I'll hold her proudly on my lap and we'll watch Paw play his fiddle. Paw's an old man now, fifty-five, but maybe he'll live to teach my baby to play the violin just like her grandpaw!

Poor Papa. He had to die right here before Christmas. He'll never see my baby. He would have spoiled her rotten. Mama tries to be happy. When I get my baby, she'll be glad, and I'll let her help me all the time. Maw's old, too—past fifty—but she can still rock her some.

In the distance, Paw was humming tunelessly. He wound the Seth Thomas clock and banked the stoves for the night.

At last, the girls were breathing the regular breath of sleep.

Maw came through from finishing up in the kitchen. "Wrap it up boys; put away your game. It's time to go count the stars." She wouldn't let them stand on the porch and wet off the edge in ordinary weather. It had to be sleeting or snowing; that's the only way Maw would put up with it.

Out the two went. They ran their fingers along the top of the porch railing, scraping off slices of snow. They were soon back, shaking like wet dogs from the cold. "There ain't more'n six inches of snow on the railing," Glen reported as he measured with his thumb and fingers.

Thelma awakened Christmas morning to the sound of her grandfather raking ashes from the kitchen cookstove, building up the sleeping fire. The morning air was already sharp with wood smoke from the living room stove. She could see her breath as she pushed her face up from the covers. A glow of light was coming through the transom.

Then a baby cried. *A baby cried!* Thelma's eyes flew wide open and she lay perfectly still. Was it a dream? She didn't make a sound. Again. A baby cried! Thelma threw the covers back, hopped out of bed, gave a skip the length of the icy bare floor and then tiptoed into the sitting room. Why hadn't anyone else heard the baby, and why was Paw the only one up stirring about? The red-patterned wool Brussels carpet was cozy under Thelma's feet.

Then she saw her ample-bosomed grandmother rocking contentedly by the stove with a blanket-wrapped baby in her arms. The heater was already ablaze and warm—babies must always be kept good and warm.

Thelma, exhilarated, crept to her grandmother's side, then peeked in at the newborn. Her smile widened and her cheeks grew pink with excitement. Already her heart went out to it and she reached to touch, wanting to take it in her arms. *My baby, my own sweet baby!*

Maw felt a sudden uneasiness as she looked into Thelma's sweet upturned face. She spoke in a soft voice that was just above a whisper. "Honey, look what Aunt Della and Uncle Omer got last night after you went to bed. It's a new baby boy. Isn't he precious?"

Maw's voice broke into Thelma's dream and, immediately, her smile began to fade. She stood there with a look of utter disbelief on her face. Then she gave a nervous little laugh. "I wanted a girl, but I don't mind. I like boys, too. But, Maw, 'member? I'm the one who asked Santy for a new real baby, not Aunt Della."

There was a shaking in her voice. She nodded for her grandmother's approval, trying to catch and hold Maw's eyes with hers. "Aunt Della, she has Little Opal. She didn't ask for a real baby for Christmas. This is mine!"

Thelma caught the swift exchange of looks between her grandparents. The moment hung in space . . . hung and hung. The very climate of the room changed. Thelma's eyes were full of tears. Desperation moved in, heavy and oppressive. "You mean . . . ?" she cried, swaying on her feet.

It went into Maw's heart like a knife. She shook her head. "For mercy sakes. Mercy, mercy." Maw's whispered words and her tear-filled eyes gave the answer.

Thelma was pleading for denial. It's all a mistake—will soon be corrected. "But . . . but . . . he'll be lonesome without me, Maw. Aunt Della hasn't seen him yet. She has Little Opal. Can't I have him? Then she can ask Santy for a real baby next year!" She hoped her argument sounded convincing.

Paw had kept quiet except for closing or opening the damper on the stove. He saw the slow stubborn setting of Thelma's under-lip as she walked to him. Now she understood the downcast look on his face.

He took a deep, heavy breath, sat down and stretched his legs toward the fire, then he pulled Thelma onto his lap. He was thinking, *We will not haggle with her. She'll be all right. I know full well how it is with a woman when she gets her head set—even little ones.* Then he rubbed his chin thoughtfully and looked at Thelma in kindly concern. She seemed to be passing into another world, a strange dream world where she was alone. He gathered Thelma closer in his arms and kissed her with unmistakable understanding, avoiding her eyes. Drawing her legs up, he wrapped them warmly in the tail of her gown.

Thelma folded up like a hurt bird and settled herself in the curve of Paw's arm. He had never seen her look so forlorn—so in need of comfort. "Now, don't take on so, Honey," he said in his kindest voice. "Thelmie, listen to this. Maw is right. This is Uncle Omer's and Aunt Della's baby. Let's name him Chris, 'cause it's Christmas. Did you look in your stocking?" His suggestion was small balm for her injured heart.

Paw studied her: She had her father's coloring and her mother's determination. The hot coal fire was scorching one side of her face, and she was drawn closer into the lock of his arm. His long, soft beard soothed her hot face but in spite of it, the tears rolled down her cheeks. She stared soulfully at her baby, dodging Paw's reasoning. She was so alone—*so all alone*.

As she watched her daughter, Orpha's face began to crumble. Tears ran down her cheeks. She wanted to say something, but mere words were not enough. Nothing seemed adequate at the moment. Paw mentioned naming the baby Chris, but Della said they had planned to use Ralph Edward.

Deep convulsive sobs rankled Thelma's pathetic little body as she hung in Paw's arms like a rag doll. The picture of dejection. The hurt, the piercing ache. After a while the pitiful moans thinned to a thread. It was just no use to cry.

By now, the others in the household had been aroused and were wandering in—one by one. Maw whispered to each of Thelma's disappointment.

Little Opal came into the room singing, ". . . not a preacher was stirrin', not even a mouse . . .When I waked up, I didn't know where I was. Who tooked me back to Thelmie's and Mabie's bed 'ast night?"

Both boys were buttoning up shirts and tying shoes. Paw wagged a finger and gave them a withering look.

Mabel looped her arm through Thelma's. "It's all right. Here now, here now—come with me. You have a dolly like mine over there under the tree, and look what's in your stocking!"

Breaking the awkward pause, Paw leaned way forward—almost sliding Thelma from his knees—and fished his red bandanna handkerchief from his hip pocket. "There, there, crying never mends anything," he said. "It just makes your eyes an ugly red. Blow. Blow hard!" He almost covered her face with his muscular hand, then he dabbed at her eyes to soak away the sad little puddles. It wrung his heart for one so young, so very young, to have this despair.

Up on the wall behind the stove, Thelma saw the navy blue, gold-trimmed, velvet plaque: GOD BLESS OUR HAPPY HOME. She remembered how she'd prayed to Jesus for the baby. Sobs welled inside her again. "Jesus . . . oh, Jesus . . . why?" This time, Santa and Jesus both had made the mistake. Then she stretched out, stepped down and slowly walked away. There are some things you have to face alone.

Paw Pheanis rolled his thoughts around in his mind as he looked at his new grandson. *What helpless creatures you babies are. You, Chris, came into this world a month early—yes, a full month early—you pure and innocent little lamb. Already, just a few hours old, you have witnessed unhappiness. It's a crazy quilt of a world—the cross-currents of life—it is.* Paw fumbled for an answer. It just made no sense.

Thelma will never forget, even if she lives to be a hundred, the wracking torment of the scene yet so vivid, that Christmas morning, December 25, 1908. She had a lifetime of love, but by some strange set of circumstances, she never knew the most sacred of all experiences—of becoming a mother and holding her own baby in her arms. That touch of melancholy will go with her to her grave.

Tri Town Topics, Christmas Special, December 24, 1970

Dr. Perry Pentecost

Oh, My Achin' Tooth!

I had a phone call one day from a lady. "Lois," she said, "you must get acquainted with ninety-year-old Dr. Pentecost. But wait . . . he's in the hospital." I thought, the obituaries will get him before I do! She continued, "He's not sick. It's just a broken leg." He and his wife, Mae, brought happiness to me and my whole family for his six remaining years.

I REMEMBER WATCHING the century turn over—1899 to 1900. How exciting it was! Not many living now, in 1974, can say they witnessed that!

People are always asking me, "What's it like to be ninety?" I tell them, "Well, I have good health, enjoy three meals a day, can eat anything, and I never gain or lose a pound. I take vitamins and sleep well. My mind is extremely alert. I enjoy all my African violets, a huge garden and mowing our big yard on the riding mower. Best of all, my loving wife, Mae, takes extremely good care of me and our home. What more could a fellow ask?"

I've always loved people and my chosen profession, dentistry. For the last several years, since I retired, I've had my office here at home. I wear a white starched coat, just like I did in my town office. I have patients who come from all the neighboring towns and even as far as Arizona. Yes, folks who've moved away still come back and look me up. I do keep busy!

For as long as I can remember, there have been dentists. The techniques or procedures weren't the same as we have today, but they did very good work.

When I was a little fellow in school, I was thinking about being a dentist. Boys, from first grade on, always carried a pocketknife. They were forever gouging holes on desk tops. I'd tear up bits of scrap paper real fine and tamp it into a hole, as if I was filling a cavity in a tooth. At recess I'd take a lilac whip, bend it around, and I'd pretend it was forceps a-pulling my little friends' teeth.

Folks, back then, weren't as dedicated to good mouth hygiene as we are today. I found some real old clippings Mama had saved—they were probably her mama's.

> TO CURE TOOTHACHE: *Heat two tablespoonsful of vinegar. Dip a little absorbent cotton in this and apply it to the gum at the root of the aching tooth. Also, a wad of Pa's chewed tobacco is the handiest antidote at times when a person's cavity pains him horribly.*
>
> BLEEDING GUMS: *Use a dogwood twig to clean your teeth, or rinse your mouth daily with water and a bit of quinine.*
>
> CUTTING BABY TEETH WITHOUT PAIN: *Boil the brain of a rabbit and rub the gums of the child with it, and the teeth will grow in healthy and without pain.*
>
> PLAQUE: *Cooked or raw rhubarb cleans all the plaque off the teeth while it cleans out the system in early spring.*

Yes, I remember Mama using these cures from time to time—all except the rabbit's brain!

Rare and expensive were the marketed toothpaste and powders. Mama mixed our own powder in a half-pint Mason jar: one part salt, two parts soda. The whole family brushed their teeth religiously with it.

A friend of ours had a dentist living in her home. She thought his was a pretty nice profession. That's what got me to thinking about dentistry. Next thing I remember, I was walking along with my father, telling him what I'd decided. "Yes, Son, I'd like for you to be a dentist," he said.

I graduated from Cicero High School in 1900.

Just the other day I heard of a dentist who quit and changed professions. He said, "Nobody loves a dentist. For hearing the very word 'dentist,' a person thinks of the man's fingers in his mouth or of saliva spilling down the corner of his mouth and dripping from his chin or cotton soaking it up. He gets cross-eyed watching the drill, and his nerves go erratic listening to its steady drone. He'll sit on pins wondering if the instrument will slip and rip into his tongue or cheek. Dentists talk all the time or tell jokes, and you can only reply with a grunt and a lifted eyebrow."

But there comes the time when everyone loves his dentist! In the middle of the night, abscessed teeth send out distress signals. You'll look at him with deep respect when he's pulled the bad old ones and refitted you with perfect, beautiful shiny ones. Or when you have bleeding gums—when every bite of food brings you agony, or the smile to a friend is painful and your breath is bad—your friendly dentist is right there to put everything right.

A man came in one evening holding his swollen, aching jaw. Doubled over with pain, he said, "I never had nuthin' hurt me so bad in me life, Doctor! I been stove up as a rusty pump with this arther-ritis—m'shoulder's been a-givin' me billy-hill. This danged cough keeps hangin' on. So, m'old woman gives me a big dose o' caster erl to git rid of the pizen from m'teeth in m'system, she says. Well, if I thought th'tooth was bad, I should've knowed 'bout the cure! I'm 'bout t'th'end of m'tether, Doc, what with durn rotten teeth, financial worries, an' a-tryin' to scrape up 'nough fer fall taxes.

"M'wife's been under th'weather fer some time —weak as a cat an' her legs limber's rags. I tole her she needed a good tonic. I'm jist like poor ol' Job. All m'troubles have come down at once. But as th'Lord has promised to provide fer His lambs, I dare t'hope He will do a little somethin' fer this ol' fleeced ram." He went on and on. Patients became my close friends. I know all their illnesses, deaths, family, everything.

So I said to him, "Trials and sadness comes into almost everyone's lives at one time or another, Buddy. I remember this old proverb: *You can't keep trouble from coming, but you needn't give it a chair to sit upon.*" Then I said, "If you can laugh at your troubles you will never run out of something to laugh about!" He still had a long, disturbed face. After I'd taken care of him, we chatted a while longer, and he left with a grin on his face.

Folks paid me—sometimes with cash, sometimes with food, sometimes with promises. Most often I came out ahead. Occasionally I lost.

Reminds me of what a patient told me the other day when he asked the cost of his new dentures. He laughed and said, "A doctor dropped a note to his fully recovered hospital patient: Just pay me half of what you offered to pay me when you thought you were dying!"

One old fellow, with the unmistakable odor of Watkins Salve, sat down in the chair. Poor guy, he not only had a severe toothache but also a horrible cold. The swollen jaw was tied up with an old sock, and his forehead was as hot as the lids on Mama's old cookstove used to be. His red farmer's handkerchief was used up, and a lamb's leg bobbed in and out of his nose as he tried to breathe. Said he'd kept using cloves of garlic or tobacco juice in the cavity holes, and he put hot salt packs on it, but nothing worked.

Try as he would, he couldn't stop trembling. He wasn't only in terrible pain, but he couldn't accept the possibility of losing his teeth. He complained, "I've heard that eatin' ain't quite the same once a body's teeth is falsified." I opened my mouth wide and showed him my dentures. I picked up an apple, started eating it, and said, "Corn on the cob, nuts, popcorn—but I won't try taffy!"

I told him what to do to get the swelling down and gave him medicine for pain. I asked him to come back in a few days so I could extract the bad ones. Maybe, by then, he'd feel much better from his horrible cold.

When I next saw him, I said, "Your cough sounds better this morning." He grunted, "It should be. I been practicin' fer weeks. I still feel like I been run through a corn sheller."

One very old lady came with a terrible cold. She apologized, afraid I'd catch it. Then she laughed and said, "It's the only thing left I have to give to anybody."

As I said before, I graduated from Cicero High School in 1900. In September 1972 I was honored as the oldest member present at the Cicero School reunion and banquet, graduating seventy-one years ago. As I was introduced, I was laughing and I said, "A lot of funny things happened back then, but most of it was before or after school."

The Indiana Dental College was at the corner of Delaware and Ohio in Indianapolis. It took me three years to graduate—with no vacation in the summers. It didn't cost too much to go. I worked at my boarding house for room and board and at a restaurant waiting tables and washing dishes. I stacked them in two big metal basket-racks, then plunged them up and down with my arms in the big sinks of very hot, sudsy water until they were clean. I bought my meals at the same place. For ten cents I could get a steak as big as my hand, three slices of bread, butter, two sides, and coffee tea or milk.

There were three very nice ladies in my class. It was rare for females to go to college back in the early 1900s, much less dental college. We had our dental school class reunion in 1950. I mentioned in my speech how nice these women were. They demanded kind attention and always acted ladylike.

My first office was in Cicero, up over the old Bank Building. I did a lot of gold fillings. It was a badge of importance and affluence to have a gold tooth in front. No one does that anymore. Some gold molar fillings I put in back then are still in the teeth of persons living today. One lady, before she died, had worn hers for forty years!

There were many stories of robbers digging up graves to get this gold. Grave robbers—or ghouls as they were called—were a constant worry. They even dug up fresh graves and sold bodies to medical schools for research.

When one young handicapped fellow died, an older family member planted a bomb above his corpse. He knew students at med school would want to study the body and they'd send ghouls to dig him up. I never did hear the outcome.

Over at Deming, this couple lived way back off the road. There was a big thump on their front porch one night. They went out to see what it was. Someone yelled to them, "We dug this up by mistake!" There, in a gunnysack, was the body of the couple's only child who had died sometime earlier. How could anyone be so heartless? Why hadn't they re-buried it?

In the late 1800s and early 1900s, Cicero, Arcadia, and Atlanta were boom towns. People moved in from all over. The glass factories in each town paid huge wages. There was a big demand for glass—bottles, dishes, drinking glasses—just everything glass. Then the essential gas wells went dry. Cicero's glass factory burned. Most folks thought it was arson—set so the company could claim insurance. After that, families moved away in droves. There went my practice. So I moved to an office in Tipton in 1909.

One day a little boy and his parents, riding in their horse-drawn buggy, started to Tipton for an appointment with me. The horse got scared at an approaching automobile and turned right around in the shaves, breaking them. The three walked on to town to get help. I made that lady a set of teeth, and she's been wearing them for sixty-one years!

False teeth were made by the vulcanite process. They don't do that anymore. I had a little woman come to have me repair her teeth. They were constructed in 1896. They set right on top of her gums and were made of red and pink rubber. Red was the substantial kind. We used the pink, the color of gums, for a veneer around where it showed.

I made a relative set of dentures off her old ones, and mailed them to her in Illinois. They fit her fine. I've always made dentures. Still do. I buy individual teeth from suppliers and match size and color to patient's own teeth. I pulled mine and made dentures for myself.

For extractions I give anesthetic to numb the gums in many places. I never deaden nerves for fillings, however. Never! I've taken as many as twenty-eight teeth out at a time, and that patient got along just fine. Mostly I don't take more than eight or ten—it's too hard on a body's constitution. After the extractions, I tell the patient to go home, wash his mouth out with warm salt water, and use the rinse after meals and at bedtime for several days to avoid infection.

I learned the technique of putting on braces in dental school. I've done more of that in the last few years than I did in my early practice. I usually put them on a child when he's around eleven years old.

Once in a while a spoiled kid crawls up in the chair; sometimes he's just nervous. I'm kind to him, telling him it isn't going to be nearly as bad as he thinks it is. I'll be real patient. After I'm all finished, I let him go out and play with my new baby kittens!

If the child keeps being naughty, I ask him to go home and to have his mama call me when he gets real brave. No, they don't usually kick, but they'll jerk away, cry and carry on, and that bothers me. I'm afraid the drill will slip and really cause trouble.

One little girl in our church, she comes around and talks to me every Sunday. Such a darling! She had a tooth that had to come out. She never whimpered, never even flinched. It isn't necessary to have much pain if they'll cooperate. When I was all finished, she ran to her mother a-laughing. She said, "I was a good girl and didn't cry. Now can I have my ice cream cone?"

Then she brought her dolly to me and asked, "Will you see if my baby needs a tooth pulled too, Doc-tor Penny? She cries a lot." Kids have a hard time pronouncing my name. I said, "Let me give her a good look, Sweetie. No, no she doesn't have a bad tooth today, so I guess she's got pain in her sawdust." She gave me the cutest smile, hugging the dolly close to her, and said, "You are teasing me, Doc-tor Penny!"

A mother brought her little fellow in. He was green as that grass out there in the yard and so weak his legs shook when he walked. He was crying with the pain from an abscessed tooth. Mama lifted him up into the chair. I bent closely over him, then pulled out my handkerchief to mop up the tears and the sweat that was running in rivulets down his face.

When he calmed, I said quietly, "Open wide now. Open wide." Just then he gave a quick cough. Up came his dinner—spaghetti, tomato sauce, everything—all over himself and me. Mae came running with a washpan of hot soapy water and a rag to clean up the mess. His mama kept saying, "I'm so sorry! I'm so sorry!"

One little boy jumped excitedly into my dentist chair. I said, "Open wide!" and out came a big *burrrp*! He gave a hearty laugh, wiped at his mouth with his hands and said, "I should never have et all them radishes!"

Women and young ladies would avoid eating raw onions or radishes before their appointment. Men? Sometimes they'd forget, and after brushing their teeth good before coming (at the wife's insistence), they'd take a big chew of tobacco. Oh well, too late now, so he'd enjoy it all the way into town. At my office, he'd ask for a glass of water to rinse out his mouth before we started in. I never did smoke or chew, but I kept ashtrays and a cuspidor handy for those who did. Mae called it a stinking habit and refused to clean the spittoon. I had that to do.

In the wintertime, most kids came to me with their asafetida bag suspended from a string around the neck. I had to wear one when I was small, and I never did get used to that horrible odor. It was supposed to keep the contagious diseases away. Oh yes, it worked because kids didn't get close to each other!

A mother asked me, "My Johnny grits his teeth something awful every night. He has nightmares—sees spiders, snakes, big bugs crawling the walls. What can we do for him?" I don't know if there ever was a satisfactory answer to that complaint. Some claimed they needed a good dose of worm medicine, and usually that did help. A child going through difficulties in school or home will often grind his teeth when he sleeps.

My wife's nephew, a soldier, got real sick. He vomited his uppers; they just slipped right down that commode with the rest of it! You've heard of this happening to drunks, but he wasn't a drinking man—just very, very ill. The army dentist couldn't get to him for two months, so he gave me a call. He came by bus, arriving at three in the morning. I hurried and took off my pajamas and put on my clothes.

The first thing I did was to take the impression. Until I needed him each time, he stretched out on the davenport and slept. After being on the road so long and being so sick, he was dead tired. Mae could hear his snoring clear to our upstairs bedroom! At three that afternoon, twelve hours later, I had his upper plate made. Then he was on his way back to Ft. Sill, Oklahoma, his face still bearing the marks of the couch's pillow.

Doctors often sent me their anemic patients and those with aching joints and muscles. Usually they looked for two sources of the cause: infected tonsils or teeth. I'd frequently find bad teeth and gums full of puss. One fellow was scheduled for back surgery. A neighbor mentioned he'd better go to his dentist first—bad teeth can cause all kinds of aches and pains. Sure enough, he had several bad teeth. A few weeks after I pulled them, the back pain was gone. He told me he felt better than he had in years.

Just a while back, it took me four hours to pull a young fellow's wisdom tooth. The roots had grown around his jawbone. It didn't make me nervous, but it was tiresome. Most of the young dentists now don't do that kind of work. I've never had to turn one over to an oral surgeon yet.

I was married to Grace Thompson in 1905. God didn't bless us with children of our own. We adopted three from the same family: a boy and two girls—ages four, two, and three weeks old. A terrible tragedy brought all this about.

The young family lived in Cicero. Neighbors and fellow workers of the husband assumed that the stove started the fire that killed the children's parents. The baby girl, Laurann, had colic. She cried constantly—night and day. The doctor finally found something that would settle her down, so the exhausted mother and babe finally got the sleep they desperately needed. The mother probably overslept that morning. She had been accustomed to waking up early, to have the fires built, the house warm, and her husband's breakfast ready when he returned from his overnight job.

She wouldn't have given a second thought to sleeping in that morning, even as tired as she was, or to have him fix his own meal and let her sleep. So folks figure she had rushed to the kitchen to build up a quick fire. She probably put in wads of paper, kindling, and sticks of wood, but forgot to light a paper first—she was still overcome with sleep. She must have thrown coal oil into the stove, so the fire would quickly ignite. But folks always knew never to do that. If there happened to be live coals down inside, it would all blow up.

Just then, there was a loud explosion! The husband, seeing the flash of fire through the kitchen window as he was returning home, rushed into the house and grabbed her. She died instantly from the blast. He caught fire and died soon afterward, crying, "My wife! My wife! Oh, Lord, save her and our babies!" Their babies: John, Ruth, and Laurann.

I'll never, ever forget it. Town people had heard the early morning *boom* and were rushing outdoors from their homes. Some were half-dressed, hastily drawing coats about them, faces full of alarm, and crying, "Oh my God! Oh my God!" Men, half-asleep, ran in and out in their long underwear, some still pulling on their pants and coats, trying to be of help to rescue the couple and the children and to put out the fire.

The horse-drawn fire engine arrived too late. The house burned to the ground. The children, thank God, were safe.

The doctor came running with his black bag. Cicero preachers, as soon as they heard of the woeful situation, came and gathered together those who were standing around, and they were praying. For days, the whole community was filled with shock. It was like a dreadful dream. I kept hoping to wake up and all would be normal again.

It was so pitiful—both parents gone. Crying tots. What would happen to the children? Kin on both sides wanted them to grow up together, but none were in proper circumstances to take all three. Most had big families.

Their preacher and the doctor talked to the relatives a few days later. They then came to Grace and me to see if we'd adopt them, which we did, happily. I had the most benevolent feeling! God works in mysterious ways.

It was quite an adjustment for Grace and me—three little children to start with all at once. We felt so confused. Nothing was left of their home but ashes—everything gone. There was so much to be done.

Family and friends came to our rescue with food, diapers and baby things, clothing for John and Ruth, toys, bedding, a baby bed for Laurann, and beds for the older two. Different neighbors and family members took turns helping with the laundry and the meals and gave us much-needed advice. I wanted to take a couple weeks off to help Grace, but she insisted that I work. With three more mouths to feed, money was needed more than ever.

With so much commotion, people coming and going all day long, the children had their minds distracted during the daytime. After supper, when it got dark, we'd hear their pitiful cries, "Mama? Mama? I want my mama!" And since their father had worked nights, they missed him coming home for breakfast, so they had morning crying spells.

Grace tried to comfort them by saying, "Mama's gone to be with Jesus in Heaven. She and your papa are up there looking down on you all the time." Grace taught them their prayers, but still, they cried themselves to sleep.

I don't know when it happened, but after a while the crying stopped, and it was replaced with happy laughter. Soon we were living like any other five-member family. We were so blessed!

These children were always a great joy. Never any trouble. I give Grace the credit for making life so full and meaningful for us all. She had been a music teacher, but she gave that up. She saw to it that the children could all play instruments. We had our own musical group—piano, violin, clarinet and cello. I sang. Many harmonious hours were enjoyed together. We spent a lot of time with those children. I was Scout Master for fourteen years. That was before they were organized like they are now.

Thinking back to that time in our lives, two of my favorite adages come to mind: *When you educate a man, you educate an individual. When you educate a woman, you educate a whole family.* And the other: *Good family life is never an accident but always an achievement by those who share it.*

Grace died in 1952. Our three were grown and living in their own homes. My greatest thrill: John is a dentist, a captain in the Navy. John's son, Robert, also graduated from dental college. Our two very beautiful daughters married and are now Ruth Richter and Laurann Neary. And we have seven grandchildren.

Some years after Grace's death, I married Mae. She'd lost her husband about the time Grace died. Mae was childless. She loved mine as her own, and they adored her.

For a long time, I raised prize gladioli—twenty acres of them a year. I sent the long blooming spikes to Chicago, Cincinnati, St. Louis, all over. I have a box full of ribbons from prizes I won at fairs.

Sitting around visiting with friends, many funny anecdotes come about during an evening: there were the old men whose teeth spent most of the time in their pockets, the farmer who put his teeth in the toolbox on the tractor all day long, and the housewife who had to always hurry to find hers when there was a knock on the door. Do you remember reading that the one item most often left behind on passenger trains in Britain was false teeth?

That reminds me of the time a train engineer came to me to have his teeth relined. He said he was laughing real big at a joke a fellow was telling him when he lost his teeth out the locomotive's window. What did he do? He stopped the train, slowly backed it up, got out, picked them up out of the weeds, brushed them off with his hanky and put them back in.

Down on the Ohio River a great big catfish was caught. When it was cleaned, they found a set of false teeth in his stomach!

Most folks around Cicero have seen the six-pound bass that Johnny Knotts caught. He had it mounted, then he hung it up over the west door of Jut and Katherine Durnell's Back Lash Restaurant. In the bass's open mouth, Johnny anchored an old set of his wife Avis's dentures. Jut added this inscription: BASS SNAPPER—A RARE FISH

Mr. and Mrs. Elmer Ripley, Cicero, were fishing off the bridge west of Cicero when Elmer, eighty-two, spied a set of dentures lying in the sand in the sun, way down below. He crawled the steep bank carefully to get them, then took the teeth to the Back Lash. Jut placed them with a sign: FREE—MUST PROVE OWNERSHIP!

Sometime later, a man from Perkinsville, fifteen miles from

here, came in to eat. He saw the sign and said, "I know a fellow who had a most unsettling experience. He pushed his boat away from the bank down here, ready to go fishing near the bridge. He took a violent fit of coughing, and his teeth went flying right out of his mouth! He was unable to find them anywhere. After the high water of the early spring rains receded, he felt that maybe they'd show up. Well now, Mr. Durnell, I'll have him come by and see if these belong to him. He's been worried sick about the replacement expense." The owner soon happily reclaimed his set of teeth.

That reminds me. A bride of two years was complaining to her husband, "Now that we're married, you don't give me any more presents." The husband said, "My dear, does a fisherman give bait to the fish he's already caught?"

One morning I left to be gone all day. I had no more than pulled away, my wife said, when a car drove in. A man in his best bib and tucker, all spit and polish, jauntily walked up to my office door. Mae let him in. He complained, "Am I in a pickle! I know I'm a few days early, but I've just gotta have my new teeth today!" Mae nodded her head in a gesture of understanding as she looked the toothless, well-dressed man up and down. She said slowly, "I'm so sorry, but the doctor is away for the day."

His face went sour and he began mumbling to himself, but then he perked right up when he saw a row of dentures I'd just finished. He stood with his thumbs in his vest pockets, looking over the seven sets lying out there on the table. He said eagerly, "I'll just take mine. They're ready." Then he proceeded to try on each of them. As he took one set, then another, Mae became annoyed. *He'll try them all on, just like pairs of shoes?* she thought. *But, someone else's teeth?*

The man gave a yell out the door to his wife, who was waiting for him in their car, "Come in and help me decide which are mine!" Mae said she was dressed fashionable, too, and so beautiful.

When he picked up, first one set, then another, it dawned on the wife what he was doing. With arms akimbo, she stood looking at him and said sternly, "If that doesn't beat all. What's gotten into you, anyhow? You don't have the faintest idea which ones are yours! People's mouths are like fingerprints—no two alike!" He chuckled and she continued disapproving.

Finally, he said happily, "Ah-ha, these seem to fit! Aswan, I just plopped them in and they stuck like a scab on a sore. These'r them, you betcha!" He clamped his molars together and curled his lips up and ogled at them in the mirror. He looked at Mae, "What's your opinion?" Mae nodded amiably. He stood there with a serene smile on his new face, then dug deep into his pocket and pulled out a roll of bills and laid them on the desk. "Hot ziggity," he shrieked and slapped his leg. He grabbed his wife by the arm and waltzed her out the door.

Uncertainty slid into Mae's thoughts as the car drove away. *What if those teeth weren't his? I've let him take them and now what?* But the teeth did belong to that man and I laughed at the episode—one you're not likely to read about in the manuals of dental college!

A man was asked, "Why do you carry those false teeth around in your pocket?" He replied, "I'm trying to break my fat wife from eating between meals."

I guess the most trying experiences I had was with this man who had a droopy mustache. When I filled his teeth, it kept getting in my way. I was so afraid the drill would get in it and tangle—think how that would hurt. When I pulled his teeth, I was tempted to use some of Mae's hair clips to keep that mustache hair pulled back.

Now, this actually happened: Dick was always making excuses for not wearing his teeth to his friend, Tom. "My store teeth never have fit too awful well, and when I smoke or chew I don't take no comfort with 'em. So I takes that crockery out and puts 'em down 'side me ever-where I be." Tom knew Dick wouldn't leave them in long enough to adjust to them.

Well, Tom and Dick had left their wives behind to go shopping. They were to meet them later to eat at the Back Lash. Both men were in the boat over very deep water, rowing to the other side for some early-morning fishing. Dick's teeth lay beside him as he puffed on a cigar.

Tom thought he'd have some fun. He slipped his own teeth down beside Dick when he wasn't looking, and he put Dick's teeth in his own jacket pocket. After a while, Dick picked up an apple, then remembered he'd have to put his teeth in to eat it. Tom was suppressing a laugh. *Just watch when he tries to wear my teeth,* he was thinking.

Dick tried to put in the uppers first, saying, "An apple is one thing you can't gum!" He struggled to work it into place but the upper plate resisted and sat there whopper-jawed in his mouth. He got choked, then coughed. It flew out of his mouth!

Both men tried to reach way overboard for it, then watched it float away and gradually drop out of sight. Dick shuddered as he watched. Disgusted, he reached down and picked up the lowers and flipped them overboard, too. "Here's the rest of ya. Danged things no good noway!"

Rowing back, the men were thinking of a big meal they'd looked forward to and, now, *What will our wives say?* Sometimes a practical joke backfires.

Children didn't like giving up their baby teeth. They'd let each one hang by a thread and defy anyone to touch it. Usually, only a slight tug with the mother's or father's thumb and forefinger pulled it loose. But after a while, the child wanted it out, so the Tooth Fairy would leave a penny under his pillow. Most mothers had a pair of forceps to pull their children's baby teeth.

Some used a different method. Six-year-old Angie John kept worrying a front tooth back and forth, but it wouldn't come loose. Her grandma said, "Here, I'll show you the way Mother took care of my first baby tooth." Grandma proceeded to tie one end of a string around the doorknob and the other to the tooth. Angie looked on amazed, then, realizing what was happening, she swung around real fast to take off running! Out came the tooth!

Usually, the string was tied to the tooth and to the doorknob on a half-opened door. Mother would tell the child to slowly step backwards until the string was taut. Then the mother would give the door a swift kick shut. The child, hearing the slam, wouldn't realize what had happened until he saw the string and tooth hanging down almost to the floor.

A mother often had to force her children to brush their teeth. Some would use their brush until it wore down to a nub. One brush was shared in big, poor families. A boy, at school, would insist his mother said all her kids didn't have to brush their teeth cause they drank milk.

They tell about the preacher who preached on and on one Sunday—well over the allotted one-hour limit. Next week, the same. The trustees warned him to cut it shorter. When the preacher went to have his teeth checked, the dentist looked in the man's mouth and said, "Land sakes alive. I've made a big mistake. I gave you women's teeth!"

I've had a wonderful life. Yes, I've had my ups and downs and my share of troubles, like everybody, but the good has far outweighed the bad. I just can't help but think how tragic life must be for the person who has plenty to live on, but nothing to live for.

Author's note: Dr. Perry Pentecost practiced dentistry until two weeks before his death, at age ninety-six.

Tri-Town Topics, March 27, April 3, 1975
The Indianapolis Star, March 7, 1974
Tipton Tribune, March 22, 1974
Cicero, Indiana, 1834-1984

Index

An asterisk (*) indicates a photo on that page.

Lois Kaiser Costomiris' books

Rail Fences, Rolling Pins & Rainbows

MORE *Rail Fences, Rolling Pins & Rainbows*

and

Windmills, Washboards & Whippersnappers

may be ordered from

GUILD PRESS OF INDIANA, INC.
435 Gradle Drive
Carmel, Indiana 46032

Cost is $20.00 per book. If shipping in Indiana, add $1 per book Indiana State Sales Tax. Shipping and handling is $3.50 for the first book, plus $.50 for each additional book.

Credit card orders may be placed by calling 1-800-913-9563.

Be sure also to check the Guild Press of Indiana web site at
WWW.GUILDPRESS.COM